DTP'S 2019 NFL DRAFT GUIDE

DANIEL PARLEGRECO

TABLE OF CONTENTS

Chapter 1 Introduction 1

Chapter 2 QB's 3

Chapter 3 RB's 16

Chapter 4 FB's 37

Chapter 5 WR's 39

Chapter 6 TE's 67

Chapter 7 OT's 80

Chapter 8 Interior Offensive Lineman (Guards or Centers) 93

Chapter 9 Edge Players (4-3 DE's and 3-4 OLB's) 109

Chapter 10 Defense Tackles (Includes 3-4 DE's) 128

Chapter 11 Middle Linebackers 147

Chapter 12 Outside Linebackers (Strong Side or Weak Side) 157

Chapter 13 Cornerbacks 167

Chapter 14 Safeties 186

Chapter 15 Conclusion 201

Chapter 16 Glossary of Terms and Top 50 Big Board 202

Chapter 1

Introduction

Here we are, the 2019 NFL Draft is officially here! What do we have to look forward to in this years' draft? A lot! If you've never read my draft guide in the past, here is what you'll have to enjoy in this year's version:

- Detailed evaluations of 300+ of the best prospects entering the draft
- Reports written in 'easy to understand' language for the average or the diehard NFL Draft fan
- Why I like or don't like a particular prospect, and where they would best fit
- Scouting glossary of terms used

Maybe you're asking, 'who am I and why should you listen to me?' Both honest questions. The truth is I'm a regular guy, just like you who loves football. The only difference is I've been doing this for the last 5 years and each year I've developed more and more of a love for it and have gotten better. I come at these evaluations from the average fan's perspective and not an NFL GM.

I write all my reports in an easy to understand way without utilizing extreme scouting lingo or hard to understand words or concepts. If you do have any questions in regards to certain words I utilize, you can simply use my scouting glossary of terms in the back of the guide. Why am I different than the average fan? And why am I different from all the other "scouts?"

To answer the latter question first, I rely on the film, and the film only! Rather than being overly reliant and overly affected by pre-draft workouts in underwear, I base my evaluations STRICTLY on the tape. I generally watch anywhere from 2-6 games on every single prospect in this class.

Doing it this way prevents me from overvaluing guys who can run impressive times or can win athletic competitions. We know football players play football, and the best way to evaluate them is by watching them play it. While this is risky, I'm the only one who stands completely by his convictions of 'watching the tape' only.

In fact, I release this guide earlier than any other draft publications! Some might say that's suicide because things change in the weeks leading up to the draft, I don't believe it is. In fact, rather than be swayed by other media talking heads, I let the tape start and finalize my evaluations. That's what makes my evaluations more accurate than most.

Why can I say that? Here are a few examples:

- When everyone else was ranking Carson Wentz as a late Day 3 prospect early on in the draft season back in 2016, I had him graded as a Top-5 player by November.
- When some said Patrick Mahomes was a system QB who won't succeed due to his "college offense," and that he was a MAJOR reach by the Chiefs, I had him graded as a Top-3 player in the draft.
- When Levi Wallace was considered slight and not an NFL CB last season, I had him graded as a Day 2 corner. He went undrafted. But… he ended up being one of the best rookies in the league this past season.

I could go on and on. These are just 3 examples. With that being said, I'm not always right, and sometimes I'm really wrong. But I'm not afraid to stand behind my convictions whether they are popular or unpopular. I refuse to simply state what the majority believe.

Once again, in this draft season my evaluations are very different from the others. You might be surprised or you might HATE my viewpoints. But I can promise you that I didn't have any preconceived notions about any of these players. Nor did I rank my hometown or favorite college programs players higher as many TV personalities do. You would be astonished if you knew.

With that being said, let's dig deep into these players. Read this with an open mind and you won't be disappointed. I put everything I have into all of this for you guys. Here we go, the 2019 NFL Draft!

Chapter 2

QB's

1. Drew Lock QB Missouri 6'4 223 lbs

Strengths: Lock possesses a long and well-built NFL QB build with prototypical height, length, and adequate build. Production levels have been outstanding in the SEC, throwing for 96 touchdowns and only 39 interceptions with a 63% completion percentage his senior season. Lock is a tremendous deep ball thrower. He shows the ability to stand tall in the pocket, possessing outstanding deep ball accuracy with the ability to hit guys in stride from 40-60 yards away. Lock is a 4-year starter who took the reins as the starter in his final 8 games of his freshman season. Lock shows ideal arm strength with easy velocity, making all the tight window and sideline throws necessary. Lock is a fearless gunslinger and is a threat to constantly attack the back half of a defense. He is comfortable making down the field passes with proper touch and trajectory. Lock does a nice job of utilizing his eyes and looking off targets, rarely locking onto the first target. An overall good athlete who shows some functional movement skills within the pocket to create and extend plays both inside and outside the pocket.

Weaknesses: Has some accuracy concerns on the shorter to intermediary routes having very subpar completion percentages. Plays in a very simple 1-read offense where he throws mostly digs, screens, slants, and deep routes. Takes some bad blind-side hits due to his failure to see the blitz and feel the rush bearing down. His internal clock lacks necessary sophistication holding onto the football for far too long. Plays in a very pass-happy offense where he was set-up for big numbers despite his low completion percentages. Has struggled against the better defenses in college football completing less than 50% of his passes against Top-25 schools. Some might have concerns he needs to put a bit more weight/muscle on his frame. Has major issues with his footwork. Can be a little careless with the ball at times, throwing off his back foot and putting too much air under the ball.

Best Fit: Starter Immediately

Player Ranking (1-100): 88.9 – Lock is an incredibly talented thrower of the football but is going to need some time to learn the finer details of the game. His accuracy concerns are a tiny bit troubling but he did also throw the ball downfield a lot more than most other QBs, and he had a poor supporting cast. He's gotten better and shown improvement in each season. He's a 1st round player with serious starter upside.

2. Kyler Murray QB Oklahoma 5'10 195 lbs

Strengths: Murray, the Heisman trophy winner this past season, is an unbelievable 2-sport athlete who excelled for the Sooners after finally getting his chance.

He was drafted in the 1st round for the Oakland A's before finally choosing football over baseball. Murray had a stellar 1 and only year starting with over 4300 yards passing, 42 touchdowns, 69% completion percentage, and only 7 interceptions. He's always a threat to run, running for an additional 1,000 yards and 12 touchdowns. His acceleration and quickness are unreal, getting to top speed in a flash. An outstanding athlete who shows ridiculously quick feet as well as long-speed to take plays to the house. Patient post-snap, scanning the field, never getting hooked on his 1st target. Excellent poise and awareness within the pocket, showing veteran movement skills. Excellent with his eyes, showing the ability to look off targets, rarely staring down intended targets. Fearless, not showing any level of intimidation with tight windows throws. Very accurate in short/intermediate routes. Understands where to place the ball on back shoulder throws or on timing-based routes, always giving his receiver a chance to make a play on the ball. An accurate thrower on the move (right or left), his ball placement never suffering. Easy ball velocity which makes it look effortless. Really impressive arm talent, showing the necessary skills to make all the throws. Feels the blitz and often times has an escape plan. Smart, never trying to do too much, despite his athleticism. Rarely takes big hits, looks completely comfortable getting to the ground.

Weaknesses: Murray is a 1-year starter with limited starting experience. Has obvious size/frame limitations, and will have difficulty reading and seeing over the line of scrimmage within the pocket. His lack of size is apparent when he fails to always see the cheating safety in the middle of the field. Murray's accuracy seriously wanes when he attempts to throw the ball inside the hashes. A low arm trajectory combined with his lack of height, lead to a lot of knockdowns at the line of scrimmage. Rarely sets his feet in the pocket, always holding onto the ball, too reliant on his feet. Can be a bit too conservative, tending to go the safe route with the football. Slow decision maker.

Best Fit: Playmaking QB who needs to be paired with a smart offensive coordinator

Player Ranking (1-100): 86.1 – I get all the concerns with the player, most notably his size. With that being said, he's still my 2nd favorite QB in this draft class. He's a flat-out playmaker who has better arm intangibles than former athletic quarterbacks, such as Lamar Jackson (Whom I never loved). It's rare to see an athletic quarterback with such great accuracy like Murray. Murray is just a stud who has impressed me in so many big-time games for the Sooners this year. Despite his lack of experience, he still shows some advanced understanding of playing the position. 1st round player.

3. Dwayne Haskins QB Ohio State 6'2 220 lbs

Strengths: Haskins is an impressive redshirt sophomore for the Buckeyes who finished 3rd in the Heisman this year with outstanding production. Had 4580 yards passing, 47 touchdowns, and only 8 interceptions. Still very young and will only be 21 years old on draft night. Despite his 1-year of starting experience, it was very clear Haskins gained more and more responsibility and improved throughout the campaign. Haskins possesses a prototypical NFL frame with great height, length, and broad shoulders. Haskins is a natural and effortless thrower of the football with an efficient set-up and an elevated, natural release. An above-average athlete, he displays the ability to tuck the ball and run when nothing is open downfield. Good footwork within the pocket as well, showing the ability to create for himself, or step-up in the pocket to make a tight-window throw. Haskins has a live arm, with top-notch velocity, showing the ability to alter speeds depending on the situation/route. Good anticipation on timing throws, perfectly leading and timing the ball. Impressive eye-manipulation to set-up teammates on screens or play-action type plays. Veteran pocket movements and poise, always keeping his vision downfield. Despite playing in a college spread offense, he showed the ability to make both horizontal and vertical reads and was required to read the entire field. Excellent accuracy on short to intermediate routes.

Weaknesses: Haskins is a 1-year starter and lacks adequate experience. Despite his outstanding production, his receivers had some terrible drops, resulting in a couple of his interceptions. Haskins offense was extremely simple, mostly predicated on slants, screens and swing passes to his running backs. Has a tendency to see things late, with too many late throws on his resume. Accuracy is below average to bad on deep-ball throws, or when asked to hit a moving target past 10 yards. A bit conservative, lacking the gun-slinger mentality to get the ball downfield consistently. His internal clock still lacks sophistication, as he held onto the ball far too long in critical situations, taking some unnecessary blind-side hits. Inconsistent footwork when asked to move off his spot, causing most of his throws to be high, forcing his receivers to consistently catch everything outstretched over their heads.

Best Fit: West-Coast QB

Player Ranking (1-100): 84.2 – I'm sorry but I can't be 100% behind Haskins as a franchise QB. There's no doubt he's ridiculously talented and is an excellent thrower of the football, but he's very frustrating at times as well. He absolutely has the highest upside in this draft class, but it's "potential" at this point. Expecting him to be ready from Day 1 at the next level is going to be very upsetting for a team. I think Haskins really needs to go to the right team that can utilize him in a west-coast offense. He needs more time and experience. It's true he seems like a great kid on and off the field, but I would feel more comfortable taking him in the 2nd.

4. Daniel Jones QB Duke 6'5 220 lbs

Strengths: Jones is a 3-year starter for the Blue Devils and has improved in each season. Was mentored for 4-years by the same guy that mentored Eli/Peyton, Duke's head coach David Cutcliffe. Outstanding toughness, returning to practice 9 days after his shoulder surgery. Jones is a smart kid who possesses prototypical NFL height and length. Jones is tremendous between the hashes, almost always putting the ball right in the numbers on in-breaking routes. Gets rid of the ball quickly with a quick release. His deep ball accuracy is really good showing the ability to perfectly place the ball against both zone and man coverage. His best trait is his touch, showing the ability to alter speed and placement at all levels of the football field. Good mobility, showing fearlessness in the open field to pick up yards when the play breaks down. Also shows very active feet within the pocket, creating extra seconds. Always keeps his vision downfield, making some outstanding sideline throws at the last second. Excellent pocket-presence, showing the durability and toughness to take hits while delivering strikes down the field. High-football IQ with an advanced understanding pre-snap of what the defense is doing. Goes through his progressions quickly, displaying the ability to make full field reads.

Weaknesses: Jones biggest area of concern is his decision-making, throwing some brutal interceptions right to the defense. High interception to touchdown ratio each season. Has had good college production, but not top-tier. Seems to have a lot of communication issues with his receivers, throwing the ball when his receivers have their backs to the ball A LOT. Had shoulder surgery to his non-throwing shoulder this past season, causing him to miss a couple of games. Lacks elite arm strength, and seemingly wouldn't fit in an attacking downfield passing offense. Has had serious fumble issues in all 3 seasons with 9 fumbles. Takes too many unnecessary hits when running, failing to get down adeptly. Needs to put on additional muscle, has a tall, lanky frame.

Best Fit: West-Coast QB

Player Ranking (1-100): 83.8 – Jones is an ultra-competitor who shows tremendous toughness. He's not a great or natural thrower of the football who is going to WOW with his arm. But he makes up for it with his advanced ability to read defenses and his terrific touch and placement down the field. He runs a lot of RPOs (run-pass options) that require him to quickly read the linebackers and are extremely effective in today's NFL. I think he's going to be a solid starting QB in this league for the right offense, not elite. 2nd round player.

5. Ryan Finley QB NC State 6'4 208 lbs

Strengths: Finley is a Boise State transfer who possesses a long and rangy build with outstanding height and length for the position. Finley is a pro-style QB, he is a very comfortable passer of the football, having a nice combination of proper touch and trajectory. Finley is very calm and collected showing veteran pocket movements and outstanding poise. Shows the ability to accurately throw to all levels of the field. Had a 64% completion percentage this year, 2nd in the ACC. Outstanding and quick release, showing the ability to get rid of the ball quickly. Had some of his best games against the best defenses, including against Clemson, in his junior year. Advanced understanding of the game, going through his route progressions, rarely settling on the 1st target. Plays with a certain fearlessness, not afraid or intimidated by tight window throws. Can throw receivers open or throw anticipatory throws on comebacks or timing-based routes. Shows above-average mobility, not afraid to run for the 1st run and displayed some nice open-field ability when given a chance. Good pocket presence, feeling the blitz and often has an escape plan. Shows great poise at crucial times, keeping composed and has had some nice game-winning drives at the end of games. Has nice touch and ball placement on balls down the field, has really shown in his senior season the ability to throw the deep ball. Shows the ability to throw with precision and accuracy when on the move. Can create space for himself and avoid the sack to make a throw.

Weaknesses: An older prospect who is going to be 25 during his rookie season. Offense is predicated on short to intermediate high percentage throws, including a ton of screens. A little careless and overly confident with the football, leading to some questionable decision-making. Average arm strength who really struggled in certain games against defenses that granted very little separation. Decent athlete, but not great. Accuracy really struggles when throwing near the sidelines. A lanky frame, he needs to add some body mass to his frame. Hung up on throwing to his first target despite double coverage, needs to do a better job of going to his 2nd and 3rd options. His biggest issues are with training his eyes, failing to see blitzing linebackers and safeties over the top.

Best Fit: Pro-Style QB that can play immediately

Player Ranking (1-100): 82.5 – Finley is a really talented thrower of the ball without any glaring weaknesses. He's played in a pro-style system and understands the mental side of the game. His accuracy is outstanding and he shows enough arm strength and mobility to win at the next level. Going to be a solid starting QB at the next level, but not elite. 2nd round player.

6. Jarrett Stidham QB Auburn 6'2 214 lbs

Strengths: Stidham is a 3-year starter for the Tigers, displaying above average size for the position. He's a tough and really athletic kid who isn't afraid to sacrifice his body to pick up additional yards. Plays in a read-option style of offense where he frequently tucks the ball and runs. Shows good movement skills both in and outside of the pocket, even picking up yards running against athletic defenses like Georgia and Alabama. Doesn't lock onto receivers, and understands how to go through progressions before getting rid of the football. Has experience taking the ball under center at times in Auburn's offense. Shows to be a good decision maker, rarely giving the defense an opportunity to turn the ball over. Has nice arm strength with the ability to fling the ball all over the field. Made his name backing up Seth Russell and then taking over for him at Baylor after Russell got hurt. Transferred to Auburn the following year. Stidham has outstanding leadership qualities and is known to be a really hard worker. Has shown success against some of the best defenses in college football. Really impressive in his ability to throw the ball on the move, rolling to his right or left. Reliable accuracy when throwing within the pocket and throwing balls under 15 yards. Really impressive play-action passer, going all-out on his ball fakes.

Weaknesses: Plays in an option-style offense where his offense is predicated on a lot of screens and short throws. Intimidated by tight windows, frequently throwing the ball out of bounds rather than giving his receiver a chance. Gun shy, takes far too many coverage sacks. Doesn't feel the rush and lacks a great internal clock, lacking the pocket presence or the awareness. Doesn't set his feet in the pocket, always looking jittery and uncomfortable. Accuracy concerns on the deep-ball. Safe QB, rarely taking a risk. Far too late on many of his throws. Has kind of a clunky side-arm type of delivery. Needs to speed up in his recognition and mental processing time.

Best Fit: Starting QB

Player Ranking (1-100): 81.1 – Stidham is a solid QB who does most things well, but nothing great. He's a really good athlete but was never required to read the field or consistently have to go through his progressions. I like that he has success going up against big-time college defenses and in big-time games. He reminds me of a slightly less talented Mitchell Trubisky. 2nd round player.

7. Will Grier QB West Virginia 6'2 218 lbs

Strengths: Grier, another transfer who played for Florida as a true freshman before transferring to WVU. Has started the last 2 seasons in all 11 games for the Mountaineers. Had an outstanding final season, completing 67% of his throws, 3864 yards passing, 37 touchdowns with only 8 interceptions. Grier is a winner, seemingly turning around 2 different college programs quickly. Grier displays the adequate size and traits of an NFL pocket QB. A quick deliverer of the football and a quick decision maker which allows him to avoid too many sacks. Does a nice job of utilizing different pump and ball fakes to disguise his throws, allowing his receivers to beat corners on double moves. Comfortable in his ability to roll out to the right or to the left and make throws on the move. Despite not having great deep-ball arm strength, he throws with tremendous velocity. Really does a nice job of working between the hashes and utilizing the right amount of touch and placement. Impressive in his ability to lead receivers, and even place it in a spot (back shoulder) where only the receiver can make a play on the ball. Fearless in his ability to patiently stay poised in the pocket while pressure is bearing down. Overall, he has very reliable accuracy especially from within the pocket.

Weaknesses: Grier plays in a typical college spread offense, rarely needing to read a full-field or go to another receiver outside of his 1st intended option. Struggles against pressure and blitzes when he doesn't have a perfectly clean pocket. Needs continuous training of his footwork, as he has the tendency to get 'happy feet' when pressure bears down. Lacks terrific deep ball arm strength. Really struggles to make tight window throws when on the move. Has a tendency to be very erratic and can be a hot/cold player who needs to get into a rhythm. His down the field accuracy can be very off. Received a 1-year suspension for performance-enhancing drugs when he was at Florida. Going to need some time to learn to work under center at the next level.

Best Fit: Starting QB potential. Needs a year of seasoning in an NFL offense.

Player Ranking (1-100): 80.2 – Grier reminds me of a more athletic Andy Dalton. Lacks great physical tools, but is a 'smooth' QB. He will never be a top-5 type of QB at the next level, but he can certainly be a middle of the road NFL Quarterback with good coaching. Worth a late 2nd round pick.

8. Jordan Ta'amu QB Ole Miss 6'2 212 lbs

Strengths: A 2-year starter for the Rebels, Ta'amu had an outstanding senior season throwing for almost 4,000 yards. Despite being a senior, Ta'amu just turned 21 in December and will be a younger prospect. Good athlete displaying quickness and the ability to pick up yardage with his feet. Throws with nice touch and placement on his passes down the field. Displays impressive arm strength, throwing with plenty of velocity, making it look easy at times. Comfortable downfield passer showing little hesitancy. Not intimidated by tight windows, has complete confidence in his zip/arm velocity. Really impressive ball placement at all levels of the field. Can create additional time inside/outside of the pocket with his footwork and movement skills. Impressive completion percentage numbers, showing accuracy and reliability against SEC defenses. Coaches love him, showing that he's wired right and possesses mature work habits and an unselfish attitude.

Weaknesses: Many will argue that Ta'amu was helped by the fact that he had the best receiving core in college football which helped pad his statistics. Only has 1 full year of experience as a starter. Lacks the ideal prototypical QB size and has a smaller frame with limited ability to put additional pounds on. Inconsistent with his ability to go through progressions, at times gets fixated on the 1st target. Pocket presence and awareness is still a work in progress, as he often gets "happy feet" when pressure is bearing down. Accuracy wanes while on the move. Can be overaggressive when he sees 1 on 1 matchups, failing to account for cheating safeties. Needs to learn that sometimes a 5-8-yard gain is OK and doesn't always need a big play. Overthrows a lot of balls down the field.

Best Fit: Developmental QB

Player Ranking (1-100): 76.8 – I really like Ta'amu and I think he can be a starter in this league down the road. He's only 21 and has limited experience as a starter and will continue to get better with more time in a system. Give him a year or two of seasoning. Impressive arm, intangibles, smart, and a real gunslinger. Yes, he was helped by good receivers but that's not the full story. He's a little bit smaller than I typically like for my QB's but he's not 'SMALL' per se. This kid is really talented. 3rd round is where I would take him.

9. Brett Rypien QB Boise State 6'2 202 lbs

Strengths: Rypien is a 4-year starter for the Broncos with some outstanding stats and production, breaking some of Kellen Moore's records at the school. Has shown improvement in each of his 4 seasons. Really impressive TD/interception ratio. Has thrown for over 60% completion percentage in each of his 4 seasons, with an almost 70% completion percentage his senior season. Rypien is a comfortable downfield passer showing outstanding touch and placement on balls. Highly intelligent kid both on and off the field and is loved by his teammates and coaches. Reads the game well, going through his progressions. An outstanding release, getting rid of the ball quickly and efficiently. Shows good anticipatory skills in leading his receivers and knowing exactly where his receivers are going to be. Plays in a pro-style offense. Really impressive in his ability to use play-action and ball fakes to manipulate coverages.

Weaknesses: Rypien is a bit of an undersized guy who lacks necessary body armor. Fails to feel the blitz or any outside pressure, lacking ideal pocket awareness and taking some unnecessary coverage sacks. A statue in the pocket who rarely likes to move off of his spot. Very average arm strength, failing to put necessary velocity on balls past 15 yards. Makes his living on short/intermediate routes on simple high percentage routes. Doesn't throw the prettiest ball with the ball constantly fluttering and floating in the air. Has thrown many inopportune red-zone interceptions.

Best Fit: Ideal for a West-Coast Offense

Player Ranking (1-100): 73.1 – I really like Rypien and I think he has starter potential. He's a better NFL QB prospect than former Boise State great Kellen Moore. He's really accurate and can be an ideal QB in a West-Coast offense. He's a 4th round player.

10. Gardner Minshew QB Washington State 6'1 224 lbs

Strengths: Minshew was a 2-year starter for East Carolina then transferring to Washington State before his senior season. Had a ridiculous senior season with 4500 yards passing and 36 touchdowns. Impressive down the field passer, showing outstanding touch and trajectory at all levels of the field. Stands tall in the pocket with impressive pocket presence, rarely looking rattled and always keeping his eyes down the field. Good with his eyes, never locking onto his targets and rarely settles on 1st target. Utilizes body/head/pump fakes to create separation for his receivers on crucial downs. Not intimidated by tight windows, showing the confidence in his arm to fit the ball in. Will make the tough throw while pressure is bearing down. Shows veteran movements and poise within the pocket. Functional athleticism showing the ability to create inside and outside the pocket to buy additional time.

Weaknesses: Lacks the ideal prototypical size for a QB and is a bit on the shorter side. Between his height and his arm trajectory, he gets a lot of balls batted down at the line of scrimmage. Needs to learn to alter his ball velocity depending on the situation, can be a little too carefree when needing to add velocity in tight situations. Needs to speed up his internal clock and decisiveness, taking far too long to go through progressions and find a target. Struggles seeing and accounting for the safety over the top pre-snap. Hesitates to utilize throwing across the middle of the field, a little too reliant on the sidelines and "safe" throws. His accuracy wanes tremendously when his receivers are running horizontal routes, failing to hit them in stride. Serious arm strength concerns, ball flutters in the air when throwing past 20 yards. 5th year senior who will be 23 in May.

Best Fit: Developmental QB who can progress to backup

Player Ranking (1-100): 71.4 – I like Minshew as a prospect and prefer him over Falk. I think he has more upside and a slightly stronger arm. Minshew absolutely has limitations but I don't think he has a noodle arm. Really good athlete who shows veteran poise. Might be a career backup, but has starter potential. 4th round player.

11. Tyree Jackson QB Buffalo 6'7 249 lbs

Strengths: Jackson is a 3-year starter who had a really good final season as a junior for the Bulls with over 3,000 yards passing and 28 touchdowns. Jackson possesses a huge frame, with outstanding size and length. Keeps his feet moving within the pocket, showing the ability to sidestep and create additional yardage behind the line of scrimmage. Jackson throws a terrific deep ball, showing beautiful touch and placement down the field, always giving his intended receiver an opportunity to catch the ball. Jackson isn't intimidated by narrow windows, throwing the ball with tight zip and velocity in contested situations. An effective thrower on the move going to both the right and the left, showing good accuracy when forced off his spot. Shows the ability to alter his arm trajectory on different types of routes. A good functional athlete who moves when he needs to both in and out of the pocket, rarely relies on his feet. A big, tough guy who will refuse to go down easily in the pocket, fighting through tacklers.

Weaknesses: Has only played in 1 full season, missing a number of games during the earlier part of his career, due to nagging injury concerns. A simple 1-read offense where he almost always throws to the 1st intended target. Jackson plays in a run-first offense, where he wasn't relied upon heavily in the passing game. Locks on his intended target the entire snap, making it easy for safeties and linebackers to cheat to one side of the field. Has had accuracy concerns throughout college, only completing 55% of his balls this past season. An erratic passer who shows good accuracy on short throws as well as deep balls, but when asked to throw the intermediate routes, his ball placement and timing is all over the place.

Best Fit: Developmental QB

Player Ranking (1-100): 70.1 – Jackson is an upside player. He reminds me quite a bit of Cardale Jones a few years ago. A big, strong guy who has RARE arm talent and is a good functional athlete. The problem is, he's very raw. He needs continued refinement with his passing mechanics and footwork. His accuracy is so hit or miss and can go long stretches while making very few accurate passes in games. My guess is he's going to need at least 2 more years of development with a good quarterback coach. There are certainly some traits to work with, and teams will absolutely like his upside. I wouldn't feel comfortable taking him until the 4th round.

12. Clayton Thorson QB Northwestern 6'4 225 lbs

Strengths: Thorson has prototypical size for an NFL QB, showcasing a tough and durable build. Thorson is an above average athlete, showcasing good footwork and athleticism to extend plays and even run for TDs. Thorson shows veteran pocket movements and awareness and poise in the pocket. Thorson understands ball placement and puts the balls in good locations especially on short to medium routes. Thorson is a highly intelligent guy, both on and off the field. He has a good understanding of defenses and shows an ability to read and react promptly. Shows the ability to make NFL throws, throwing timing routes and tough, contested balls to the center of the field. Thorson shows the durability to take punishment, scrambling or in the pocket. He's wired well with outstanding work habits and a very unselfish attitude. Has led Northwestern to many big-time wins in his career, including against top 25 teams where he's carried the team on his back in overtime.

Weaknesses: Thorson is a bit of 'above-average' at almost every aspect of the game, but not great at anything. His delivery is elongated and it takes him a bit to get rid of the football. His arm strength is adequate, but not elite. His down the field accuracy isn't great, and he rarely tests the back half of a defense. He's a safe QB who rarely takes risks throwing the ball down the field. Thorson tore his ACL in the bowl game during his junior season but recovered quickly to play in his senior season. Questionable decision maker, frequently throwing the ball into double coverage.

Best Fit: Backup NFL QB

Player Ranking (1-100): 68.5 – Thorson is a career backup QB at the next level. He makes his living on dink and dunks. I think he can be a solid backup QB, but he doesn't have the "traits" to get scouts excited about his long-term growth or his ceiling. I wouldn't take him until the 5th round.

13. Jake Browning QB Washington 6'2 210 lbs

Strengths: Browning is an impressive pro-style senior QB who has started all 4 years at Washington. In each of his 4 seasons, he has thrown for over 62% completion percentage. Browning is a smart kid who reads the game very well, both pre-snap and after the snap. Shows good footwork within the pocket, shuffling and sliding horizontally to create that extra second. Reads and processes things very quickly, and is a known film-room junkie who works very hard on his craft. Similar to Mayfield last year, Browning is the definition of a hard worker. He plays with incredible swagger and competitiveness that is unparalleled. Makes very few bad mistakes, and when he does, he usually rebounds quickly not making another major mistake throughout the rest of the game. Patient thrower, waiting to go through his progressions before settling on a target.

Weaknesses: Had 2017 shoulder surgery during the offseason but showed no ill-effects from it. The offense is based around simple 1-read throws, many of them being screens and short routes. Rushes throws when the pocket collapses, leading to some poor interceptions. Has a bad habit of allowing the ball to float in the air and lob it up hoping his receiver makes the play. Very average arm strength, failing to fit the ball into tight windows or have the necessary velocity to get the ball on time. Holds on to the ball far too long, leading to way too many unnecessary coverage sacks. Loses accuracy when having to move off his spot. Telegraphs his throws, locking his eyes onto his intended target. A very average athlete who hesitates to run when given space. Struggles in 3rd and long situations, tending to play it safe and hope his receiver get can extra yards after contact. Lacks ideal QB size and is a bit small and lanky.

Best Fit: Backup QB

Player Ranking (1-100): 66.2 – A solid QB but likely won't be anything other than a backup at the next level. Competitive and tough, but lacks the necessary passing fundamentals to be a success as a starter. 5th round player.

14. Easton Stick QB North Dakota State 6'2 221 lbs

Strengths: Stick is a 4-year starter who took over during his freshman campaign after Carson Wentz' injury, and has greatly impressed during all 4 seasons with the Bisons. The definition of reliable, he hasn't missed a start, posting some outstanding production with 88 touchdowns and 28 interceptions. The first thing you'll notice with Stick is he's an outstanding athlete who can create, showing tremendous escapability both inside and outside the pocket. Once in the open-field, Stick shows quick feet and shiftiness to make guys miss, resulting in additional yardage. Stick plays in a pro-style system where he has experience taking the ball under center. Stick is a gunslinger who is fearless throwing the deep ball, placing the ball in good spots to allow his receivers the opportunity to make a play on the ball. Smart and disciplined, Stick understands when to throw the ball away or when to tuck the ball and run. Outstanding at utilizing pump/head fakes to sell routes and create spacing downfield for his receivers. Keeps his eyes down the field at all times, rarely locking eyes with the first intended target.

Weaknesses: Holds onto the football far too long, taking some unnecessary sacks. Questionable decision maker who routinely floats the ball into the air, hoping for the best. Has not competed against top-flight competition and when he did in the East/West Shrine game in January, he really struggled. Arm strength overall is average, lacking the necessary zip to fit the ball into tight windows. Underthrows and throws behind intended targets quite frequently.

When running, Stick is complacent with the football, leading to some fumbles.

Best Fit: Backup QB

Player Ranking (1-100): 60.1 – There are traits to work with in Stick. He impressed me in a number of throws he made at the college level. Granted, he wasn't competing against top-flight competition but he doesn't possess a noodle arm. And he's a really good overall athlete with decent size. He won't impress in open air workouts with his throwing ability, but there's upside here as a player. 6th round player.

15. Nick Fitzgerald QB Mississippi State 6'5 230 lbs

Strengths: Fitzgerald is a 3-year starter for Mississippi State and has had a really impressive college career. Fitzgerald is a big, sturdy and powerful kid who has the ideal next-level QB body frame with broad shoulders. He's a 2-way threat with outstanding rushing ability, running for over 3,000 yards in his career breaking SEC rushing records for a QB. Really impressive athlete showing outstanding game-breaking speed and open field ability. Tough kid who shows all the intangibles and toughness of a leader. Will battle and fight on every play of the game. Despite playing in a college-spread offensive system, he still shows the ability to look off targets and go through his progressions rarely getting fixated on the 1st option. Not afraid to stand tall in the pocket, showcasing the durability to take punishment.

Weaknesses: Fitzgerald is a more athletic Tim Tebow. His passing mechanics are severely flawed and his accuracy is all over the place, resulting in completion percentages around 50% each season. Has a bad habit of releasing the ball on his heels, causing too much float in the air. Rarely puts the ball in the numbers for a receiver, the receiver almost always has to adjust to his throws.

Best Fit: Backup QB, Special Teams' Player

Player Ranking (1-100): 57.4 – 7th round player. Fitzgerald is the definition of a college football player. I don't see his game translating to the next level. He absolutely can compete for a backup QB spot and play some special teams for an NFL team.

16. Trace McSorley QB Penn State 6'0 200 lbs

Strengths: McSorley is a 3-year starter for the Nittany Lions who has proven to be a BIG game QB, playing some of his best games in the bowl games and against other Big-Ten rivals. Really good athlete showing an ability to run and create while on the move. Also shows that he can be moved and potentially be used as a receiver at the next level if teams desire. Really impressive TD to INT numbers in each of his seasons as the starter. Has shown improvement in his accuracy during each of his seasons at Penn State. Comfortable downfield passer showing impressive touch placing the ball in a spot where only his receiver can make a play on the ball. Impressive in his ability to feel the blitz and create an escape plan for himself to buy more time. Effective when escaping to his right or left side and throwing accurately on the move. Quick release, gets rid of the ball rapidly.

Weaknesses: Undersized QB who lacks the prototypical size teams want in a QB. Erratic footwork, he rarely sets his feet, frequently adding unnecessary steps between his set-up and his release causing inaccuracies. Always tries to get outside the pocket, refusing to attempt to win from inside the pocket. Very average arm, choosing to play the dink/dunk game.

Best Fit: Backup QB or Developmental WR

Player Ranking (1-100): 54.3 – A good athlete who lacks the basic fundamental skills and size to play QB at the next level. I would imagine he will transition to WR at the next level due to his athleticism and movement skills. He's an undrafted free agent.

17. Taryn Christion QB South Dakota State 6'1 225 lbs

Strengths: Christion is a 4-year starter for South Dakota State who has really impressed at the FCS level, putting up 100 touchdowns to only 32 interceptions. Outstanding athlete who shows the ability to tuck the ball and run. Good ball handler showing the ability to create spacing for his receivers down the field by utilizing head/pump/ball fakes. Impressive in his ability to throw accurately on the move. Tough kid who shows the willingness to take a beating and put his pads into a defender. Understands how to utilize his eyes, rarely locking onto the first target and keeping his vision downfield at all times.

Weaknesses: Poor internal clock and lacks great pocket awareness, failing to feel the pressure around him. Doesn't always set his feet when throwing, which leads to severe inaccuracies. Saw a major drop in production after Wieneke and Dallas Goedert left in his senior season. Competed against FCS competition, will be a big jump up for him at the next level. Gets into 'FLIGHT' mode too quickly, always looking to ditch the pocket and utilize his feet. Lacks a great live arm, with just a marginal throwing arm with poor mechanics. Footwork is either completely stationary or "happy" with no in-between. Panics when under pressure.

Best Fit: Developmental QB

Player Ranking (1-100): 52.1 – Christion is a developmental type of prospect who lacks any great traits other than his athleticism. He will likely be an undrafted free agent, in hopes of having some backup ability.

QB Top-10 Rankings
1. Drew Lock
2. Kyler Murray
3. Dwayne Haskins
4. Daniel Jones
5. Ryan Finley
6. Jarrett Stidham

7. Will Grier
8. Jordan Ta'amu
9. Brett Rypien
10. Gardner Minshew

Chapter 3

RB's

1. Josh Jacobs RB Alabama 5'10 216 lbs

Strengths: Jacobs is a 3-year contributor for the Tide who has never been the primary bell-cow back, but has been given significant snaps since his freshman season. Built with a power-packed frame, he has continually added muscle, weight, and strength each season without sacrificing his explosive makeup. He's also the teams' primary kick return specialist, showing excellent return ability, returning one for a touchdown this season. Jacobs is one of the best creators I've seen as a back, showing outstanding feet and agility, with the ability to consistently create something out of nothing. He utilizes explosive hips to generate the outstanding change of direction with his jump-cut ability. Not simply a 'speed back,' Jacobs is physical and tough! He routinely runs behind his pads, delivering powerful blows to tacklers, rarely going down in head-on collisions. Shows patience behind the line of scrimmage, quickly scanning for openings, and then waiting for just the perfect time to explode through. Routinely hits the hole with conviction, dropping his pads, planting his feet and exploding. Possesses the vision to almost always pick the right opening. Does a nice job of minimizing his surface area through contact, keeping his pads down? Really good contact balance, quickly regaining momentum and getting back to top-gear. Jacobs is a dual-threat back with tremendous upside as a receiver, reminiscent of Alvin Kamara. Possesses experience in running routes, reliable hands, and yards after catch ability. Was a rotational back at Alabama, meaning he doesn't have a lot of wear and tear on his frame in comparison to most other Alabama backs that have come out.

Weaknesses: Needs to show better awareness against ankle swipers, far too often goes down by simple ankle tackles at the 2nd level. Has never been relied upon as the primary back to carry the load. Has very little experience in pass protection, Alabama used their other backs when they needed someone to pass protect. Had some nagging hamstring issues early on in his career.

Best Fit: Zone-blocking scheme to utilize his vision/movement

Player Ranking (1-100): 89.1 – Jacobs is a tremendous talent and the best back in this draft class. I've seen countless runs on film where he literally has 3 guys on him, and somehow, he gets out of it to create extra yardage for himself. He's a rare combination of size, strength, physicality, explosiveness, receiving ability and special teams return experience. The only real "knock" on him is that he has little experience in pass protection, and will likely need some time to develop in that arena. But in most instances, due to his receiving ability, he won't be needed much as a pass protector, similarly to Alvin Kamara. I can see teams and scouts being leery of him due to the fact that he was never relied upon heavily, and was simply a change of pace back who took advantage of tired defenses. But they shouldn't be, Jacobs is a stud. 1st round player.

2. David Montgomery RB Iowa State 5'11 216 lbs

Strengths: Montgomery is a 2-year starter who has had tremendous production in each of the last 2 seasons with over 1100 yards rushing in each season and 24 touchdowns combined. Montgomery has also greatly impressed in the receiving game with 71 catches combined, showing his versatility and 3-down ability. As a receiver, Montgomery shows ball tracking skills with the ability to adjust to poorly thrown balls. Montgomery is a physical specimen, built with thick limbs and a mature man's physique. A determined runner who shows competitiveness and fight, finishing runs and showing the forward lean to pick up short yardage runs. Outstanding after contact, Montgomery is one of the most elusive and shiftiest backs in this class. Montgomery runs balanced, keeping a lower center of gravity, showing the ability to escape tackle attempts. Senses his surroundings well, anticipating spacing in his runs at all levels. Quick-footed athlete who gets to top speed in an instant, showing very good acceleration. Montgomery follows his blocks, hitting holes with conviction, wasting very little movement. Displays the fluidity and movement skills to easily change direction without losing any built-up speed. Has outstanding start/stop quickness to smoothly and easily redirect and regain momentum. A willing blocker who shows good awareness and recognition skills.

Weaknesses: Despite his compact size, Montgomery isn't exactly a physical finisher who delivers punishment upon contact. Reliant on his jump cutting ability and quickness then utilizing his lower body drive to push piles forward. Tries to do too much on every snap, very often getting caught in the backfield. Lacks a 5th gear to be able to take it to the house. Needs to learn how to utilize and engage his lower body as well as his hands in pass protection failing to reliably anchor. Played against weaker Big 12 run defenses, where he often got to the 2nd level before he was even touched. Inconsistent hands, having some poor concentration lapses while the ball is in-flight.

Best Fit: Zone-blocking scheme

Player Ranking (1-100): 81.4 – Montgomery is a really good runner who shows excellent explosion and quickness. His ability to make guys miss both at the line of scrimmage and at the 2nd level is tremendous. He offers upside as a receiver as well, showing good routes and separation quickness. I believe he will get better as a pass protector with more experience. He will be a really good starting back at the next level and should be a 2nd round pick.

3. Devin Singletary RB Florida Atlantic 5'9 200 lbs

Strengths: Singletary is a 3-year starter for Conference-USA program Florida Atlantic. Production-wise, very few runners have reached the levels of Singletary, rushing for over 4200 yards and 66 touchdowns the last 3 seasons. Singletary is still young and will be 21 years old for the NFL draft. Built with a compact build and low center of gravity, Singletary utilizes his natural leverage advantage to bounce of tacklers, rarely going down to the 1st guy. His contact balance is rare, staying on his feet through traffic and somehow, someway still on his feet. A quick-footed athlete who shows terrific open-field ability, almost always creating for himself and making defenders miss. Shifty and change of direction abilities are Singletary's forte, utilizing subtle jump cuts to redirect his frame. Has shown good games and success against big-time college programs. Really patient behind the line of scrimmage, scanning the openings and then digging in with his plant foot and exploding forward. While limited in opportunities, Singletary has shown upside and potential catching the ball out of the backfield with crisp, smooth routes. Don't let Singletary's size fool you, he's strong and he will break through uncommitted tackles with ease. He's also violent in space, showing physicality and a nasty stiff arm to gain additional yardage.

Weaknesses: Singletary has a small frame and will be exposed if he's asked to do significant damage between the hashes. He is too reliant on bouncing his runs to the outside to utilize his quickness and burst to beat tacklers to the edges. When used in pass protection, Singletary's lack of size and blocking ability is noticeable, and he's a liability at this point. Attempts to do too much on every play, at times taking negative yardage. Quick but not especially fast and lacks the necessary long speed to be a 'take it to the house' kind of back

Best Fit: Zone-blocking scheme RB

Player Ranking (1-100): 80.1 – In an ideal world, Singletary should be a complementary back to an elite # 1. He's not a bell cow and will struggle if asked to handle short-yardage situations or be used in pass protection at this point. But Singletary is an extremely good football player who possesses rare contact balance and open-field ability. He's going to be a dynamic offensive weapon who hopefully will get drafted by a smart and creative offensive mind. He's a chess piece who can afford an offensive coach a lot of really great tactical options. At the very least, he should be getting 10-15 touches a game. Late 2nd round player.

4. Trayveon Williams RB Texas A&M 5'9 200 lbs

Strengths: Williams is a 3-year contributor for the Aggies who has practically started every game of his career. He had a phenomenal final season as a junior with 1760 yards rushing and 18 touchdowns. Williams plays far bigger and tougher than his size would indicate. Solid and tenacious in pass protection, Williams shows the ability to utilize solid leverage, to anchor his body and completely stop blitzers dead in their tracks delivering good POP in his hands. Minimizes his surface area through traffic, showing good contact balance to get through tiny little creases. A direct runner, who plants his foot and gets upfield in a flash, wasting very little motion. Williams is an explosive, game-changing back who shows outstanding short-area bursts in addition to the long speed to take it to the house. An excellent and experienced dual-threat back with very good receiving abilities, running solid routes and good hands. Williams has tremendous instincts and reads situations very quickly, understanding when to stay in to assist in pass protection or to quickly get in the flat to bail his QB out.

Weaknesses: The debate will be if Williams has a big enough frame for the next level. I tend to think he lacks adequate ideal body armor to be a consistent hammer for most offensive systems which will require him to run between the tackles. Fails to deliver any kind of movement in short-yardage situations, lacking necessary leg drive. His running ability is minimized as an inside runner, failing to have the power to fight through contact, relying on his quickness/shiftiness at all levels. Not a fall forward guy, generally goes down pretty easily in head-on collisions. Has had some ball security concerns during his career.

Best Fit: Change of pace back who should touch the ball 10-15 times a game

Player Ranking (1-100): 79.2 – Williams is one of my favorite backs in this class who offers tremendous 3rd down upside. It's rare to see a guy as small as Williams who is as good in pass protection as Williams is. Williams routinely picked up blitzes, anchoring and hunkering down against SEC defenses. In addition to his pass protection, his receiving abilities are excellent as well. He shows tremendous versatility and dual-threat ability with his explosiveness and athleticism. While his pure running ability is good, he's a bit too reliant on kicking his runs to the outside and lacks true 'in-between the tackles' experience to be an effective 20+ carry a game guy. 3rd round player.

5. Damien Harris RB Alabama 5'11 220 lbs

Strengths: Harris is a 3-year contributor for the Tide who displays a well-built frame and compactness with outstanding strength throughout his body. Brings a real punch to the table, especially between the tackles where he brushes aside tacklers like they aren't even there. Strong hands that show reliability in ball security with 0 career fumbles lost. Harris plays with outstanding contact balance showing the ability to stay on his feet after impact. Plays with a low center of gravity keeping himself skinny through narrow and quickly closing windows. Has shown some improvement in his ability to protect the QB throughout his career. Harris constantly bounces off tackles and gets 6-8 yards in a blink of an eye, even when it appears nothing was open. Rarely gets stopped in the backfield, showing the ability to keep his legs moving at all times. North/south runner who really runs behind his pads, keeping his body low and square and delivering powerful blows to tacklers. Shows potential in pass receiving when given opportunities, utilizing soft hands and the ability to pluck the ball away from his frame. Gets the majority of his yardage by running between the tackles and not reliant on winning outside the hashes. Plays with outstanding vision, showing the ability to see things quickly before they happen.

Weaknesses: Harris is a north/south back who has little experience in attacking the outside edges. Erratic pass protector who needs to continue to improve, preferring to deliver a big blow rather than anchor and sustain for the duration of a play. Had one of the best offensive lines in football. A bit of a disappointing senior campaign where his numbers and production were down. Good speed, but lacks the true game-changing speed to affect a game every time he touches the ball.

Best Fit: Power back in a man-blocking run system

Player Ranking (1-100): 79.1 – Harris is a good back who will never WOW anyone but will be consistent and a constant chains mover for an offense. 3rd round player.

6. Justice Hill RB Oklahoma State 5'10 185 lbs

Strengths: Hill is a tremendously talented and explosive back who had a stellar college career with over 3500 yards rushing. A lean and muscular physique that shows surprising power and toughness throughout his frame. Rarely goes down upon the first contact, Hill competes at all levels of the game. An impressive pass protector, Hill shows the ability to sink his hips and absorb contact rarely getting pushed back. As a runner, Hill shows tremendous initial quickness, exploding off the ball and quickly running through closing windows. Shows the coordinated feet to start, stop and redirect quickly. An elusive athlete who can make defenders miss in a phone booth. Outstanding body control and instincts in his jump cuts to create. Hill isn't a typical 'scat' back where he's limited to outside zone runs or tosses, he's effective when used inside as well. He shows fluidity and agility in his hips, crossing the field with ease. Displays patience and field vision, waiting for the right hole and then hits it with conviction.

Weaknesses: Been some concerns and reports about Hill's maturity. A very slight runner who possesses a very lean physique making him prone to injuries as was evidenced in his injury to his ribs, causing him to miss the last few games of his junior year. Lacks the lower body power or drive to push piles forward or be effective in short-yardage situations. Despite having receiver traits, Hill has had some struggles catching the football. Hill has a lot of wear and tear on his body, carrying the load the last 3 seasons.

Best Fit: Zone-scheme

Player Ranking (1-100): 78.8 – Hill is a change-of-pace back but holds added value as a receiving back as well. I wouldn't hesitate using him in pass protection either despite his smaller frame. He could definitely handle 15 touches a game, and will absolutely make defenses pay. Love this kid, as long as his maturity isn't a major concern for teams during the interview process. 3rd round player.

7. Darrell Henderson RB Memphis 5'9 200 lbs

Strengths: Henderson is a smaller, but compactly-built runner that finished 10th in the Heisman this year. Henderson had an absolutely ridiculous season with 1900 yards rushing and 25 touchdowns this past season. Henderson reminds me quite a bit of Dalvin Cook. Possessing outstanding start/stop quickness, Henderson quickly goes from 0-60 upon the snap of the ball. His fluid hips, agility and coordinated feet allow him to cross-field with ease without losing any built-up speed. Keeps himself really small through contact, playing with a low center of gravity. This allows him to limit his surface area making it extremely difficult for defenders to get 2 hands on him. Henderson is an outstanding athlete with tremendous lower body explosiveness, utilizing jump cuts in the open field to create. One of the best open-field runners you'll see, showing tremendous shiftiness and change of direction. Plays tougher than his size indicates, running behind his pads and running over defenders. Shows a real eagerness and toughness when used in pass protection. A plus receiver who shows good routes and the ability to separate.

Weaknesses: Henderson didn't compete against top-tier competition or defenses in college. A smaller back who lacks ideal body armor to be a bell-cow in most offensive systems. Comes from a spread system where his runs were often manufactured preventing him from utilizing his eyes. Not a dirty yards runner who will pick up or be effective in short-yardage situations.

Best Fit: Zone-system

Player Ranking (1-100): 77.3 – Saying Henderson is a scat-back is vastly underestimating his abilities. He's a tremendous athlete who shows traits to be effective on all 3-downs. A perfect target in today's NFL who can be the next great Alvin Kamara and influence multiple aspects of the offense. 3rd round player.

8. Jalin Moore RB Appalachian State 5'11 205 lbs

Strengths: Moore is an outstanding back for App State who has had tremendous production in his career with over 3500 rushing yards and 33 rushing touchdowns. Willing blocker who shows toughness, fearlessness, and awareness pre-snap maintaining a strong anchor and delivering powerful blows to oncoming blitzers. Maintains a low center of gravity and balance through impact, limiting his surface area for defenders. Despite being a small-school guy, Moore had some success against Top-25 defenses. Dangerous with the ball in his hands at 2nd level, showing a knack for creating for himself with his shiftiness. A tough kid who will fight and battle to pick up additional yardage. When used in the receiving game, shows reliable hands, snatching the ball out of the air. A elusive guy who can create for himself, he makes it extremely difficult for defenders to get 2 hands on him. An agile guy who displays the fluidity in his hips to cross field and change directions with ease. A team leader who is known to hold his teammates accountable.

Weaknesses: Fractured and dislocated his ankle on October 9th causing him to miss most of his senior season. Has had some other minor injury concerns, suffering some ankle and foot issues in 2017. Limited production as a receiver with less than 200 career receiving yards in his career. Tries to do too much at times with the ball in his hands, having some bad negative yardage plays. Quick from 0-10, but lacks the deep speed and will occasionally get caught from behind in open-field scenarios.

Best Fit: Any offensive system

Player Ranking (1-100): 77.0 – One of my favorite players in the whole draft. He's a complete running back who can do everything well. Impressed by how well he held up in pass protection. He will continue to get better with coaching at the next level. Only concerns are his injury history and the fact that he isn't a take it to the house runner. 3rd round player.

9. Myles Gaskin RB Washington 5'10 192 lbs

Strengths: Gaskin is a low center of gravity back for the Huskies with very little body fat and a tapered midsection. A 4-year starter for the Huskies who has had tremendous production in each season. He's the definition of elusive, showing the ability to make guys miss in a phone booth with explosive jump cuts and shiftiness at all areas of the field. He does a tremendous job of keeping his balance upon contact, rarely going down to the first guy around him. His agility and short-area quickness are 2nd to none in this class, making him such a hard guy to get 2 hands on. Uses his vision nicely, following his blockers and taking what the defense gives him. Outstanding anticipation abilities, sensing his surroundings well and anticipating spacing quickly. Very direct with little-wasted movement. Aggressive and willing in pass protect, showing good effort and toughness when being used to hold up. Keeps his body low and utilizes a wide base to sustain blocks. Has a real nose for the end zone, and will find a way to get there when you least expect it.

Weaknesses: Gaskin lacks an ideal starting running back frame without the necessary body armor to hold up through the duration of an NFL season. Despite his toughness as a pass protector, he lacks suitable girth and lower-body anchor to sustain at the next level. He's a quick runner, not necessarily fast and is generally a 1-speed runner who doesn't have the ability to switch on another gear. Wins more with effort than he does power, and lacks a punch with the ball in his hands to deliver blows. Despite his athletic ability, he hasn't really caught the ball much in the Huskies offense. Some inopportune drops when going out in the flat. Good senior season, but production dropped off a bit from his previous 2 seasons.

Best Fit: Zone-blocking scheme

Player Ranking (1-100): 76.6 – Gaskin is a very good and valuable player in today's NFL, showing the quickness, toughness and overall movement skills to succeed in 15-20 offensive snaps a game. He needs to continue getting stronger, but he's a talented runner who won't be a bell cow, but more of a change-of-pace back who can be more than simply a #2 back for a team. A good offensive coach will make good use of his overall abilities. He should be taken somewhere in the 3rd round.

10. Jordan Scarlett RB Florida 5'11 210 lbs

Strengths: Scarlett is a 2-year starter and a 3-year contributor for the Gators who averaged just under 6 yards per carry this year. Scarlett is a compactly-built runner with outstanding lower-body strength. Scarlett is a hard-nosed back who shows toughness, lowering his pads always looking to deliver a hit. Scarlett possesses good contact balance, staying on his feet through contact, with an impressive ability to keep or regain his momentum quickly. Scarlett follows his blocks and runs with good pad level, keeping his center of gravity low through contact points. Utilizes good forward lean to always fall forward and pick up additional yardage. Scarlett is a decisive runner who does the majority of his damage between the hashes. Displays some impressive open-field ability, showing quick feet with loose hips to evade tacklers. A competitive runner who shows toughness and finishing ability, rarely allowing himself to get tackled for negative yardage. Excellent body control and instincts, showing the ability to anticipate spacing in his runs. Breaks ankle tackles with ease, easily shrugging them off. Outstanding vision, coupled with good initial acceleration out of his stance.

Weaknesses: Needs serious timing, technique, and awareness work as a blocker, failing to reliably see free rushers. Has improved as a receiver during his career, but still has some poor untimely drops where he has to catch the ball outside of his frame. Teams will need to look into him off the field, as he was suspended his entire sophomore season after credit card fraud charges.

Best Fit: Zone-blocking scheme

Player Ranking (1-100): 74.7 – Scarlett has really impressed me as a runner. If he checks out OK off the field during the interview process, then he should absolutely be drafted in the early part of Day 3. I believe he's a 4th round back and absolutely has NFL starting potential. Utilizing his vision and open-field ability, putting Scarlett in a zone-blocking offensive system would make the best use of his traits. Scarlett has very few concerns besides off the field issues and is truly an all-around back.

11. Bruce Anderson RB North Dakota State 5'11 209 lbs

Strengths: Anderson is a 4-year contributor for 3-time National Champion in the FCS, North Dakota State. Anderson has had outstanding production, running for over 2100 yards the last 2 seasons in addition to showing great production in the receiving game as well. Anderson was an outstanding kick off return guy his first 2 seasons, showing upside for the next level. Anderson is an explosive back who gets from 0-60 in a flash, showing terrific initial acceleration. Also shows the speed and the fluidity to beat linebackers to the edges, threatening both between the tackles and outside the hashes. Dynamic in the open-field showcasing his quick and shifty frame, fully utilizing his loose hips to change direction without gearing down. Good vision and decisiveness behind the line of scrimmage, picking the right hole and running behind his blockers. As a blocker, Anderson shows willingness and instincts, just needs more experience. Keeps his legs moving through impact. Maximizes his frame, showing terrific physicality for his size. Tremendous upside as a receiver, utilizing his soft hands to catch the ball and be effective once he receives the ball to do damage post-catch.

Weaknesses: While Anderson certainly maximizes his frame, he isn't exactly a power back, and fails to adequately deliver punishment to head-on tacklers. Struggles to push piles forward, lacking ideal forward lean. Had an offensive line that opened up mountain-sized holes, where he didn't make contact with a defender until the 2nd level. Overly reliant on bouncing runs to the outside edges. Played against FCS levels of competition. Would like to see him gain additional functional strength in his lower body to better sustain in pass protection.

Best Fit: Zone-style back

Player Ranking (1-100): 74.2 – Anderson is one of my favorite FCS prospects in this draft class. I was blown away by his film, and he has 3 or 4 runs in every game that made me go "WOW!" His explosive characteristics and his upside in the receiving game make me really love his potential. I wholeheartedly think he can be a starting running back in this league going forward. Maybe give him chances on special teams early on, and progressively give him carries. 4th round player.

12. Darwin Thompson RB Utah State 5'8 200 lbs

Strengths: Thompson is a community college transfer prior to transferring to Mountain West Utah State for 1 season. His 1 season was outstanding though, rushing for 1044 yards and 14 touchdowns and another 351 yards receiving with another 2 touchdowns. Don't let Thompson's lack of size fool you, he's incredibly strong and is known to be a work-out warrior on campus with ridiculous strength and power throughout his frame. Thompson never stops moving his legs through contact, getting good push and movement in traffic. Possesses rare contact balance, showing the ability to stay square, keep his pads down and remain on his feet through walls of traffic. An outstanding receiving option, showing strong hands to finish catches in heavy traffic. An explosive lower body, showing the ability to make quick jump cuts to make defenders miss in the open field. His lower body power allows him to carry defenders on his back for additional yards, refusing to go down easily and upon the first contact. Shows fluidity and looseness in his runs, with the ability to cross field without losing any built-up speed. An elusive athlete who can make defenders miss in tight spaces.

Weaknesses: A 1-year wonder who lacks much experience in college. Very little experience in pass protection, and was usually asked to run routes as a receiver in passing situations. Quicker than fast, lacks elite top-speed to take the top off the defense or threaten the back half. Struggled in games against upper-echelon defenses including Michigan State and Boise St this season. More of an elusive runner than a physical finisher upon contact.

Best Fit: Change of pace back

Player Ranking (1-100): 74.0 – Thompson is a tremendously powerful and explosive back. While he doesn't have great height or length, his quickness and explosive nature make him a solid receiving threat out of the backfield. Coupled with his ability to create and make the 1st defender miss, he could be a solid # 2 or change of pace back at the next level. I would feel comfortable taking him in the 4th round.

13. Elijah Holyfield RB Georgia 5'11 215 lbs

Strengths: Holyfield, the son of famous boxer Evander, really came onto the scene this year after a stellar junior season with over 1,000 yards and 7 touchdowns. Holyfield is a compactly-built bowling ball who shows good overall size and toughness. Holyfield consistently runs behind his pads, never stopping his feet upon contact, and showing real finishing ability. His best attribute is his full-field vision, showing an excellent ability to read/process things quickly. He then patiently awaits an opening and plants his foot in the grass and wastes little time or motion. He utilizes his explosive hips to jump-cut in the hole and evade while finding any tiny crease. Shows controlled athletic movements in the backfield. Quickly accelerates showing outstanding initial quickness. Solid lower-body strength, showing the ability to square his shoulders and widen his stance to anchor down when asked to pass protect.

Weaknesses: I've noticed that Holyfield goes down quite a bit to simple ankle tackles, failing to avoid them and getting tripped up rather easily. Very little experience in pass protection and in the receiving game at this point. A 1-season wonder that has only had 1 year of production. Was arrested prior to his sophomore season for multiple misdemeanor drug charges. Quick but not exceptionally fast, Holyfield lacks the 2nd gear.

Best Fit: Either offensive scheme

Player Ranking (1-100): 73.4 – I really like Holyfield as a runner. He had to back up Michel and Chubb in previous years and got very little experience or carries. But this year, he showed his true potential! He's an explosive back who shows good toughness and physicality as well. While his level of physicality is a bit inconsistent considering his size, Holyfield will get better and better. His explosive jump cuts to create for himself are outstanding! He almost always makes the 1st guy miss. He has true starting RB potential at the next level. He just needs to prove he can be a 3-down back since he has very little pass catching or pass blocking experience. 4th round player.

14. Bennie Snell Jr RB Kentucky 5'11 222 lbs

Strengths: Snell Jr is an incredibly productive college running back who dominated SEC competition for 3 straight years, running for over 1,000 yards in each year. Snell is a compactly-built guy who is an absolute load to have to handle at all levels. A punisher with the ball in his hands, Snell is always looking to lay the wood and commit defenders who want to tackle him. He's a direct runner who wastes little movement in the backfield. Snell does the majority of his damage between the hashes, where he utilizes good forward lean, leg drive and competitiveness to pick up the necessary yards in short yardage situations. As a pass protector, Snell is one of the best in the class showing 3-down value. Perfectly squaring his shoulders and anchoring his legs, he shows the lower body strength to absorb. Tough as nails runner who runs through arm tacklers. The best attribute of Snell's game is his ability to break tackles and pick up additional yardage after contact, showing tremendous competitiveness, concentration and toughness.

Weaknesses: Snell Jr is a slow-footed athlete who lacks the 2nd gear to be able to finish runs or to take runs to the house at the next level. A 'take what's given runner' who fails to have the shiftiness or creative ability to gain anything more then what's given. As a receiver, he shows limitations and is simply a last resort. Lacks the explosive lower body to quickly cross-field or be utilized on outside the hashes runs. Simply a power-blocking fit for a team. A 3-year starter that has a lot of wear and tear on his body getting beat up in the SEC.

Best Fit: Power or Man blocking system

Player Ranking (1-100): 72.0 – Snell Jr has had an excellent career against really good defenses. He lacks athletic components to be an elite #1 RB at the next level. But his pass protection ability and toughness will make him an attractive player for some teams. He's not going to light the world on fire as a starter but could be an excellent #2 for a team. 4th round player.

15. Rodney Anderson RB Oklahoma 6'1 220 lbs

Strengths: Anderson is a well-built and compact running back who displays the thickness in his limbs to play as a bell cow at the next level. He came onto the scene after impressing in his sophomore year with almost 1500 yards from scrimmage and 18 touchdowns. One of the most talented and intriguing talents in this draft class. Really loose-hipped athlete, he possesses outstanding movement and change of direction ability. Impressive balance to be able to keep or regain his momentum when crossing the field or cutting back. A solid receiving option with the strong hands to finish catches in traffic. A tough runner who shows the ability to drop his pads and move bodies picking up additional yardage. Excellent open-field skills creating extra yards in the open field with his cut-back ability and elusiveness.

Weaknesses: Anderson has only played 1 full season in college and has limited experience and game tape. Has had an injury-plagued career. Broke his leg his freshman year then had a neck injury the next year causing him to miss the entire season. And in his junior season he tore his ACL causing him to miss all but 2 games. Has benefited from Oklahoma's spread offense allowing him to play against lighter boxes and fewer defenders. Not a great pass protector, failing to even attempt at times. Needs technique and recognition work before he can even be considered as a reliable blocker. Not a power-back per se and can struggle in short yardage situations.

Best Fit: Starting RB if healthy

Player Ranking (1-100): 71.1 – I wouldn't feel comfortable taking Anderson until the 4th round. His ceiling is through the roof but he certainly has some flaws as a back. But his injury concerns are the most troubling thing for me. I can't take a guy in the first 100 picks that hasn't proven the ability to stay on the field.

16. Bryce Love RB Stanford 5'10 200 lbs

Strengths: Love is a small, athletically built back with a slim torso and little body fat. Despite being a smaller guy, Love is fearless in pass protection, showing the willingness, good instincts and the physicality required. Above average in pass protection, showing good technique and an ability to sustain rushers keeping his body low and square. Stronger than his size indicates, shows the ability to pick up short yardage 3rd and 4th downs by keeping his legs plowing and moving at all times and rarely going down easily. Will not get tackled in most instances by simple arm tackles. Patient runner who waits for the right time before exploding through the opening. Very shifty and nimble, utilizing outstanding footwork and subtle little body movements to keep defenders off his frame. A ridiculously productive guy who ran for an average of 164 rushing yards a game his junior campaign. Highly productive as a return guy for Stanford on both kickoffs and punt returns. One of the most explosive backs in the class, showing both outstanding short area quickness and deep long speed. Shows flexibility in his movements, displaying fluidity and loose hips which allow him to utilize jump cuts and spin moves to create openings in space.

Weaknesses: Lacks the experience in catching the ball out of the backfield as Stanford rarely uses him to catch the ball. Is that due to the system or that he can't do it? Above average in pass protection, but not always showing necessary awareness and power. Lacks ideal body armor to handle the rigors of the NFL level. A very disappointing senior campaign where he battled an ankle issue most of the season. Huge drop in his production went from 8.1 yards per carry (junior season) to 4.8. (senior season) Tore his ACL in the final game of his career in the bowl game. His ankle, ACL and injury history will be major concerns for teams.

Best Fit: Starting back if can stay injury free

Player Ranking (1-100): 70.9 – Love is a tremendously gifted back who is so explosive and difficult to deal with in the open field. The thing that is a bit concerning is that he doesn't catch many balls for a smaller back. But he possesses tremendous movement skills, vision, and production. If he didn't return for his senior season, he would likely have been a 1st round pick. Now with the ankle and ACL injuries, I wouldn't take him until the 4th round.

17. Tony Pollard RB Memphis 6'0 200 lbs

Strengths: Pollard is a hybrid RB/WR combination who has shown versatility and solid production for the last 3 years. As a runner, he averaged over 7 yards per carry and 6 touchdowns this past season. As a receiver, he added another 39 catches and 458 yards with 3 touchdowns. Pollard is one of the most dynamic return specialists in college football and has returned 7 kickoffs for touchdowns the last 3 seasons. The very definition of versatility, displaying success lined up all over, including as an outside receiver, slot receiver, or a running back. Pollard is dynamic in the open field, utilizing a variety of moves involving his explosive hips to smoothly and efficiently change direction. As a running back, he possesses the vision to see narrowing holes and explode through, utilizing his outstanding acceleration. Tremendous short-area bursts, showing suddenness and contact balance through the 1st level. Runs balanced with a low center of gravity to escape tackle attempts. As a receiver, Pollard's athleticism and explosive characteristics are evident in the way he smoothly gets downfield. A willing blocker who shows toughness and peskiness, generating some good torque and power from his lower body. An effective move blocker who does a nice job of making 2nd level contact.

Weaknesses: Lacks a clear position or identity as a football player, will need to be drafted by a coaching staff that has a plan to utilize his traits. If he plans on taking more snaps as a running back, he needs to add additional weight and muscle to his frame. Has the traits to be an effective route-runner but looks inexperienced, failing to see openings or how to operate and consistently run his routes. Struggles in head-on run situations, failing to have the lower body strength and power to deliver punishment upon impact. Despite his willingness, he gets overpowered in protection situations when he doesn't have build-up speed.

Best Fit: Versatile hybrid RB/WR

Player Ranking (1-100): 70.5 – There's certainly a role for a guy like Tony Pollard at the next level, someone who can be an effective receiver, as well as merit some carries as a runner. He's an explosive back with serious open-field ability. His agility and short-area explosion is top-notch and he will be an exciting NFL player. 4th round player.

18. Miles Sanders RB Penn State 5'11 215 lbs

Strengths: Sanders is a 1-year starter for the Nittany Lions who had a tremendous final season with just under 1300 yards rushing and 9 touchdowns. Sanders is built tough with a large, compactly-built frame. A finisher who lowers his shoulders upon impact delivering blows to head-on tacklers. A quick-footed guy who plays with some elusiveness down the field, showing good looseness with cut-and-acceleration skills. Didn't have a lot of production as a receiver, but he did line up quite a bit in the slot, showing some experience and soft hands when called upon. Outstanding suddenness and start/stop, displaying the ability to quickly redirect his frame and cross field. Excellent body control and instincts in his jump cuts with an explosive lower-half, showcasing the ability to create in space. Tremendous at fighting off ankle-tackles, routinely running through them like they aren't even there. A decisive runner who hits the hole with conviction.

Weaknesses: Sanders is a bit of a 1-year wonder who got his first chance to start this past season after Saquon Barkley left for the NFL. Reliant on bouncing his runs to the outside to pick up yardage. A backward runner who tends to run horizontally rather than vertically behind the line of scrimmage. Far too often, Sanders delivers shoulder bumps in pass protection, rather than utilizing solid fundamentals and anchoring with his lower half. Quicker than fast, Sanders lacks the second gear speed to pull away. Quite a few times this year he had nothing but green in front of him, but he ran out of bounds.

DTP's 2019 NFL DRAFT GUIDE

Best Fit: Any offensive scheme

Player Ranking (1-100): 70.0 – Sanders is a solid runner who will be a good all-around back at the next level. While he isn't a top-notch athlete, he's a solid back who is built with toughness and will have an impact on 10-15 snaps a game as a rookie. He's a liability at this point in pass protection, but he can help spell a primary bell-cow runner for a team. 4th round player.

19. Dexter Williams RB Notre Dame 5'11 215 lbs

Strengths: A 4-year contributor for the Fighting Irish who finally got his chance to start full-time this year. He didn't disappoint with 941 yards rushing and 12 touchdowns, averaging 6.6 yards per carry. Williams is a between the tackles 1-cut runner. He's a chain-moving running back who utilizes his outstanding patience to wait for a tiny crease to open. Once he finds that crease, he utilizes his explosive nature to quickly explode through it. Utilizes his forward lean upon contact to always push forward, rarely getting pushed backward. Maintains good leverage and contact balance through contact, staying on his feet. Good vision and knows when to kick his runs outside or when to take what's given through the hashes. Impressive long-speed that shows the ability to take it to the house without getting caught from behind. An agile guy who plays with controlled and athletic movements in the backfield wasting very little time.

Weaknesses: Received a 4 game suspension after getting arrested for marijuana possession. A complete liability in pass protection, he needs major technique and recognition work before he can be relied upon as a blocker. Far too often goes down upon the first contact, allowing simple ankle tackles to bring him down consistently. Doesn't play with the physicality or deliver the punishment you would expect for a guy of his size. Limited experience as a receiver. Has no 3rd down or passing value.

Best Fit: Zone-system

Player Ranking (1-100): 69.7 – I really like Williams as a pure runner. If he wasn't such a liability in pass protection and offered some upside as a receiver, he would be a Day 2 selection. But because he offers little 3rd down upside, he should be a 5th round pick. He's a really good athlete with good size, vision, and patience.

20. Travis Homer RB Miami 5'11 195 lbs

Strengths: Homer is a 2-year starter for the Hurricanes who has posted almost identical numbers statistically in each season with just under 1,000 yards rushing in each. Homer is a 3-down threat with dual-purpose abilities as a pass catcher. A solid receiver who shows impressive movement skills, route-running ability, and soft hands out of the backfield, notching around 200 yards receiving in each season. Offers some additional upside as a return guy, has experience doing it. As a pass protector, Homer shows toughness and competitiveness, quickly recognizing things pre-snap. Homer is at his best in the open-field showing the ability to flash a 2nd gear and threaten the back half of a defense. He shows the change of direction abilities and the elusiveness to make defenders miss in a phone booth. Keeps his pad level down through contact, running hard, keeping his feet moving at all times. A quick-twitch guy who not only shows the 0-60 acceleration abilities but also shows the long-speed to take runs to the house. Despite being undersized, Homer shows better than expected toughness as a runner.

Weaknesses: Homer is not a power back and fails to be able to break many tackles, far too often going down to the first contact. Lacks adequate size and body frame to be an every-down back at the next level. Fails to deliver any kind of physical finishes at contact and lacks the lower body explosiveness to push piles forward. Homer is overly reliant on bouncing his runs outside the hashes, attempting to utilize the sidelines. As a pass protector, Homer is a major liability at this time, lacking anchoring skills to sustain blocks, keeping his frame far too upright. Despite Homer's receiving ability, he still has some very inconsistent hands, sometimes leading to some really poor drops.

Best Fit: Change of pace back

Player Ranking (1-100): 69.3 – I like Homer and he's a great combination of size, speed, elusiveness, vision, and versatility. He's not truly a great 'between the hashes' runner, he's a guy that offers upside as a receiving back, presenting true 3-down potential. He's a 5th round player because I'm not completely sold on his pure running ability. Fails to blow me away, frequently getting easily tackled and taken down by the 1st defender who makes contact with him. 5th round player.

21. Alexander Mattison RB Boise State 511 211 lbs

Strengths: Mattison is a well-built and compact back with monstrous legs who has had 2 tremendous years of production. His final season as a junior he rushed for over 1400 yards and 17 touchdowns. Impressive when used this year in the receiving game, showing to be a reliable target with good soft hands. Gets from 0-60 really quickly, showing good acceleration with little-wasted movement in the backfield. Hits the hole with conviction, following his blocks. Shows some explosiveness in his legs with jump-cut ability, rarely losing any built-up speed. Really good contact balance, showing the knack for staying on his feet and regaining his momentum quickly. A physical finisher at contact who lowers his shoulders and punishes defenders. Has the good vision to identify openings immediately and makes quick decisions. Shows good awareness as a pass protector, quickly identifying blitzers.

Weaknesses: A liability at this point in pass protection, tending to go for a knockout block rather than actually sustaining through contact. Immediately loses speed when kicking his runs outside the hashes. Quicker than fast, lacks the 2nd gear ability to take runs to the house. At his best at the 1st level, failing to have any kind of ability in space to create for himself or pick up additional yardage. Doesn't always play with the physicality and power you would expect for a compactly-built guy like Mattison.

Best Fit: Zone-style runner who would fit in best as a change of pace guy

Player Ranking (1-100): 68.9 – Mattison is a solid runner who would be an outstanding change of pace back at the next level. He has the size and frame NFL teams love. He's a direct back who shows decisiveness and gets what's given by his blockers. I would take him in the 5th round.

22. Alex Barnes RB Kansas State 6'1 227 lbs

Strengths: Barnes is a 4th year junior who had a tremendous final season with Kansas State with 1355 yards and 12 touchdowns. Built with prototypical next-level size, Barnes possesses suitable body armor. As a runner, Barnes possesses impressive contact balance, showing the ability to follow blocks and run though narrow spaces with conviction. A tough runner who displays tremendous upper-body strength to finish plays. Also displays the lower-body explosion to push piles forward. Runs with a violent streak at the 2nd level, utilizing an impressive stiff arm to fend off tacklers. Better athlete than you would expect for a guy his size, showing break away speed and impressive stop/start quickness. An agile guy who shows the ability to cross field and change direction without losing much built-up speed. Senses his surrounding well, showing good vision in open-field situations.

Weaknesses: Inconsistent decision maker that shows some hesitancy when there isn't a large lane to run through at the line of scrimmage. Despite his good balance, he leaves too much of his frame upright and exposed through contact. Needs to utilize his size and power more against smaller defensive backs, losing his balance easily to ankle tacklers. Far too passive in pass protection situations and needs technique and recognition work before he is considered reliable. Far too often doesn't run behind his pads.

Best Fit: Versatile and can play in any offensive scheme

Player Ranking (1-100): 68.3 – A good player who has a chance to compete as a #2 back immediately for a team. Possesses the size, athletic abilities and power teams covet, I'm just not of the viewpoint that he is a starting NFL quality back. 5th round.

23. LJ Scott RB Michigan State 6'1 230 lbs

Strengths: Scott is a filled out and compactly built guy who displays a power-packed frame. Scott is a physical guy who is a real finisher, picking up quite a few yards after impact. Keeps his pads down and looks like a hammer in search of a nail that is just waiting to deliver punishment to a tackler. Shows a surprising amount of speed and athletic ability despite his size. Shows nice patience in waiting for a hole to open up and then exploding through it. Flashes the 5th gear once he hits the 2nd level. Possesses the ability to blow through arm tackles and ankle swipers. Has the power and the bruising style that wears out defenses over the course of a game. Runs balanced, keeping a low center of gravity to escape attempted tackles. When given a chance to run routes or catch the ball, he shows reliability with soft hands.

Weaknesses: Scott has had off the field concerns with 7 arrests due to a suspended license. Scott poses little threat as a receiver with very minimal receptions during his career. Has had some ball security concerns, losing the ball at inopportune times. Had a great 2016 season with over 5 yards a carry, but had a bit of a down 2017 season running for just over 4 yards a carry. Rarely used in pass protection and will need some technique and recognition work before he can be considered a reliable blocker.

Best Fit: Power blocking scheme

Player Ranking (1-100): 66.0 – I personally wouldn't take Scott until the 5th round. He's a talented kid but between the off the field concerns and the fact that he has limited experience in pass protection or receiving, I personally would wait until the 5th.

24. Devine Ozigbo RB Nebraska 6'0 235 lbs

Strengths: Ozigbo was a limited role player until his senior season where he took over as the main starter for the Cornhuskers and really impressed with 1100 yards rushing and 200 yards receiving. Built with an incredibly thick physique, Ozigbo looks like a bowling ball in search of pins. He's a decisive runner who wastes little time in the backfield. Has really improved in his career in his ability to make the 1st guy miss and create for himself in the backfield. Good vision, frequently picking the right hole for himself. Understands how to utilize his size and strength to fall forward when pushing the pile. Really impressive as a receiver, frequently catching the ball in traffic or contested situations. Plays with a good natural pad level, keeping his pads low and playing downhill. Follows his blockers, keeping his body square. Good instincts and awareness as a blocker, showing toughness, anchor ability and physicality to sustain.

Weaknesses: Ozigbo is a take what's given guy who rarely has the ability to get much more. Despite his size and toughness, Ozigbo far too often looks to bounce his runs outside the hashes and lacks the athleticism to effectively do that at the next level without losing yards. A 1-speed runner that lacks the quickness to hit closing lanes. Questions will be asked about his lack of game time until his senior season. Has had some ball security concerns and bad fumbles at inopportune times.

Best Fit: # 2 back change of pace back or in goal-line situations

Player Ranking (1-100): 65.4 – Was really impressed with some of his games from this year. He's going to lose some yards and rarely is a threat to take it to the house but he's a physical, downhill runner who can be used in the running or receiving games. 5th round player. Will need to prove on special teams that he deserves a spot on a team.

25. Mike Weber RB Ohio State 5'10 215 lbs

Strengths: Weber is well-built with good compactness and size. Good body frame and strength to fight and carry the ball 20+ times a game. Weber is a north/south runner who does a nice job of hitting the hole quickly. He does the majority of his damage between the hashes, where he wastes very little movement. Direct runner, who routinely follows his blocks. Shows coordinated feet and good agility to cut and cross-field without losing much speed. An impressive receiver who shows the ability to run polished routes and finish his routes with reliable and soft hands. Shows home-run ability in the open field with the long-speed to take the ball to the house. Willing blocker who demonstrates the ability to play square and sustain blocks.

Weaknesses: Despite Weber's size, he doesn't always play with great physicality. Lacks the ability to push the pile due to his inconsistent and high pad level. Constantly raising his pads far too high mid-play, resulting in an inconsistent ability to move piles forward or gain additional yards upon contact. Not much of a finisher, and generally goes down upon the first impact with a linebacker or safety. A build-up speedrunner who lacks great acceleration and can't get up from 0-60 quickly.

Best Fit: Backup back

Player Ranking (1-100): 63.4 – Weber is a 6th round player who lacks any 'great' qualities but is well-rounded. He has a chance to be a solid # 2 back, but I believe isn't starter quality for the NFL.

DTP's 2019 NFL DRAFT GUIDE

26. James Williams RB Washington State 6'0 205 lbs

Strengths: Williams is a dual-purpose back who is built with a lean, athletic frame. Williams is a 3-year contributor who has had over 875 yards from scrimmage (receiving/rushing) in each season and almost 1200 yards in his final season. He also offers upside as a kick returner. Williams is one the best-receiving backs in college football and made his living catching little swing passes and making guys miss in the open-field. Williams always plays downhill, getting from 0-60 in a flash. Williams is an angle-killer in the open-field showing the ability to quickly shuffle and redirect his feet. The definition of an elusive athlete who can make defenders miss in a phone booth, showing outstanding body control and instincts in his jump cuts. A tougher runner than you would expect, fighting through ankle tacklers, rarely going down upon 1st contact.

Weaknesses: Williams is a far better receiver than he is a runner. As a pure runner, Williams lacks the ideal body armor to be a consistent hammer at the next level. Lacks the physicality/toughness to finish runs and deliver punishment. Struggles to engage his lower body and push piles forward, rarely getting any kind of forward lean. An upright runner who fails to keep his pads down when going through contact. Lacks the ability to offer anything in pass protection, lacking the strength or the experience.

Best Fit: Receiving back / Special Teams

Player Ranking (1-100): 62.9 – Williams is an outstanding receiving back who shows tremendous open-field traits. One of the most explosive backs in the country who shows true game-changing ability in the open field. He understands how to alter speeds to truly break-away at any given time. Also shows the slipperiness to elude tacklers, rarely allowing himself to get tackled on initial contact. I don't believe Williams offers much in the running part of the game, but absolutely a special teams' and 3rd down back. 5th round player.

27. Karan Higdon RB Michigan 5'9 203 lbs

Strengths: Higdon is an impressive senior back for the Wolverines who has played valuable snaps each of the last 3 years, but only completely starting his senior season. Had an incredible senior season with over 1200 all-purpose yards. Possessing a low center of gravity physique, Higdon plays with natural leverage ability. A smooth accelerator who glides through any tiny creases he spots. Despite his smaller stature, his lower body power coupled with his leverage, make him a very difficult guy to take straight on. Plays with coordinated feet to start, stop and redirect. A balanced runner who lowers his pads into tacklers. Keeps his feet moving upon contact getting additional yards after contact. Follows his blockers and runs with conviction. Has a good understanding of his surroundings, does a nice job of anticipating space.

Weaknesses: Used a bit as a receiver split out wide or in the backfield, but fails to have much production when doing it. Looks completely overmatched when asked to pass protect and pick up blitzers, lacking the necessary pop in his upper body. Tends to go low and cut block on every blocking snap, which sometimes works and sometimes fails miserably. Doesn't have a "GREAT" attribute as a back, just OK at a lot of things. Fails to deliver any kind of punishment as a runner, isn't an overly physical guy. Quicker than fast, not a great home-run type of player who is a threat to break off a big run at any moment. Gets caught from behind on quite a few occasions.

Best Fit: Backup/Special Teams'

Player Ranking (1-100): 62.1 – Higdon is a good back who has shown really good production in the Big-10 against some really good defenses the last 3 seasons. I just worry he doesn't have the "IT" factor. Good at a lot of things, but not great as any 1 thing. Has a chance to make it as a backup runner and try to prove he can contribute on special teams in the preseason. 6th round player.

28. Kerrith Whyte Jr RB Florida Atlantic 5'10 200 lbs

Strengths: Whyte is a 4th year junior who had an impressive junior campaign with 866 yards rushing and 8 touchdowns. A smaller, athletically-built runner who offers upside and value as a dynamic return guy as well. Played in a niche role behind Devin Singletary, sharing carries. An explosive runner who runs behind his pads and follows his blocks while wasting very few steps. Whyte's best attribute is his contact balance keeping a low center of gravity, maintaining outstanding leverage with good pad level staying skinny through contact. Utilized controlled, athletic movements in the backfield. It's amazing at times how he stays on his feet through tight windows and heavy traffic. Tremendous athlete who plays with suddenness and shiftiness, constantly causing defenders to miss tackles. Displays coordinated feet to start, stop and redirect quickly. Has the 2nd level speed to pull away.

Weaknesses: An east/west runner who far too often tries to bounce his runs outside, getting him in trouble behind the line of scrimmage. Not a forceful runner who is going to utilize any kind of forward lean to pick up additional yardage at contact. Lacks the finishing or punishing ability to offset tacklers or push the pile. Lacks the ideal body armor to be a consistent hammer and carry the ball 20+ times a game. Limited experience in catching the ball out of the backfield or pass protecting.

Best Fit: Change of pace back, special teams'

Player Ranking (1-100): 61.9 – I really like Whyte as a change of pace back who offers upside on special teams as well. He's a really good # 2 back who is so shifty and quick in space. His contact balance and ability to stay on his feet is outstanding! A really good little player and valuable piece to any offense. 6th round player.

29. Nick Brossette RB LSU 5'11 217 lbs

Strengths: Brossette is a 1-year starter who had a stellar senior season for the Tigers, running for over 1,000 yards and 14 touchdowns. Brossette is built with a power-packed frame, showing thickness and strength throughout. When Brossette runs behind his pads, he's a load to handle in 1 v 1 situations. He shrugs off ankle biters and low-body attempts with relative ease. Does the majority of his damage between the hashes, playing with a low center of gravity and great contact balance, bouncing off tacklers. Good patience and vision, picking the right lane, rarely running into a straight wall. A better than expected athlete who shows really good straight-line speed, rarely getting caught from behind. Possesses the body armor to be a consistent hammer at the next level. A direct runner who wastes very little movement in the backfield. Good short-yardage back who displays the lower body strength to push piles forward.

Weaknesses: Brossette needs major recognition and timing work in pass protection, far too often attempts to cut block instead of accurately anchoring. Very limited experience as a receiver. Only has 1-year of experience and offers little 3-down upside. A 1-gear runner who has good build-up speed, but lacks the quick-twitch and short area bursts to explode at the 1st level. Despite his size, he's not a violent runner who consistently runs behind his pads.

Best Fit: Power-blocking system

Player Ranking (1-100): 61.5 – Brossette is a good change of pace power back for the next level. He's not a next-level starter, but he offers upside in short-yardage and goal-line situations. He's a tough as nails kid who will offer some special teams' ability early on. Coaches will love Brossette. 6th round player.

30. Wes Hills RB Slippery Rock 6'1 209 lbs

Strengths: Hills was a 2-year year starter at Delaware who had really good production with over 1800 yards rushing during his 2 years there. This season after transferring to Slippery Rock had an incredible 1700 yards rushing despite missing 2 games. Hills has remade his body quite a bit, opting to play with a leaner physique. Hills plays physical, lowering his shoulders upon impact, almost always generating some good forward lean. Not afraid of contact, in fact, just the opposite, he looks for it. A sudden runner who plants his foot and goes, then shows the ability to alter speeds at all levels of his runs to create for himself. Strong and violent, shrugging off ankle biters with ease. A direct and fast-hitting runner who wastes very little movement or timing in the backfield. Elusive in the open field, showing quick feet and change of direction ability to sidestep 2nd level defenders. This past season, has shown some ability to utilize his soft hands to catch the ball out of the backfield.

Weaknesses: An older prospect who will be a 24-year-old rookie. Was deemed academically ineligible to remain at Delaware and transferred to Division-2 Slippery Rock for his final season. Broke his foot his last season at Delaware, and had some other minor injury concerns. An upright back who leaves the ball and his frame far too exposed. A bit too quick and reliant on bouncing his runs to the outside.

Best Fit: Scheme-versatile

Player Ranking (1-100): 60.5 – Hills is a solid back who shows good overall ability. Physical and athletic, Hills possesses plenty of upside to continue to develop. Scouts loved the way he was competing at the Senior Bowl practices, showing toughness and receiving ability. 5th round player.

31. Jacques Patrick RB Florida State 6'3 234 lbs

Strengths: Patrick is a senior RB for the Seminoles who is compactly-built with broad shoulders and a filled-out frame. Patrick is your typical power back with outstanding power and strength. He rarely goes down on initial contact, keeping his legs moving and plowing through defenders. Excellent short-yardage back maintaining momentum and picking up needed yards. He's a direct 1-cut runner, rarely losing any yards, taking what the defense gives to him. Plays in a pro-offense and has some experience and reliability both in pass protection and being a friendly target in the receiving game. Teams like him as a # 2 back due to his decisive nature and his ability to finish runs and hit the hole with conviction.

Weaknesses: Missed half of his junior season due to torn cartilage in his knee. Didn't look to be quite the same player in his senior season as he was as a junior, losing some of his production and yards per carry. On many occasions, you'll notice he could break away and get 40+ yards on a run but fails to have that home-run ability. An upright runner who leaves himself too big and too much of his body exposed. Lacks the 2nd gear and only has 1 gear all the time. Doesn't have the movement skills or the flexibility in his lower half to change directions or cross the field.

Best Fit: # 2 back for a team

Player Ranking (1-100): 60.2 – He's a solid runner who might end up being a better pro-RB than college. He reminds me a bit of Christine Michael and is kind of a 'what you see is what you get' type of back. He's a tough, physical and hard-nosed back. 6th round player.

32. Ryquell Armstead RB Temple 5'11 223 lbs

Strengths: Armstead is a 3-year starter who possesses outstanding compactness and physicality throughout his frame. Armstead's had a really nice career, most notably his senior season with 1100 yards rushing and 13 touchdowns in only 10 games. A tough runner who maintains good pad level through heavily congested traffic, minimizing his contact area. Armstead has excellent vision and patience, sensing his surroundings well and anticipating spacing in his runs. Runs behind his pads, showing power and punishment when taking on tacklers head on. Shows good acceleration after planting his feet, wasting very little movement. A highly competitive runner who demonstrates toughness. Follows his blocks and hits the hole with conviction, demonstrating good timing before exploding through vacated openings.

Weaknesses: Tries to do too much on every snap, causing him to get tackled behind the line of scrimmage quite a bit. Very minimal receiving experience in college. While he has improved in pass protection, still gets overwhelmed quite a bit lacking suitable awareness and technique. Battled a toe injury in 2017 minimizing his production levels his junior season. Lacks the second level speed to pull away, simply a 1-speed runner. Saw multiple plays where he was tracked from behind in open-field situations.

Best Fit: Backup RB

Player Ranking (1-100): 58.2 – A good all-around back who will compete for a backup spot at the next level. His size and his vision are his two best traits. He will likely get drafted, but I believe it shouldn't be until the 7th round. Between his injury history and his lack of value on 3rd down, due to his ineptitude in pass protection and in the receiving game, will likely cause him to drop in the draft.

33. Damarea Crockett RB Missouri 5'11 225 lbs

Strengths: Crockett is a big, bruising back who has played in a committee backfield the last 3 years. As a freshman, Crockett had his best season, running for over 1000 yards and 10 touchdowns. A powerful guy who utilizes his size/lower half to consistently get good forward lean through contact, rarely falling backward. An elusive target, who shows good agility and quick-feet to redirect and bounce runs outside.

Explosive hips when jump-cutting, showing above-average change of direction and lateral movement ability. Consistently blows through ankle swipers, showing good balance and power in his legs. Solid in pass protection, showing good awareness and understanding pre-snap. Demonstrates the ability to anchor and square his shoulders, anchoring down and delivering a POP to blitzers.

Weaknesses: Crockett's main concern has been his propensity to fumble . Dealt with a nagging injury in his final season as a junior which disrupted his production and lowered his yards per carry average. Fails to get his pads down through contact, causing him to leave his upright frame exposed through traffic. Despite his size, he doesn't always show it, failing to break many yards in space, almost always going down upon 1st tackler. An indecisive runner who wastes too much time/movement in the backfield before deciding. Quicker than fast, lacking top-end speed to break off big runs.

Best Fit: Rotational back

Player Ranking (1-100): 55.8 – Crockett has very good size and offers upside as a pass protector. I would be worried about giving him too many snaps due to his constant and nagging fumble concerns. It's a shame because there is absolutely some ability here as a runner. His quickness and agility are pretty surprising considering how big he is. Obviously possesses a very explosive/strong lower-half that assists him. He's worth a 7th round flyer.

RB Top-10 Rankings

1. Josh Jacobs
2. David Montgomery
3. Devin Singletary
4. Trayveon Williams
5. Damien Harris
6. Justice Hill
7. Darrell Henderson
8. Jalin Moore
9. Myles Gaskin
10. Jordan Scarlett

Chapter 4

FB's

1. Alec Ingold FB Wisconsin 6'1 247 lbs

Strengths: Ingold is a 4-year contributor who has played in over 50 games during his career at Wisconsin. Productive in both the running and receiving game, totaling over 21 touchdowns during his career. Ingold is an effective short yardage back who plays with great determination and effort. Truly a versatile back, he shows the ability to play in a wide variety of roles, including on special teams. Fearless in his ability to lead block, showing no hesitancy against bigger linebackers or blitzing defensive backs. Strong in his lower half, showing the anchoring ability and functional strength to reliably step into gaps and stop blitzers in their tracks. A surprisingly nimble athlete who generally is a good route-runner, selling out his routes at the top. A reliable target who generally has good hands.

Weaknesses: Ingold is a limited athlete who doesn't possess much of an ability to create for himself or gain additional yardage after the catch. An average runner who besides his physicality, doesn't offer much else as a runner, possessing little vision.

Best Fit: A true versatile FB

Player Ranking (1-100): 62.4 – Ingold is the best overall 'TRUE' FB in this draft. He's not an elite athlete, nor is he an outstanding receiver but he's a bit of a 'DO EVERYTHING' guy that offers a bit of everything. 5th round player.

2. Trevon Wesco FB/TE West Virginia 6'4 274 lbs

Strengths: An impressive starter for West Virginia, he played a bit of a hybrid FB/TE role. Has experience playing on all the special teams' units as well. Wesco possesses a gigantic frame with a terrific wingspan, possessing heavily muscled limbs. Wesco moved all over the offensive front, playing in the backfield, out wide, in-line or as a wingback. Wesco is a beast in the open field, utilizing his power and frame to bully smaller defenders. Overall good hands, showing the ability to extend and make catches outside of his frame. Good initial acceleration out of his stance, engaging his hips and lower body to generate terrific point of attack and push in the run game. Has made some impressive circus catches.

Weaknesses: Wesco isn't necessarily a "FB" and is more of a move player that has some experience playing in the backfield. A limited athlete who isn't going to generate much separation when running routes. Is prone to some poor concentration drops. Limited production in his career with out 14 career catches and 2 career touchdowns.

Best Fit: Hybrid offensive weapon

Player Ranking (1-100): 59.4 – Wesco is a talented offensive threat who has the size and wingspan to threaten all over the field. He had a really nice Senior Bowl week showing his ability to compete against top-flight competition. He's a good move blocker who can be used in the backfield. 7th round player.

3. Winston Dimel FB UTEP 6'1 242 lbs

Strengths: Dimel is a stout and compactly-built Kansas State graduate transfer who went to UTEP for his final season. Dimel excelled as a sophomore for Kansas State, posting his best individual season with 12 touchdowns, showing his toughness in red-zone situations. A good lead blocker who shows physicality and finishing ability, frequently digging out linebackers at the 2nd level. Excellent in space, showing terrific latch on ability and strength to sustain blocks. Moves all over the line of scrimmage, playing both as an H-back, in-line tight end or a wingback. Possesses good overall vision when running, showing the patience and decisiveness to pick the correct gap.

Weaknesses: Had a really disappointing final campaign for UTEP after only playing 5 games and requiring shoulder surgery which caused him to miss the final 2 months of the season. Dimel is ineffective when running the ball outside of the red-zone, lacking the explosiveness to quickly accelerate or to threaten breaking off big runs. A limited receiving threat who has t-rex arms which shows an inability to consistently catch the ball outside of his frame.

Best Fit: Blocking FB

Player Ranking (1-100): 56.9 – The nice thing about Dimel is he's a FB through and through. A physical finisher who looks like a hammer in search of a nail looking to make contact. Could be an effective special teams player immediately and get some snaps in running situations. 7th round player.

FB Top-10 Rankings
1. Alec Ingold
2. Trevon Wesco
3. Winston Dimel

Chapter 5

WR's

1. Kelvin Harmon WR North Carolina State 6'3 214 lbs

Strengths: Harmon is a tall possession-based receiver with an impressive wingspan and filled-out frame. Has posted tremendous production each of the last 2 seasons with over 2200 yards receiving combined. Plays with some sharpness in his routes, utilizing clean footwork at the breakpoint to creates spacing. Runs his routes with wiggle and manipulation, utilizing head/body fakes to create on shorter routes. Shows the flexible body control to utilize his length and track the ball mid-flight to adjust. As a blocker, Harmon shows good awareness and a real willingness to WANT to block. Impressive in his ability to utilize his hands to play physical within the first 5 yards to create separation off the line. Effective in using his body to shield corners on comeback and sideline routes. A trustworthy target in contested situations, Harmon wins the majority of 50/50 balls showing the ability to hold onto the football. A true chain mover who was often times relied upon in crucial 3rd down situations. Smart guy who works his butt off on every snap and demonstrates the ability to play every receiver position.

Weaknesses: Harmon isn't always the cleanest catcher of the ball, and had some serious struggles with his hands his freshman season. Has seemingly improved each season. Not an elite speed athlete who is going to consistently separate at the next level on up-the-field routes. An upright athlete who takes a second to build-up speed in his routes. Not an overly effective runner with the ball in his hands, tending to go down far too often on first contact. Good athlete but isn't an elite athlete.

Best Fit: An 'X' receiver

Player Ranking (1-100): 86.9 – Harmon is probably the most complete and most polished all-around receiver in this class. Does virtually everything well. He isn't going to light the world on fire athletically, but he's just a SOLID SOLID guy that will continue to develop. Hardworking, smart, and ridiculously effective. Late 1st round player.

2. D.K. Metcalf WR Ole Miss 6'3 225 lbs

Strengths: Metcalf is a 2-year starter for the Rebels who possesses prototypical size, power, and muscularity for a wide receiver. Metcalf was only a redshirt sophomore at Ole Miss and just turned 21 in December. Metcalf is an absolute beast and will dominate the ball at the high-point. He shows toughness and willingness to catch the ball through highly-contested traffic and then maintain control through contact. Bad ball catcher, showing the ability to adjust and contort his body to bad throws by his quarterback. Impressive top-gear showing the ability to run past defenders in straight-line situations. Does a nice job of utilizing his head in conjunction with his footwork to sell his routes down the field to create spacing. Impressive post-catch to be able to pick up additional yardage through contact. Explosive athlete who is a threat to reach the end-zone at all levels of the field. Understands how to use proper jam-technique to disengage and release at the line of scrimmage from press corners. Good blocker who understands how to utilize his length to engage defenders, showing willingness and toughness to seal the edges.

Weaknesses: A build-up speed runner who takes a while to get to top gear. A bit of a clunky route-runner who fails to run sharp routes, tending to round off the top of his routes instead. The last highly regarded Rebel receiver Treadwell has had a difficult time in the NFL with a similar problem of not being able to consistently separate or run precise routes. Very average production in college considering his level of talent and ability. Has only played in 21 games in his college career. Bad injury history including a neck injury his final season, causing him to miss the final 5 games of the season. Strictly an outside receiver at this point, rarely playing in the slot during his career. Is prone to some concentration drops on occasion.

Best Fit: An 'X' receiver

Player Ranking (1-100): 86.1 – The most 'purely talented' receiver in this class and is the full package of what you want in a receiver, possessing athleticism, physicality, and toughness. My only concerns are the mental side of the game and his injury history. The interview process is going to be huge for him to demonstrate he has a football mind and can handle more complicated offensive systems. If he does that and impresses, I'll be shocked if he isn't a 1st round pick.

3. Marquise "Hollywood" Brown WR Oklahoma 5'10 168 lbs

Strengths: Brown is a 2-year starter for the Sooners who has been an absolute production machine in each season with over 1,000 yards. His final season as a junior, Brown posted one of the best years for a receiver in the country with 1318 yards and 10 touchdowns. Brown is an explosive receiver and the definition of a big-play guy, eating up zone-cushions with ease down the field. While playing man-to-man, Brown shows the deep-speed to consistently create separation against speedier defensive backs as well. Brown understands how to alter speeds at the top of his stems to create spacing down the field. Good quickness, balance, and wiggle at the line of scrimmage to beat press coverage and get a clean release. Flexible body-control and concentration when the ball is in flight, showing the ability to get outstretched and extend, adjust to the ball with a defender on his back. Possesses the hip flexibility and lateral quickness to separate on in-breaking routes, creating separation and not having to gear down. A QB-friendly option who always works back toward the QB down the field. Dangerous with the ball in his hands, showing open-field elusiveness and shiftiness.

Weaknesses: Brown is slight, and I mean very slight, lacking suitable body armor to take NFL hits consistently. He might be limited to strictly slot duties at the next level, due to his lack of height/length. Inconsistent hands, lacking the strong hands to consistently come away with contested catches when the defensive back disrupts the catch point. A bit of a body catcher, needs to have more of an "attack mindset" when the football is within reach, being overly patient waiting for it to reach his frame. Lacks the physical makeup to break tackles and elude defenders, tending to go down on first contact.

> **Best Fit:** Z-receiver who can also play the slot

Player Ranking (1-100): 85.7 – Brown is an explosive down the field threat who is one of the best big-play guys in this entire draft. His separation quickness, smoothness in his routes and long-speed make him a dynamic offensive weapon. He's a mix of Tavon Austin and Desean Jackson in the way that he plays. He's not a guy you want consistently lining up as the 'X' receiver because he will get manhandled against bigger corners at the line of scrimmage. Late 1st round player.

4. Deebo Samuel WR South Carolina 5'11 216 lbs

Strengths: Samuel is a senior receiver for the Gamecocks who has had a really impressive college career doing practically everything for his offense. A compactly-built guy showing the muscularity and compactness to play at the next level. Samuel has, for the most part really good hands and has made some remarkable circus catches during his career. Always a threat to do damage with the ball in his hands, one of the best yards after catch receivers showcasing his ability to break tackles and fight for additional yardage. Used as a return guy early in his career, showing versatility and upside if used again. Showed his ability to recover from his broken leg during his senior campaign with a really impressive final season. Samuel is an outstanding ball tracker, showcasing his ability to find the ball deep and adjust his body mid-air. Samuel is a quick-footed guy who accelerates in and out of his breaks quickly. An all-around receiver who can win in a variety of ways, showcasing outstanding footwork and route-running fluidity. Versatile guy who has played both outside positions, as an H-back, and in the slot. Despite his teams inept QB play this year, he was still very impressive in his senior year. Impressive in his ability to sell routes and use body/head fakes to create spacing.

Weaknesses: Samuel broke his leg early in his junior season, causing him to miss most of his junior campaign. Can make the circus catches but is prone to some simple concentration drops. Quick but not exceptionally fast, lacks the home-run ability to get behind the defense. Serious durability concerns throughout his career. Lacks ideal size and height, and can get beaten on jump-ball situations in the red zone.

> **Best Fit:** All-around receiver who is best as a move or a 'Z'

Player Ranking (1-100): 84.9 – I love Samuel and I think he can be an absolute stud at the next level if he stays healthy. Can be used in a variety of different ways for an offense. Smart kid who will improve any football team he goes to. Should be drafted somewhere in the 2nd round.

5. A.J. Brown WR Ole Miss 6'1 225 lbs

Strengths: Brown has been arguably the most productive wide receiver in college football the last 2 seasons, totaling over 2500 yards receiving and 17 touchdowns. Built with a power-packed frame, showing tremendous girth and thickness throughout his frame. A versatile weapon who lines up at all the wide receiver positions, showing the ability to win outside or in the slot. Brown runs his routes with precision, savvy and snap, showing outstanding start/stop quickness. Tremendous on the shorter to intermediate routes where he can utilize the middle of the field and shield defenders with his huge frame. Physical at all areas of the game, showing a nasty stiff arm and physicality with the ball in his hands. Outstanding and sticky hands, showing complete comfort to extend and snatch away from his frame. Knows how to utilize his wingspan to routinely out-compete and outmuscle at the catch point. Fearless in contested situations, showing reliability and terrific concentration. Good releases when playing against press coverage, showing good jam technique and physicality. Relentless in his ability to work back towards the QB, presenting a friendly target on broken down plays. Good ball tracker, showing the body control and awareness to win 50/50 balls, or make difficult over the shoulder catches look routine. A physical point of attack blocker who shows tenacity and the ability to lock on and sustain his position.

Weaknesses: Brown is a high-volume guy but isn't a deep threat vertically down the field, possessing average long speed and separation quickness. Shows inconsistent effort and appears to lose interest during some games. Due to his size, he can struggle a bit when it comes to changing direction. Is best used as an oversized slot and his size can be offset when playing against bigger, longer corners.

Best Fit: Oversized slot

Player Ranking (1-100): 84.6 – There is no denying Brown's levels of production in the last 2 seasons despite playing with 2 other NFL receivers. To say it's impressive is putting it lightly. Brown is a high volume guy who excels at the physical areas of the game. He reminds me of Terrell Owens with the ball in his hands, showing explosiveness and a downhill nature. 2nd round player.

6. N'Keal Harry WR Arizona State 6'4 213 lbs

Strengths: Harry is a 3-year starter for Arizona State who has completely dominated the Pac-12 the last 2 seasons with over 1,000 yards in each season. He's a long and rangy WR with outstanding size and length. His length and catch radius makes it extremely hard for most college corners to cover. Not just a possession receiver, Harry is a speed threat, showcasing the long-speed to run past corners on up the field routes and 9-routes. Harry is used by the Sun Devils coaches in every imaginable way, including in the return game. A red-zone nightmare, Harry possesses the jumping ability and the high-point ability to get up and snatch the ball. Wins the majority of 50/50 balls. A classic 'X' receiver, but can also line up in the slot or play in-motion as a 'Z.' Stays on his feet through contact, keeping his legs moving at all times. A true deep-ball threat who finds a way to come down with the ball on most occasions. Good jam-technique, understanding how to utilize his hands to quickly beat press-coverage.

Weaknesses: Takes a while to get into top gear. Struggles and loses speed when asked to cross the field, change direction or run horizontally. Needs to improve his aggression, timing, instincts, and awareness in his blocking ability. Raw in his route-running skills, instead relying on contested catches vs. smaller cornerbacks. Not a guy who is going to consistently separate at the next level, struggled in some games maintaining or getting spacing down the field.

Best Fit: Outside receiver who can play as an 'X' receiver

Player Ranking (1-100): 84.4 – I like Harry I just am not convinced he should be a 1st round player. He possesses outstanding size and length, but little in the way of consistent separation or route running. That was especially evident when going up against better defenses where he really struggled. The way he 'WINS' in college is going to be a lot harder at the next level. 2nd round player.

7. Riley Ridley WR Georgia 6'1 200 lbs

Strengths: Riley, the younger brother of Falcons wide receiver Calvin, is a tremendously gifted receiver. Built with good overall size, very lean with an impressive wingspan. Ridley is a versatile target who shows experience and ability to play both on the outside and in the slot. The best adjective to describe Ridley is smooth. A smooth accelerator who shows good initial movement out of his stance, running his routes with precision and savvy. Impressive start/stop quickness, showing the ability to frequently get corners turned around with good change of direction, suddenness and fluid hips. Ridley is an outstanding ball tracker, showing the ability to utilize his body control and strong mitts to snatch the ball at the high point, or track the ball for a beautiful over the shoulder grab. Understands how to attack and beat zone coverages, quickly finding soft zones and sitting in. Really good separation quickness, showing the ability to alter his route speeds at the top of his stems to create spacing. Attacks the football with an aggressive mindset, perfectly shielding the ball with his frame. Outstanding hands which shows jump-ball reliability, snatching the ball away from his frame. A physical blocker who shows an understanding and willingness to assist in run support.

Weaknesses: Ridley was a rotational player prior to his final season at Georgia, and only had 26 career catches prior to his junior season. Was arrested for marijuana possession in March 2017. A limited route-tree in college. Needs to learn how to utilize his hands at the line of scrimmage against press-man physical corners. Not a threat after the catch, generally going down upon 1st contact. Quicker than fast, and doesn't appear to create loads of separation on vertical routes.

Best Fit: An 'X' receiver who can also play in the slot

Player Ranking (1-100): 84.1 – Ridley is a really effective, smooth receiver who will be a solid #2 receiver at the next level. His upside is huge as he gains additional experience. A team needs to be patient with Ridley because he has had limited receptions and production in college. He has very few 'downsides' to his game and has very little risk of busting in the NFL. 2nd round player.

8. Emanuel Hall WR Missouri 6'2 195 lbs

Strengths: Hall is a highly productive 2-year starter for the Tigers who has proven to be the definition of a big-play guy during his college career. Hall possesses above-average NFL height and length. An outstanding athlete who possesses really good long-speed as well as initial quickness off the line of scrimmage, showing the ability to get vertical on very good SEC cornerbacks. Also shows the quickness to be able to separate at the line of scrimmage or at the breakpoint of his routes and create. An incredibly agile guy who shows tremendous start/stop skills as well as the ability to flip his hips and change direction without losing any built up speed. Has a good understanding of how to utilize the sidelines on 'out-routes.' Runs routes with such nuance showing subtle manipulation with his eyes/body/feet to create for himself. Plays bigger than his size, showing a competitive makeup and physicality upon arrival of the football fighting at the catch point. Shows good effort when asked to block, which is fairly rare.

Weaknesses: Battled a groin injury during the 2018 season causing him to miss a few games. Also battled other nagging injuries during his career with hamstring and shoulder concerns as well. Hall had a very limited route tree in college, running mostly on a linear plain, rarely moving horizontally on routes. Has battled drop issues during the early part of his career, but appears to have improved this season. Has a lankier frame with little muscle mass and will likely need to gain additional strength and muscle for the next level. Strictly an outside receiver with little slot experience.

Best Fit: Outside receiver

Player Ranking (1-100): 83.8 – Hall is one of my favorite receivers in this class who shows outstanding and explosive characteristics. I do worry about his nagging injuries in college and hope it isn't a sign of things to come. But his level of athleticism, nuance and route-running ability makes me so excited for his NFL prospects, especially since he did it against SEC defenses. He's a high 2nd round player for me.

9. Antoine Wesley WR Texas Tech 6'4 200 lbs

Strengths: Wesley is a long and rangy built receiver who had a tremendous season this year with 1400 yards, 88 receptions, and 9 touchdowns. A versatile threat who shows the ability to play inside or outside. Wesley utilizes his long arms to go up and snatch the football in mid-flight. His combination of body control, length, leaping ability, and hands make him a really hard guy to cover. Despite his size, he isn't a lumbering runner, he shows the ability to accelerate quickly. Shows toughness post catch, playing with physicality and shiftiness in the open-field. A dynamic red-zone target who will utilize his wingspan to outreach and outmaneuver smaller defensive backs. A fluid mover who shows the ability to drop his hips and change direction when running routes. Shows some nuance as a route-runner with good deception and footwork to cleanly separate at the top of routes. Good long-speed with the ability to separate on vertical routes. Shows the ability to catch the ball in heavily contested situations. Takes blocking seriously and shows a willingness and a toughness to engage and latch on.

Weaknesses: A 1-year wonder who came out of nowhere this season as a junior. An extremely skinny frame who will need major strength and bulking work before he can get on an NFL field. Comes from the Texas Tech air raid offense where numbers are put up in large batches and very often don't translate. Had injury concerns early on in his career causing him to miss a lot of games. Has little experience in handling physical corners which will force him to utilize his hands at the line of scrimmage. Would like to see him attack the football and utilize his length and size more, can be a bit too passive waiting for it to come into his chest or over his shoulder.

Best Fit: Can play anywhere

Player Ranking (1-100): 83.4 – There are very few receivers that have come out for the draft the last few years who are as big, as versatile and as multi-talented as Wesley is. He's a bit thin, but his traits are outstanding. His lack of bulk is never obvious and he displays tremendous toughness and physicality despite it. I am convinced he's going to be an NFL starter very quickly at the next level. He has traits that suggest he can be a # 1 receiver given some time. I would absolutely take him in the 2nd round.

10. Anthony Johnson WR Buffalo 6'2 211 lbs

Strengths: Johnson is a compactly-built and physical WR who has had a tremendous last 2 seasons for Buffalo. His junior season he had 1356 yards and 14 touchdowns coming out of nowhere. He's an excellent deep ball threat, showing outstanding ball awareness and ball tracking ability. While not possessing elite deep speed, he's an above average athlete. He utilizes his strength and strong hands to box out smaller corners to dominate at the catch point. He catches almost everything in his vicinity and is used to adjusting to badly throw balls by his inept QB play. Johnson is a real physical receiver who loves to block and shows a real toughness in all the physical aspects of the game. He's a QB's best friend with his ability to utilize his long arms and catch everything, even tough balls in heavily congested traffic. His best trait perhaps is his run after the catch ability. He rarely goes down to the first tackler, and I can't tell you how many times I saw him break off huge plays from only short 5 yard routes. He's always a threat to take it to the house no matter where he receives the ball. Versatile guy who can play outside or inside in the slot.

Weaknesses: Johnson has rarely played against the top echelon competition. While a good athlete, Johnson lacks the long speed to consistently threaten NFL corners on the back end. He is a slow accelerator and takes a few seconds to build up to full speed. Only 2 years of experience. Johnson is going to need a QB that isn't afraid to throw tight window throws because he rarely separates down the field.

Best Fit: Outside WR

Player Ranking (1-100): 83.1 – Johnson is a really good player who catches literally everything! Plus, he's so tough and so physical with the ball in his hands. I'm not of the belief he's a true # 1 receiver at the next level due to his lack of separation ability but he will be a really valuable cog in the wheel for a good receiving unit. 2nd round player.

11. Parris Campbell WR Ohio State 6'1 208 lbs

Strengths: Campbell is a well-built hybrid type of receiver. He is built with the desired muscle tone and strength throughout his body that teams are looking for. He's a ridiculously gifted athlete and splits his time running with the sprint team for Ohio State as well. He's known to be a 4.3 guy on campus and is always a threat to take it to the house every time he touches the ball. He's incredibly versatile as he is one of the best kick returners in the country. He also lines up in the backfield at times. Had an outstanding senior season showcasing his ability to be a full-time WR, and not just play from the slot. He's an impressive blocker who isn't afraid to get his hands dirty and get physical at the point of attack, showing toughness and the ability to sustain. He's got really good hands, showing an ability to reach and extend and use his entire wingspan. He's very elusive with the ball in his hands, showing shiftiness and suddenness after the catch. He's one of the best receivers in the country after the catch, picking up 13 yards after the catch on average. Tough kid who breaks tackles and rarely goes down on initial contact.

Weaknesses: Despite being a ridiculously good athlete, Campbell rarely runs routes more than 5-10 yards. He's strictly a short to medium route guy and is reliant on his yards after the catch. Catches a ton of screens, and gets a lot of his yardage on gadget type of plays. Needs to learn how to create better separation at the top of his routes. Very unrefined route runner who needs to add precision at all areas of his routes. Despite his long speed, his separation quickness is just average at best. He's still very raw and needs refinement in jam technique, route running, and adding a larger route tree.

Best Fit: Slot receiver/Kick Returner

Player Ranking (1-100): 82.4 – Campbell is an explosive guy who reminds me a bit of a slightly bigger Curtis Samuel. He hasn't had the production of Samuel throughout his career, but he's a very talented guy with a huge upside. He just needs to be around creative offensive coaches who can figure out how to best use him. 2nd round player.

12. Preston Williams WR Colorado State 6'4 210 lbs

Strengths: A 2-year contributor for Tennessee before transferring and sitting out a year and playing his last year for Mountain West Colorado State. Had a tremendous year with 1345 yards and 14 touchdowns. Williams possesses a long frame with an outstanding wingspan. A versatile receiving threat that shows the ability to line up all over the line of scrimmage, including in the slot. Physical at the line of scrimmage with good hand strength and wiggle to beat jams. A track athlete, he displays tremendous long-speed down the field. In addition to his track speed, he also displays really good initial quickness and balance at the line of scrimmage to separate within the first 5 yards. Shows some ability to utilize subtle movements with his hands, arms and body movements to gain some spacing at all levels. Excellent concentration and body control, making some tough, contested catches in traffic or down the field. Good agility on crossing routes, showing the ability to flip his hips without gearing down. Shows some open-field ability to get away from tacklers and break tackles in space.

Weaknesses: A very leanly built guy with practically 0 body fat, lacking much bulk or body armor on his frame. Would like to see him utilize his size and length more at the catch point, tending to be too passive waiting for the ball rather than attacking it consistently. Still a raw route runner who needs to continue to develop nuance with his footwork. Rarely had to compete against physical corners in college who pressed him at the line, but when he did, he showed a lack of experience and hand usage to shed. Tore his ACL while he was at Tennessee, didn't show any signs of it affecting his athleticism. Has some inconsistencies with his ball tracking abilities when his back is toward the football. Served a suspension for an off-season assault charge.

Best Fit: 'Z' receiver

Player Ranking (1-100): 81.1 – Williams is a really good football player and should improve once he fully learns how to utilize all his explosive characteristics and continues to refine his route-running skills. He's going to be an exceptional #2 receiver for an NFL team. Between his size and speed, his talent levels are through the roof. 2nd round player. That's assuming there are no questions about his health or off-the-field history going forward.

13. DaMarkus Lodge WR Ole Miss 6'2 200 lbs

Strengths: Lodge is a lean and physical receiver from Ole Miss who has shared the load with other top college receivers DK Metcalf and AJ Brown. Despite sharing the load, Lodge still had almost 900 yards as a senior and 700 yards as a junior. Lodge is a bad ball receiver, showing really impressive hands with the ability to pluck the ball off the ground. Outstanding at high-pointing the ball and tracking the ball mid-flight and then contorting his body to making the catch. Lodge has tremendous athletic ability, notably his vertical leaping. He possesses impressive long-speed as well. Combining his jumping ability and his ability to high point the ball while stretching his wing-span, it can be very difficult to stop him. Really impressed with the way he uses his hands and wiggle at the line of scrimmage to beat jams and quickly release. Physical point of attack blocker in the run game, does a nice job of extending and sustaining. Knows how to utilize the sidelines, with some nice toe-touching grabs.

Weaknesses: Will make the spectacular catches but is extremely prone to some terrible simple concentration drops. Is simply a short to intermediate route guy in college who rarely runs routes beyond 10 yards. Ole Miss rarely asked him to run lateral routes, so his route tree and what he was asked to do was very minimal. Simply an outside receiver at this point, never being asked to play in the slot.

Best Fit: Outside WR

Player Ranking (1-100): 80.4 – I really like Lodge and I think in the right offensive system he can be a really good starting NFL receiver. He displays tremendous toughness, physicality and is a really good athlete. His upside is tremendous. 2nd round player.

14. Terry Godwin WR Georgia 5'11 185 lbs

Strengths: Godwin is a 4-year contributor for the Bulldogs and is known as the "speed receiver" for the Bulldogs. A 2-sport athlete who was also drafted by the Atlanta Braves. Had his best year as a junior with 639 yards, 16.8 yards per catch average and 6 touchdowns. Makes some spectacular circus catches showcasing his concentration and ability. A versatile weapon who can be used in the slot or on the outside. Tremendous short-area quickness, but also has the long speed to consistently win on the outside. A real threat with the ball in his hands, showing the ability to find space and maneuver in the open field. For being a smaller guy, does a really nice job of competing at the catch point. Excellent body control showing the ability to adjust his body to badly thrown balls or work back towards the ball mid-flight. A real competitive guy who is always in the faces of his opponents talking trash. Shows the agility and looseness in his hips to flip them and cross-field without losing any build-up speed.

Weaknesses: Can struggle when he's asked to beat a jam at the line of scrimmage against a really physical corner on the outside. Lacks the precision in his routes but gets away with it due to his speed. Needs to learn to utilize sharper footwork at all levels of a route to create separation against NFL corners.

Best Fit: Slot receiver who can play outside in 3 WR sets as well.

Player Ranking (1-100): 78.9 – Godwin is a really impressive athlete with outstanding body control and an ability to adjust to the football. He's not just a "SLOT" receiver because he absolutely can play on the outside. But he'd be dynamic in the slot and a complete mismatch. I would imagine he'll be playing a lot of special teams' for a team as well. 3rd round player.

15. Anthony Ratliff-Williams WR North Carolina 6'1 205 lbs

Strengths: Ratliff-Williams is a 4th year junior who was a converted QB. He's been really impressive his last 2 years playing as a receiver and a kickoff return specialist with good production in each season. Ratliff-Williams possesses a compact and NFL-ready physique. Shows the flexible body control and ball tracking abilities in flight, adjusting his body and making some spectacular highlight-reel catches with arms fully extended. A versatile receiver who has lined up everywhere along the line of scrimmage, playing both outside and inside. A tough and physical player, he shows willingness, passion, and awareness when asked to block. A violent runner after the catch showing a mean stiff arm, fighting for every additional yard. One of the best 50/50 ball receivers in this class, virtually catches every one of them. A bad ball catcher who had to adjust to so many poorly thrown balls.

Weaknesses: Had a decent junior season but somewhat regressed after a stellar sophomore season with 2 special teams touchdowns and 6 receiving touchdowns. Not quite the finished product yet, and needs continual refinement and nuance with his route running, footwork at all levels and route deception. His athleticism is raw, not possessing the know-how when it comes to separating consistently and is reliant on his bulldog mentality to box out or outmuscle at the college level. Very limited route-tree in college.

Best Fit: #3 receiver immediately and kick returner

Player Ranking (1-100): 78.2 – There's something so refreshing about the way Ratliff-Williams plays football. He's not refined, but the guy battles his rear off. There are so many things he can do for a football team, and toughness is absolutely one of them. You can use him as a move blocker, return guy, slot receiver, outside receiver. I don't think he's ever going to be a dynamic offensive #1 receiver, but he will be a high-impact player for sure. Reminds me of Dwayne Harris.

16. Hakeem Butler WR Iowa State 6'6 225 lbs

Strengths: Butler is a 2-year starter for the Cyclones who had a tremendous final season, totaling 60 catches, 1318 yards and 9 touchdowns. The first thing that's obvious about Butler is his rare size. Butler has height and very long arms, making it almost impossible for smaller defensive backs to matchup against him, especially in red-zone situations. Plays like a bully in every sense of the word. Really good in contested situations, showing strong and reliable hands in traffic. A determined, physical football player who won't be stopped in short-yardage situations. Outstanding with the ball in his hands, showing some shiftiness and toughness to create extra yardage down the field. An aggressive, nonstop motor and is relentless is his attempts to block downfield for his teammates. Versatile receiving option, lining up at every single receiving position. Really impressive concentration and ball control, routinely adjusting his body mid-flight to come away with the catch. Proficient in utilizing the sidelines, knowing how to catch the ball in-bounds. Better than average acceleration off the line of scrimmage, surprising cornerbacks routinely. Understands how to utilize his hands and upper-body strength to fight through press coverage.

Weaknesses: Butler possesses a high-torso frame which makes his ability to redirect and change direction very difficult. Butler needs to learn how to utilize his length better on contested situations, rarely utilizing his length and wingspan to catch balls away from his frame. Too passive at the catch point, waiting for the ball to reach his frame. Little experience in running any kind of lateral routes, almost plays entirely on a vertical radius. Deep speed is questionable, rare that you see him generate any kind of separation on vertical routes.

Best Fit: Can play any WR position and will likely be a #2 receiver for a team

Player Ranking (1-100): 77.9 – Not as big a fan as some are. His Oklahoma game from this season was outstanding, but there are too many games in which he does little to impress. His way of dominating and outmuscling in college doesn't always translate as well at the next level, especially when doing it against Big-12 secondaries. I think he can be a solid # 2 receiving option at the next level. He's a sneaky good athlete and a really physical guy. 3rd round player.

17. Dillon Mitchell WR Oregon 6'2 189 lbs

Strengths: Mitchell is a long and rangy-built receiver with good length and overall size. Mitchell had a tremendous final season at Oregon, as a junior, with just under 1200 yards receiving and 10 touchdowns. Mitchell offers additional ability as a good kick-off return specialist as well. Mitchell is a good overall athlete, showing good burst and acceleration out of his stance. Excellent footwork at the top of his routes, showing preciseness, balance and suddenness to create spacing. Has versatility and experience playing both on the outside and in the slot. Mitchell is a reception machine and is excellent in 3rd and 4th down situations, quickly getting open. Mostly used as the 'Z' or the move receiver for the Ducks who rarely lines up on the line of scrimmage. A smart guy who understands how to find soft openings in space and adjust to his QB. Excellent in contested situations either on the sideline or in the middle of the field, showing the ability to snatch the ball away from his frame

Weaknesses: Mitchell's biggest issue is his inconsistencies with his hands, frequently having some extremely inopportune drops. Many of them being simple concentration drops, where he just loses focus. Many of his receptions are manufactured, where his coaches utilize him as a mismatch down the field against safeties, or when he's lined up in bunch formations. Has a bad habit of dropping to the ground to adjust to poorly thrown balls, leaving him with no ability to create after the catch. Lacks toughness and finish as a runner with the ball in his hands, not fully utilizing his explosiveness in open-field situations. Quick but not fast, lacks the vertical speed to frequently test the back half of a defense outside the hashes.

Best Fit: Z-receiver

Player Ranking (1-100): 77.7 – Mitchell is a talented receiver who makes his living mostly in-between the hashes. His precision, footwork and 0-10 acceleration are top-notch. He's more of a high-volume guy than a big-play guy. Seems to have a really good grasp of timing routes and being on the same page as his QB, always where he needs to be. He's a solid #2 receiver who should play as a 'Z.' He's a 1st down machine and will catch a LOT of balls at the next level. 3rd round player.

18. Terry McLaurin WR Ohio State 6'0 205 lbs

Strengths: A 3-year contributor in a loaded wide receiving depth chart, McLaurin had a stellar senior season with over 700 yards receiving and 11 touchdowns. Plays mostly out of the slot, but has outside experience as well. Shows fluidity and agility in the way that he runs. He gets terrific 0-10 yard acceleration out of his stance, showing the quickness and balance to get clean releases off the line of scrimmage. If pressed, he shows adequate hand strength to beat jams. A flexible athlete who shows fluid and flexible hips to create clear separation on lateral routes. McLaurin is a big-play guy who shows a diversified ability to run a variety of different routes, both shallow and deep. Feisty with the ball in his hands, showing toughness and physicality to fight for additional yardage. Good vision in the open-field to create for himself and fight openings downfield. Possesses flexible body control to track the ball down the field and make tough, contested plays. Possesses good overall speed, showing the ability on quite a few occasions to separate in vertical situations.

Weaknesses: McLaurin has had some really poor drops at inopportune times. A body catcher who is far too passive in waiting for the ball to arrive into his chest. Obviously doesn't trust his hands, rarely extends and makes clean catches. An inconsistent route-runner shows flashes of excellence, but far too often gives away his routes too early in the stem.

Best Fit: #2 receiver/slot receiver

Player Ranking (1-100): 77.2 – I really like McLaurin and I think he has a chance to be a better NFL receiver than college. He's a good athlete who shows toughness, physicality, and agility. He's still raw in the way he runs routes, but his hip flexibility and overall movement skills give me confidence he can get better. Give him a year of seasoning and I think a team will have a solid #2 wide receiver. 3rd round player.

19. Andy Isabella WR UMass 5'9 186 lbs

Strengths: Isabella is a 3-year starter for UMass at receiver, he has had tremendous production in the last 3 seasons with 30 touchdowns and over 3500 yards receiving. Isabella is an incredibly quick-footed and shifty receiver and shows tremendous agility and fluidity. Does the most damage after the catch, showing outstanding open-field ability. Will serve as a dual-purpose guy with the ability to play special teams and in the return game. As a receiver, Isabella displays great initial acceleration showing the ability to separate at all levels of routes. Great and sticky hands showing the ability to extend and pluck the football out of the air. A nuanced route-runner who shows good deception and manipulation. Does a lot of damage against zone-coverages understanding where to pick up soft spots in coverage. A competitive sprinter with long-speed to run behind defenses. A fun guy to watch who battles on every snap, playing with a relentless motor and effort. Despite the small-school competition, showed success against big-time college programs.

Weaknesses: Isabella is a small and undersized receiver who will be limited to a slot role at the next level. Struggles in contested situations, lacking the hand strength and wing-span to extend. Despite his track background, he appears quick but not especially fast on tape, failing to separate consistently on vertical routes. Lacks the adequate length to consistently play against bigger NFL cornerbacks.

Best Fit: Slot receiver

Player Ranking (1-100): 76.8 – An outstanding career in college but will certainly have some challenges making the leap up against better competition. He's not just a standard run of the mill "slot receiver." Isabella is a lot more and is already a nuanced, skillful player who shows an ability to really stand out from other slot players in this draft and in the past as well. 3rd round player.

20. JJ Arcega-Whiteside WR Stanford 6'3 225 lbs

Strengths: Whiteside is a big-bodied receiver with long legs and a high torso who displays outstanding size and length. Whiteside is your classic possession-based receiver, utilizing his frame to box out smaller DBs. In each of the last 2 seasons, Whiteside has had really solid production with 750+ yards and outstanding touchdown numbers each season. A real red-zone nightmare, Whiteside has strong hands and can win the majority of the 50/50 balls with his vertical leaping ability and length. He utilizes his body control and ball tracking ability to find the ball mid-flight to adjust his body to win at the catch point. Whiteside is an above average route runner who utilizes his quick feet to create some spacing at the line of scrimmage. Whiteside is impressive in his ability to use his sticky hands and body control to adjust to badly thrown balls. Does a nice job of utilizing the sidelines and has the awareness to keep his feet in bounds. Plays with a swagger and toughness about him. Rarely goes down to the first tackler and pushes off arm tackles with ease.

Weaknesses: Missed end of his senior campaign after suffering a knee injury. Struggles getting any type of separation consistently in college and will really struggle at the next level. Was a deep-play threat in college but likely won't be the same type of player at the next level and will have to win on the short/intermediate type of routes. Strictly an outside receiver at this point. Lacks great top-end speed to threaten the back half of an NFL defense.

Best Fit: Outside receiver

Player Ranking (1-100): 76.5 – Whiteside is a good prospect who is a slightly better target then Lazard was last year. Similar players but Whiteside is slightly faster and is better with the ball in his hands. Could project to be a # 2 receiver at the next level with some seasoning and refinement. 3rd round player.

21. Cody Thompson WR Toledo 6'2 205 lbs

Strengths: Thompson is a 5th year starter who started all 4 seasons for MAC conference Toledo. Had a medical redshirt his senior year after breaking his leg, so was able to play an additional year as a senior. Had his best year in 2016 with almost 1300 yards receiving and 11 touchdowns. Thompson is a well-built prospect who shows good thickness as a receiver with good height/length as well. A big-play guy who makes a living on running double moves getting behind the defense. Experience in the return game, returned a punt for a touchdown this past season. Thompson is an above average athlete who shows outstanding vertical leaping ability to out jump defensive backs in flight. Plays like a running back with the ball in his hands, rarely going down without a fight. Thompson's best attribute is his route-running ability, showing nuance and impressive footwork to create deception at all levels of his route. A versatile threat who plays both inside and outside. A physical receiver who takes blocking personally. A tough as nails receiver who plays with fearlessness, never hesitating to run across the middle of the field.

Weaknesses: A build-up speed runner who takes a second to get going and lacks great burst out of his stance. Mostly used on a vertical plain, showing some uprightness in his routes, failing to have the adequate change of direction and agility. A body catcher who doesn't extend his arms to catch with his hands. Too passive at the catch point and doesn't always attack the football, waiting for it to arrive into his chest. A solid athlete who lacks elite speed to routinely win at the next level on the outside.

Best Fit: Big slot, occasionally can be used on the outside

Player Ranking (1-100): 76.2 – Really impressed by Thompson. He's not a top-tier athlete who displays tremendous explosion or quickness, but he's just a flat-out football player and is tough as nails. A nuanced football player who is more than just a TOUGH player, and certainly has translatable skills. 3rd round player. I think he would be a great oversized slot receiver.

22. Jakobi Meyers WR North Carolina State 6'2 196 lbs

Strengths: Meyers is a 2-year starter for the Wolfpack who had a good sophomore season before really coming onto the draft scene this year with an outstanding junior season, reeling in a school record 92 catches totaling 1047 yards and 4 touchdowns. Meyers possesses good next-level size, showing necessary strength, wingspan and bulk. Meyers is an absolute reception machine, comfortable in all areas of the field. He's completely trustworthy in contested situations, showing soft hands and the ability to box out defensive backs. Meyers utilizes his sticky hands to routinely make tough, outstretched grabs, fully utilizing his entire wingspan. A bad ball catcher who can dig balls off the ground. Shows excellent and flexible body control to adjust to the ball mid-flight and catch the ball between multiple defenders. Does a really nice job altering speeds on deep-field routes, showing a 5th gear to get behind the defense. Good awareness against zone-defense to find soft spots in the defense where he patiently sits in. A tough competitor who shows fearlessness when working in the middle of the field. An above-average blocker with the strength, size and hand usage to be a solid move blocker.

Weaknesses: Meyers plays the vast majority of his snaps in the slot where he can be lined up against smaller corners, taking advantage of mismatches. Meyers is a build-up speed guy but lacks elite acceleration and short-area bursts. This affects his ability to separate down the field, relying on his frame and outstretched hands to make challenged catches. Isn't much of a " yards after catch" guy, tending to only get what's given, almost always going down upon the first contact. A little bit of a clunky runner who has trouble redirecting his frame and regaining momentum on double moves. Not much of a vertical threat, tending to do most of his damage on shorter/intermediate routes. A high-torso frame with long legs which could make him susceptible to injuries at the next level.

Best Fit: Slot receiver/occasionally used on the outside

Player Ranking (1-100): 75.5 – Meyers is a reception machine who is a better athlete than you would expect. He isn't a burner but isn't a slow methodical mover either. He's going to be a valuable #2 or 3 receiver for a team. He will be a 'move the chains' guy for a team. A bit of a poor man's Cooper Kupp with his work out of the slot as an oversized slot receiver. He will consistently catch the ball in tough situations and be a QB's best friend with his reliability. 3rd round player.

23. Tyre Brady WR Marshall 6'2 206 lbs

Strengths: Brady is a transfer from Miami who has played the last 2 seasons for the Thundering Herd. Possessing the ideal length and frame to play on the outside at the next level. Brady has had 2 really impressive seasons with 17 touchdowns and almost 2,000 yards receiving combined. Brady is a team leader and is known on campus to be a hard worker. Impressive wingspan, Brady shows the ability to utilize his big strong hands to pluck the ball out of the air. A bad ball catcher, constantly grabbing the ball out of the dirt or away from his body. Outstanding in jump-ball situations showcasing his ability to get vertical and outstretched. Very hard to cover in red-zone situations due to his ability to get up. Excellent catching the ball in heavy traffic, showcasing fearlessness, body control, and concentration. More than a 50/50 guy, just throw it in his vicinity and he will somehow/someway come down with the football. Good long-speed with the ability to run away from guys. Knows how to utilize the sidelines and consistently make sure he gets his foot down.

Weaknesses: A straight-line athlete who was rarely used to cross field or change direction. Small route-tree with most of his routes being vertical, focusing on his long speed. Lacks the separation quickness or the footwork to create consistent spacing on short/intermediate routes. A slow accelerator who takes a few seconds to get to top gear. Not a bulldozer with the ball in his hands, and can be a rather easy guy to bring down. Little experience in having to use any kind of jam technique at the line of scrimmage, almost always given a free release. Very little experience in the slot.

Best Fit: Outside receiver

Player Ranking (1-100): 75.3 – I rarely like receivers who can't consistently separate but there's something about Brady that is desirable for me. I've never seen a guy that catches more poor balls, or 50/50 balls. He catches EVERYTHING. It's unbelievable. He's still a work in progress as far as his route running and possession fundamentals but his size and hands make him worth a 3rd round pick for me.

24. Stanley Morgan Jr. WR Nebraska 6'1 200 lbs

Strengths: Morgan Jr is a 4-year starter for the Cornhuskers who has really shown up big the last 2 seasons with over 900 yards in each of the last 2 seasons. Morgan Jr is a versatile target who can lineup at any of the WR positions for Nebraska. An absolute playmaker showing the ability to be an electric offensive weapon for any offense. Impressive and smooth accelerator showing the ability to separate at all levels of a route. Morgan Jr is a fluid mover, showcasing smooth hips, coordination and flexibility to misdirect and alter course. A physical finisher with the ball showcasing the ability to run through guys or over them. Plays bigger than his size, with the ability to go up and high point contested balls. Makes some amazing circus catches showing the ability to win high-point balls in flight. Experienced and nuanced route-runner possessing a wide diversity of routes and clean footwork at the top of his routes to create spacing.

Weaknesses: Was arrested in May of 2017 for possession of felony amounts of marijuana. A bit sluggish and disinterested in his play at times, looking lethargic and slow off the line of scrimmage. Prone to some concentration drops. Lacks the ideal stature and length for an outside receiver in the NFL. Quicker than fast and lacks the elite top-end speed. Inconsistent in his ability to win 50/50 balls, would like to see him come away with more of them.

Best Fit: 'Z' move receiver for a team

Player Ranking (1-100): 74.8 – Stanley is a good all-around receiver who can fulfill so many roles for a team. At times, he looks just 'OK' and other times he's a world beater who takes over games. He's a 4th round player and can eventually be a solid # 2 receiver for a team.

25. KeeSean Johnson WR Fresno State 6'2 199 lbs

Strengths: Johnson is a 4-year starter for the Bulldogs who has had tremendous production the last 2 seasons, with over 1,000 yards receiving in each. A reception machine who catches so many big and crucial 3rd downs for his offense, and had 95 catches this past season. Johnson is a physical point of attack blocker and takes it seriously, showing the willingness to do the dirty work. A versatile threat, he plays both in the slot and on the outside. Has punt and kickoff return experience as well. Johnson's best attribute is his hands, he catches absolutely everything. It doesn't matter if he's draped over by multiple defenders, in contested situations, or making routine 1-handed catches. Excellent at utilizing the sidelines and getting his feet in-bounds. Has outstanding ball tracking skills to contort his body to adjust to the ball in mid-flight. Utilizes his body to shield defenders from making plays on the ball at the catch point. Physical with the ball in his hands, great at fighting for additional yardage. A surprising amount of shiftiness in the open-field, rarely getting tackled by the 1st contact. Runs his routes with clean footwork and nuance, showing an impressive ability to alter route speeds to create at the breakpoint.

Weaknesses: Johnson is an average athlete who lacks any kind of special athletic attribute, causing him to get very little separation on any type of route. A slighter-framed guy who lacks adequate body armor to be a threat with the ball in his hands. Played in the Mountain West and didn't have to go up against many top-tier corners.

Best Fit: Possession receiver who can be an effective #3 receiver

Player Ranking (1-100): 74.5 – Johnson is an under the radar guy who needs to move up draft boards. Isn't going to blow anyone away athletically, but it doesn't' matter for me. Johnson is the definition of an effective receiver, who is going to be an absolute beast on 3rd down. A nuanced route-runner with some of the best hands in this draft class. I think he's going to be a really solid #3 receiver for a team at the next level. Should go in the 4th round.

26. Greg Dortch WR Wake Forest 5'9 170 lbs

Strengths: Dortch is a smaller and tremendously explosive athlete for the Demon Deacons. Only a redshirt sophomore, will only be 20 years old for the NFL draft. Tremendous production in each of his 2 seasons for Wake Forest. Some evaluators have even compared him to Tyreek Hill. A tremendously gifted athlete who shows outstanding long-speed and potential to be a big-play guy as both a receiver and in the return game. One of the best punt returners in the country, if not the best. Dortch is a flat-out playmaker who is always a threat with the ball in his hands, showing great elusiveness and open-field ability to make guys miss in a phone booth. Plays with a competitive toughness and swagger, showing fearlessness in contested situations. Brings it on every rep. A nuanced route-runner, he does a great job of selling his routes. Impressive deep-ball tracking ability, with the ability to adjust his body and utilize good body control to make the grab.

Weaknesses: Missed the final five games with a punctured intestine in 2017. A very slight physique which will limit him to strictly slot duties as a receiver at the next level. A body catcher who waits for the ball to reach his chest, rather than attacking it. Lacks the length to snatch the ball away from his frame with a marginal catch radius. More of a pesky blocker when asked to do it rather than a physical point of attack guy. Has had some bad drops, not always the most reliable in contested situations despite his incredible body control to adjust in flight.

Best Fit: Slot receiver, occasional outside rep as deep target

Player Ranking (1-100): 74.3 – A 4th round player that you absolutely should take a chance on. Dortch is a 20-year-old kid with rare athleticism and explosiveness. He's still raw and will need refinement as a receiver, but he holds outstanding value immediately as a return guy. He is limited as strictly a slot receiver, but he's a gadget that a clever offensive minded coach can use effectively in a variety of different ways. I would run to the podium to announce this player if he's still on the board in the 5th round. He's that talented. Hope he goes to the right team where he can excel.

27. Jalen Hurd WR Baylor 6'5 227 lbs

Strengths: Hurd is a big, physical receiver who shows outstanding girth and muscularity. To say Hurd's journey to this point is anything short of unique is putting it mildly. Hurd was a 245 pound running back at Tennessee who put up 1300 yards rushing his sophomore season before taking a 2-year sabbatical and transferring to Baylor to play wide receiver. Hurd greatly impressed this year for Baylor as a receiver with over 1000 yards total from scrimmage and 7 touchdowns. He's a dual-purpose player who still takes some carries in the backfield. His experience as a running back is evident in his yards after catch ability, showing outstanding contact balance and elusive traits. A natural catcher of the football, showing big mitts with the ability to extend. Fearless in traffic, Hurd shows a really nice ability to snatch the football and high point the ball. He utilizes his large frame to box out and shield smaller defensive backs. Shows impressive suddenness at the top of his routes to separate on short/intermediate routes. A QB friendly target who always works his way back toward the football, finding soft zones in coverage.

Weaknesses: There will be some concerns about Hurd quitting football, and whether he truly loves the game. Runs a very limited route tree who is almost entirely a short/intermediate route guy. Plays almost exclusively out of the slot. Needs more nuance in his route-running, and is still extremely raw as a receiver.

Best Fit: Slot/developmental receiver can be used on special teams and in the backfield at times too

Player Ranking (1-100): 72.2 – I have some concerns about Hurd as a person and whether he truly wants to be committed to football. As far as the physical traits, there's so much to love about Hurd. His size, physicality, toughness, and athleticism. I wouldn't feel comfortable drafting him until the 4th round.

28. Travis Fulgham WR Old Dominion 6'2 210 lbs

Strengths: Fulgham is a 4-year contributor to Conference-USA Old Dominion. He came onto the scene in a very big way this season with almost 1100 yards receiving and 9 touchdowns. Fulgham has an interesting story and didn't come to the US until 9th grade where he started playing football. Fulgham possesses an outstanding NFL quality frame with great length and height. Coaches love Fulgham and praise him for his work ethic. His love of football is infectious and it shows with how much he loves to block. An outstanding blocker who loves the physical aspects of the game, showing the ability to sustain and latch on. Trustworthy in contested situations, Fulgham utilizes his frame to box and shield smaller defenders out and win the majority of 50/50 balls. Outstanding leaping ability to go up and snatch the football at its high point. Has experience playing both in the slot and on the outside. A load to have to handle in red-zone situations with his jumping ability and wing-span.

Weaknesses: Even though he played against some good defenses like Virginia Tech, he still didn't compete against many. Possesses above average speed, but lacks elite separation quickness to consistently separate at the next level. Still needs refinement with his footwork both at the line of scrimmage and at the top of his routes. Would like to see him use a little more nuance and route deception to create for himself.

Best Fit: All-around receiver who can play anywhere

Player Ranking (1-100): 71.8 – Fulgham is a developmental prospect who really excelled this year. I think he's going to compete for a #3 or #4 spot on an NFL wide receiver depth chart. He's got a great frame and plays with physicality, but he's not a guy who is going to consistently separate. 4th round player.

29. John Ursua WR Hawaii 5'10 175 lbs

Strengths: Ursua is a productive little receiver out of Hawaii who had a tremendous junior campaign with 1343 yards and 16 touchdowns. He's not just your typical quick, shifty slot receiver. He possesses deceptive speed down the field as well, showing above-average deep-speed beating some defensive backs on vertical routes. He already runs a full route-tree showing the ability to consistently separate at all levels of routes. Shows nuance in his routes, utilizing outstanding balance, footwork, and wiggle. Despite his lack of ideal length, Ursua does show reliable and sticky hands showcasing the ability to consistently outstretch his arms and catch the ball away from his frame. Shifty with the ball in his hands, frequently making the 1st guy miss in space. A fearless guy who makes a living on mid-field routes showing toughness, focus and finish. Trustworthy in contested situations.

Weaknesses: Tore his ACL his sophomore season 6 games in. Due to his lack of stride length, Ursua's will still fail to separate on vertical routes against longer, faster defensive backs. Tends to need the ball on a silver platter, failing to adjust to poorly thrown balls. Strictly a slot receiver. Very thin, even for a slot receiver, lacking suitable body armor. Would like to see him gain 5-10 pounds of muscle without sacrificing his explosive nature.

Best Fit: Slot receiver

Player Ranking (1-100): 70.5 – Ursua is a really good slot receiver. As far as strictly a slot receiver, he might be the best in this class. His top-end speed is rare for a guy who is on the short side. On quite a few occasions his junior season, he showcased the ability to beat guys on vertical plains. His lack of size/body armor to withstand an NFL season is a bit troublesome. Especially for a guy who makes his living in the middle of the field. His production levels were off the charts, and I think he's going to be a really good slot receiver at the next level. 4th round player.

30. David Sills WR West Virginia 6'3 210 lbs

Strengths: Sills is a former QB at West Virginia before transitioning to a WR before his junior season. Made the transition very quickly showcasing outstanding production in those 2 years with 33 touchdowns and almost 2,000 yards receiving. Due to Sills' height, he is a difficult challenge to match up to for smaller corners. Outstanding red-zone receiver, showcasing the skill to routinely, out jump, out muscle and physically dominate smaller corners. An absolute touchdown machine for the Mountaineers offense because of his ability to finish plays and win the 50/50 balls. Attacks the football and high points the ball perfectly. Moves all over the offense, playing both on the outside and in the slot. Above-average long speed showing the ability to run past corners and safeties on '9' routes. A physical blocker down the field, with the toughness and the willingness to block for his teammates at all levels.

Weaknesses: A build-up speed guy who takes a while to get to full speed. Lacks the separation quickness to be able to create any spacing for himself at breakpoints or at the top of routes. Stiff in his hips and in his body, movements making it extremely difficult for him to play horizontally, preventing him from getting much separation on underneath routes. Very lanky frame, lacking the necessary power and strength to be a threat with the ball in his hands.

Best Fit: #4 or #5 receiver for a team

Player Ranking (1-100): 69.4 – Sills has had a really nice couple of years as a receiver. His size and long-speed make him an attractive candidate as a developmental type of wide receiver. He has athletic limitations but he's worth a 5th round pick.

31. Mecole Hardman WR Georgia 5'11 183 lbs

Strengths: Hardman is a 2-year situational contributor for the Bulldogs who has primarily been known as the big-play guy for the offense. Hardman had a good final season with 543 yards receiving and 7 touchdowns. Hardman has great speed, absolutely destroying angles by safeties in pursuit. The definition of explosiveness, one of the fastest players in this draft without question. Tremendous vertical leaping ability and short-area bursts as well. He's also the Bulldogs return guy, both on punts and on kickoffs, as well as the gunner on special teams. He shows big-play ability when used in the return game as well, returning a punt this past season for a touchdown. Reliable hands, with the ability to extend and catch the ball consistently outside of his frame. Dynamic in the open-field, utilizing his speed, agility, and vision to create for himself. Good awareness, understanding how to utilize the sidelines and keep his feet in-bounds.

Weaknesses: Hardman is very slight and will get bullied on the line of scrimmage against bigger corners. Really struggles beating jams and getting clean releases off the line of scrimmage. Reliant completely on his speed in the open-field rather than any kind of physicality/strength to break tackles. Almost always goes down upon the first contact. A very simple route tree that is designed to get him in space and mismatched, where he rarely lines up on the line of scrimmage. Most of his big plays were on manufactured plays to get him in space, either on screens, in the slot, or in bunch formations. Rarely gets a chance to show he can catch the ball in traffic or in contested situations.

Best Fit: Developmental receiver and return guy immediately

Player Ranking (1-100): 68.9 – Hardman is one of the most athletic, explosive athletes in this whole draft class without question. His short-area quickness matches his long-speed which matches his vertical leaping ability. The problem is, he's raw, VERY raw. He runs a very limited route tree, lacking the route-running ability or experience to be a nuanced wide receiver at this point. He needs a lot of work and refinement to hone in on his craft. Otherwise, he might just be a special teams' player and situational deep-threat at the next level. He's worth a 5th round pick due to his special teams' ability and athleticism.

32. Lil' Jordan Humphrey WR Texas 6'4 225 lbs

Strengths: Humphrey is a huge framed target, displaying tremendous girth and thickness throughout his body. Came onto the scene after a stellar final season, as a junior, with just under 1200 yards, 86 catches and 9 touchdowns. Was used as a kick returner in each of the last 2 seasons as well. Played as a running back in high school and shows it with his physicality and elusive ability with the ball in his hands. He shrugs off and easily breaks uncommitted tackles, always a threat with the ball. Plays solely as an oversized slot receiver and is an absolute nightmare for smaller defensive backs who he can out muscle and box out. Understands how to find small soft spaces in zone coverage. Reliable hands in contested situations, showing strong mitts. A QB friendly target that never gives up on routes, always working to find space on broken down plays. Utilizes his length to displace and angle block smaller defenders in the run game. Shows the ability to snatch the ball away from his frame and high-point the ball on occasion as well. Possesses some wiggle in the way he runs routes, creating deception towards the breakpoint.

Weaknesses: Still a very raw route runner who lacks consistent sharpness and precision, seemingly rounding off many of his routes. An average athlete, he lacks great physical characteristics other than his size. Struggles with lateral routes, or when attempting to cross-field, immediately gears down when changing direction. Lacks much experience on the outside, and is strictly a slot receiver. Ran mostly very shallow routes, rarely used down the field. Limited route tree who made a living on comebacks, screens, hitches, and slants.

Best Fit: Oversized slot receiver

Player Ranking (1-100): 67.7 – Not as big a fan of Humphrey as some are. He had a stellar year, but his actual transferrable receiving traits don't get me excited. He could be an effective slot receiver, but never a great one. Utilizing him in a very limited way will be frustrating for coaching staffs. 5th round player.

33. Penny Hart WR Georgia State 5'8 180 lbs

Strengths: Hart is a 3-year starter for Sun-Belt conference Georgia State who has had over 1100 yards receiving in 2 separate seasons. Offers upside value as an experienced punt and kickoff return specialist as well. Hart has rare short-area quickness and shows tremendous balance through all levels of his routes. Changes direction and alters route course with relative ease, showing fluidity and flexibility throughout his frame. A smooth route-runner, he shows route deception and speed alterations in all levels of his route to create spacing. A quick accelerator who gets from 0-60 in a flash. A threat with the ball in his hands, utilized on option-runs, showing terrific open-field ability and vision. Shows really good body control to contort his body in space and adjust to the football. Despite not having ideal length, Hart does show the ability to extend and snatch the ball away from his frame.

Weaknesses: Hart is a very small receiver who lacks the size to offer anything on the outside. Has some serious concentration lapses, leading to some poor drops. Didn't compete against top-tier competition and was the conference's best receiver since his freshman season. A willing blocker but lacks the length to engage or sustain any kind of blocks.

Best Fit: Slot receiver and return guy

Player Ranking (1-100): 66.2 – Hart is a really good slot receiver who displays rare change of direction and start/stop quickness. He's a complete mismatch who will generate instant separation at all levels. His size certainly limits his versatility, but he's a talented athlete who will offer upside on shorter/intermediate routes. A fun 5th round player who can be an exciting toy for an offense.

34. Keelan Doss WR California-Davis 6'2 207 lbs

Strengths: Doss is a 4-year contributor for UC Davis who played in almost 40 games in college, posting outstanding production each season, totaling 1500 yards his junior season. Doss possesses next-level NFL size with good overall weight distribution and length. Doss is a deep threat who displays terrific body control and concentration to adjust to the ball downfield in contested double-team situations. Routinely extends his frame and makes tough catches outside of his frame in traffic. A versatile receiver, he shows the ability to line up outside or in the slot. Understands how to operate in space, finding soft openings and sitting in. A red-zone nightmare with the skill to constantly out jump and fight for balls in mid-flight. A physical down the field blocker who takes blocking seriously, routinely sustaining his man or clearing 2nd level lanes. A QB friendly target who regularly works his way back towards the ball.

Weaknesses: Doss isn't overly fast or quick, and can be a bit clunky in and out of his breaks, lacking the separation quickness to consistently gain spacing. Is reliant on out jumping and outmuscling lesser competition in college. A bit stiff in his hips and core, lacking the ability to change direction without gearing down. A minimal threat with the ball in his hands, generally going down to the first tackler.

Best Fit: Versatile #3 or 4 receiver for a team

Player Ranking (1-100): 66.0 – Doss is a guy who really impressed me on tape. I think he absolutely should make an NFL roster. He catches absolutely everything! Add the fact that he had a really good Senior Bowl, and I really think he can compete against top-flight competition. He's not going to win any athletic competitions, but he's a good football player who does all the little things really well.

35. Hunter Renfrow WR Clemson 5'10 175 lbs

Strengths: Renfrow is a smaller slot receiver who really made his name in the national championship game catching the game-winning touchdown. An impressive route runner showing a nice ability to adjust his route speeds, deceptively timing his breaks to create separation. A smooth accelerator who shows really nice initial quickness off the line of scrimmage, and good separation quickness at the top of his routes. A surprisingly physical guy after catching the ball, keeping his body low and square, and always a threat to pick up significant yards post-catch. Renfrow possesses really good quickness and balance in gaining a clean release off the line of scrimmage. A smart kid who understands the mental side of the game, showing good awareness in using pick and rub type of routes to create for himself.

Weaknesses: Quicker than fast, Renfrow is a guy who is strictly a slot receiver. A really slight frame and has ridiculously small hands. Lacks any great physical tools and possesses very limited upside. Lacks the ideal physicality at the catch point, will get bullied by bigger corners who can press him at the line of scrimmage. More of a pesky than a passionate blocker down the field, lacking the suitable strength and power to assist much.

Best Fit: Slot receiver

Player Ranking (1-100): 64.3 – Renfrow is a good slot receiver who is a smooth and fluid route runner. Lacks ideal physicality and size, but can be a really good role player at the next level. 6th round pick.

36. Jaylen Smith WR Louisville 6'2 221 lbs

Strengths: Smith is a 4-year contributor for the Tigers who had an outstanding junior season with Lamar Jackson with 1,000 yards and 7 touchdowns. Smith is built with rare physical size, showing an impressively thick physique and really nice length. Smith is a smooth receiver who runs routes with precision and deception. Despite his size, Smith is a quick and fluid accelerator who displays impressive separation quickness with the ability to break quickly on his routes. Understands how to utilize the middle of the field, and eats up zone-coverages. A QB's dream, he always makes himself available and works back toward the QB, never giving up on a play. Physical blocker who takes the end of the game seriously. Has made some tremendous acrobatic catches during his career, displaying excellent hands and ball control.

Weaknesses: Smith's production dropped quite a bit after Lamar Jackson left school as a senior. Has had some nagging injury concerns during his career which he's mostly played through. Needs to learn how to utilize his size more effectively to box out and outmuscle smaller defensive backs. Does most of his damage in the slot, rarely is effective on the outside. Very limited route tree who is mostly reliant on 5-10 yard routes or eating up zone-coverages. Quicker than fast, Smith isn't a great overall athlete who is going to out jump or run past corners down the field regularly.

Best Fit: #4 or 5 receiver

Player Ranking (1-100): 63.2 – An effective receiver who can compete for a #4 or #5 spot on a team. Will need to prove his effectiveness as a special teams' player to win a spot on the roster. But his size and ability to work the middle of the field will be appealing for teams. 5th round player.

37. Darius Slayton WR Auburn 6'2 190 lbs

Strengths: Slayton is a 2-year starter for the Tigers who has played in 11 games each of the last 2 years posting almost identical levels of production in each season. Slayton is a big-play guy who made a living on attacking the deep parts of the field, averaging over 20 yards per reception during his career at Auburn. Shows some versatility having played all over the Auburn offensive front, both in the slot and on the outside. A natural catcher of the football, utilizing his big mitts and long arms to snatch the ball away from his frame. Shows vertical separation, possessing good long speed with the ability to create for himself at the top. Good footwork at the top of his routes to create spacing, showing route deception and balance. Terrific and varied releases at the line of scrimmage, using good hand strength and wiggle to quickly shed against press coverage, keeping his frame clean. Shows effort and willingness as a blocker. Plays far bigger than his size would suggest.

Weaknesses: Slayton has major strength concerns and he's constantly bullied in the run game, getting blown off the ball against downhill defenders. Far too often doesn't finish, putting himself in outstanding positions and adjusting to the ball in flight, and then failing to hold on to the football. Plays in the very simple Auburn offense where he wasn't required to have a vast knowledge of an intelligent playbook, running very limited routes. Limited with the ball in his hands, lacking the strength or the open-field shiftiness to create for himself.

Best Fit: #4 or 5 receiver

Player Ranking (1-100): 62.8 – Slayton is a good player who has good receiving traits, including speed. He's likely going to have to compete in training camp for a spot on a roster, but he displays enough athleticism and skill to absolutely compete for it. 6th round player.

38. Gary Jennings Jr WR West Virginia 6'1 213 lbs

Strengths: Jennings Jr is an impressive receiver who quietly has gone under the radar the last 2 seasons despite putting up outstanding production. Jennings Jr has the ideal size and length for an NFL possession receiver. Does a nice job of adjusting to poorly thrown balls with a defender on his back. Shows the toughness to finish plays and pick up additional yards after the catch. Trustworthy in contested situations. Jennings is a reception machine, dominating the middle of the field on short/intermediate routes. He's a 1st down maker who is frequently relied upon to pick up a big 1st down. Powerful lower half, making it very difficult for smaller guys to bring him down. Reliable and sticky hands who catches almost everything.

Weaknesses: Has a bad habit of dropping to the ground when the ball isn't right on the money. A very average athlete who lacks any ability to get into a 2nd gear. Clunky and awkward with the ball, failing to get away from defenders. Lacks separation quickness to get away from cornerbacks, the defender is almost

ALWAYS in his hip pocket. Reliant on playing solely in the slot to utilize his size as a mismatch against smaller corners. Rarely catches the ball down the field past 10 yards. Despite his size and his strength, you don't always see him play with ideal physicality.

Best Fit: Oversized slot receiver

Player Ranking (1-100): 62.1 – Jennings Jr reminds me of an Anquan Bolden Lite. He's a good player who has outstanding size and strength but I just wish he would bully and use his size more like Bolden did in the slot. He's a 6th round player.

39. Ryan Davis WR Auburn 5'9 185 lbs

Strengths: Davis is a 2-year starter for the Tigers offense who has had solid production each of the last 2 years. An absolute production machine, Davis has had 153 catches the last 2 seasons. Versatile in his ability to play on the outside and in the slot. Offers upside as a return guy, and was the teams' primary kick off return guy this past season. Has done a nice job of adding muscle and size during his college career, maximizing his frame. Davis is always a threat with the ball in his hands, showing outstanding elusive ability to create. Shows good quickness and acceleration, getting to top gear in a flash. A good overall athlete who has some separation ability to create in and out of his breaks with good, clean footwork. Deep speed to take plays to the house.

Weaknesses: Lacks ideal body size to play as an outside receiver at the next level. Will get bullied at the line of scrimmage, lacking ideal physicality and hand strength to quickly disengage. Not a bulldozer with the ball in his hands, tends to go down easily if a defender gets 2 hands on him. Runs mostly short to intermediate routes, fails to have any kind of experience on down the field routes. Gained most of his yards on screens, hitches and manufactured offensive plays designed to get him in space.

Best Fit: Special teams and slot receiver

Player Ranking (1-100): 61.0 – Davis showed his abilities to run routes and create separation during the pre-draft process. He's a guy who has a chance to far exceed where he gets taken in the draft. He should be a 6th round player.

40. Diontae Johnson WR Toledo 5'11 181 lbs

Strengths: Johnson is a smaller, athletically-built receiver who has had a fairly productive career at Toledo. Johnson is a dual-purpose player who presents tremendous upside as a return guy, having some huge returns in the punting game. Johnson is an explosive athlete at all areas of the football field, showing smooth acceleration coupled with excellent top-speed to take the top off a defense. Johnson is tougher than his size would indicate, flashing some ability down the field and battling against defensive backs in the air. Really good body control and ball tracking abilities down the field, showing the ability to adjust to the football. Tremendous open-field ability, always a threat to take it to the house with shiftiness and rare start/stop ability. Good releases both off the line of scrimmage and at the top of his routes, showing good wiggle and balance.

Weaknesses: Came onto the scene his sophomore year with a fantastic season with almost 1300 yards receiving, and had a bit of a disappointing junior campaign almost halving his production numbers. To say Johnson's hands are very suspect is putting it nicely, he drops A LOT of very catchable balls. Has had some ball security concerns, fumbling at inopportune times in games. More of a pesky than a passionate blocker down the field. Might be limited to a slot role at the next level.

Best Fit: Slot receiver

Player Ranking (1-100): 60.8 - It's disappointing Johnson didn't stay in school. After a disappointing junior campaign, it would have been nice for Johnson to show he could replicate the success he achieved in his sophomore year. Sadly, I'm afraid it's going to drop his stock significantly. He's worth taking a risk on, due to his athleticism and open-field ability. Can possibly win a spot on a team due to his return ability early on. 6th round player.

41. Jazz Ferguson WR Northwestern State 6'5 220 lbs

Strengths: Ferguson is an LSU transfer who sat out his junior season, before posting outstanding numbers for Southland Conference Northwestern State with over 1100 yards and 13 touchdowns. Possesses rare size and length, displaying his tremendous wingspan at the catch point where he frequently can reach heights smaller DBs can't. Flexible body control with the ability to contort his frame and make some circus catches down the field. A bulldozer mentality with the ball in his hands post-catch, showing physicality and toughness to gain additional yardage down the field. Shows some surprising agility and core flexibility to change direction and gain some separation on horizontal routes. Trustworthy in heavily contested situations, utilizing his frame and outstretched arms to shield the ball. A nightmare in the red-zone due to his size, jumping ability.

Weaknesses: Was suspended his sophomore season at LSU for a failed drug test. Had some academic issues at LSU causing him to need a change of scenery. A build-up speed guy who lacks initial quickness and acceleration at the line of scrimmage. Didn't compete against many big-time defenses his senior year, played against much lesser competition. A very limited-route tree guy who is strictly an outside guy that tends to play on a vertical plain, besides some slants. Fails to separate at any level of his route against weaker college competition, not a good sign for him having to face NFL defenses. A bit of a lanky high-torso frame who needs to get stronger for the next level, or will suffer some bad hits and make him susceptible to injury.

Best Fit: Outside developmental receiver

Player Ranking (1-100): 56.4 – A developmental receiver who possesses outstanding toughness, size, length, and physicality. He's very raw in his footwork, route-running and in the mental side of playing wide receiver. He will compete for a number 4 or 5 receiver on a team. Certainly possesses some traits to like, but isn't a world beater. 7th round player.

42. Nyqwan Murray WR Florida State 5'11 192 lbs

Strengths: Murray is a 2-year starter and 3-year contributor for the Seminoles who has posted solid overall production the last 2 seasons. A versatile weapon who will line up in the backfield, in the slot or on the outside. Murray is a playmaker with the ball in his hands, showing outstanding open-field shiftiness. For being a smaller guy, Murray breaks a lot of tackles, showing toughness and lower body strength. A fluid mover with terrific initial quickness and agility to turn on a dime. Shows the looseness in his hips to change direction. An impressive route runner who will create for himself against all different types of corners, displaying terrific lateral quickness and balance.

Weaknesses: Murray was ejected during the game against Clemson this past year after throwing a punch, causing him to get suspended for the 1st half of their next game. A little careless and loose with the ball in his hands, leading to some unnecessary fumbles. Quicker than fast, will get caught from behind. Runs a very limited route tree, generally running strictly shorter routes designed to get him in space. Very poor hands, rarely catching the ball cleanly.

Best Fit: Slot receiver

Player Ranking (1-100): 55.6 – Murray is a developmental prospect who has a slighter frame and will most likely will have to stick to slot duties if he makes an NFL roster. A 7th round pick.

43. Steven Sims Jr WR Kansas 5'10 176 lbs

Strengths: Sims Jr has had an outstanding career at Kansas and is one of the leading receivers in the teams' history. As a senior, he's also carved out a role in the return game as well as showcasing his open-field capabilities. Sims Jr is the definition of explosive and can take it to the house any time he gets the ball. Despite his smaller stature, he shows the ability to high point the ball and attacks the football in the air. Has experience lining up both on the outside and in the slot in college. Outstanding footwork and body control, showing the ability to adjust to the football and work backward. Sharp footwork in/out of his breaks to create spacing.

Weaknesses: Extremely slight receiver who will likely have to carve out a role for himself primarily on special teams' and in the slot. Will get absolutely manhandled at the next level if he's playing on the outside, won't be able to get off the line of scrimmage. Small route-tree and is reliant on simple comeback routes and his athleticism to get separation. Lacks any kind of ability to be physical with the ball in his hands, goes down upon the first contact generally.

Best Fit: Slot receiver/Return guy

Player Ranking (1-100): 54.3 – I think Sims Jr is a really explosive athlete but is just too slight for the next level. He's going to have to put on additional muscle and strength to even play any snaps at all. Will have to show in camp that he has what it takes. Good college player. Will likely be an undrafted free agent.

44. Jamarius Way WR South Alabama 6'4 220 lbs

Strengths: Way is a JUCO transfer who went to South Alabama after impressing in Community College. Has really impressed at South Alabama with over 750 yards in each of the last 2 seasons. Way possesses outstanding and prototypical NFL size with a long wingspan. Way really excels at the catch point outmuscling smaller defensive backs, winning the majority of the 50/50 balls that come his way. A nightmare matchup in the red-zone, Way shows the ability to win consistently in 1 v 1 red-zone matchups. A good overall straight-line athlete who can run past guys but lacks elite long-speed. Trustworthy in a contested situation, showing the ability to box-out on comeback routes and utilize his body as a shield. Has the ability to adjust to the ball with a defender on his back. Had some good games going up against the better defenses when he faced Big-5 schools.

Weaknesses: Way made most of his living beating up on lesser competition where he was clearly the biggest/strongest guy on the football field. Like most tall receivers, Way struggles with the side to side movements with stiff hips and build-up speed. Lacks the ability to consistently separate. Very limited route-tree where he is frequently used for 2 or 3 different routes.

Best Fit: Outside developmental receiver

Player Ranking (1-100): 54.0 – Way is going to have to really impress during the pre-draft process because the way he wins in college likely won't be the way he wins at the next level. I believe he's going to be a UDFA who will have to win a spot in training camp.

45. Jovon Durante WR Florida Atlantic 6'0 171 lbs

Strengths: Durante is a 4th-year junior who transferred to Florida Atlantic following 2 seasons with West Virginia. Had just OK production at West Virginia before really coming onto the scene for FAU this year with almost 900 yards receiving and 5 touchdowns. Outstanding athlete who possesses really impressive initial acceleration off the line of scrimmage, as well as long-speed to separate on vertical routes. Shows open-field ability as well, utilizing his shiftiness and agility to cross the field and make explosive jump cuts. Good change of direction, showing the ability to drop his hips. Sudden route-runner showing start/stop ability on vertical routes and double moves. Shows physicality and a willingness when asked to block. Versatile and has experience playing both outside and inside.

Weaknesses: An extremely slight built guy who will need some strength and bulk work before playing much at the next level. Very inconsistent hands and drops some really easy balls. A body-catcher who waits for the ball to reach his body. Runs a very simple route-tree with only a few routes that he was relied on to run. Not a guy who is going to routinely catch the ball in congested situations. Gets a lot of his yards from manufactured screens off the line of scrimmage.

Best Fit: #4 or 5 receiver on a team

Player Ranking (1-100): 53.7 – A good athlete who needs major refinement before ever being relied upon at the next level. His slight frame and very shaky hands make him an undrafted free agent.

46. James Gardner WR Miami (OH) 6'4 217 lbs

Strengths: Gardner is an impressively-built receiver who displays tremendous size and overall girth for the next-level. He really came onto the scene after a stellar 2017 junior campaign in which he had over 900 yards receiving and 11 touchdowns, averaging almost 20 yards per catch. Excellent at utilizing his size, competing at the catch point and positioning his frame so that defensive backs can't make a play on the ball. A natural hands catcher who catches everything in the vicinity with good overall body control. He utilizes his sticky hands and his good length to extend and routinely make catches away from his body or in contested situations.

Weaknesses: Missed most of the 2018 season due to an undisclosed reason. A very subpar athlete who lacks great athletic ability, rarely showing the ability to separate at any level of his routes. An upright runner who gives away all his routes halfway through his stem, not understanding how to sell his routes. Lacks the ability to change direction or flip his hips on lateral routes. A stiff athlete, with tightness throughout his frame. Very minimal run after the catch ability, generally getting caught from behind rather easily. A subpar blocker who looks disinterested and passive despite his large frame. A bit of a lazy player who lacks fight or desire.

Best Fit: Outside receiver

Player Ranking (1-100): 51.2 – An undrafted free agent who will need to make his mark on special teams in training camp. He has serious athletic limitations which limit his ability to create any kind of separation at all. Don't see him making an NFL roster.

WR Top-10 Rankings

1. Kelvin Harmon
2. D.K. Metcalf
3. Marquise Brown
4. Deebo Samuel
5. A.J. Brown
6. N'Keal Harry
7. Riley Ridley
8. Emanuel Hall
9. Antoine Wesley
10. Anthony Johnson

Chapter 6

TE's

1. Noah Fant TE Iowa 6'5 241 lbs

Strengths: Fant is a long and athletically-built TE who has shown tremendous production each of the last 2 seasons for the Hawkeyes with over 1000 yards and 18 touchdowns combined. A rare athlete for the TE position, showcasing the ability to flip his hips and change direction with ease. Has the vertical ability to go up and snatch the ball mid-flight, combining his long wingspan with his vertical abilities. Shows the speed and explosive characteristics to create separation even against defensive backs. A fluid accelerator who reaches top-speed within a couple of steps. Good awareness and 'WANT' when it comes to his ability to position himself at the point of attack in pass protection. A big-play guy who shows the "yards after catch" ability to consistently pick up chunks of yards. Versatile guy who lines up in-line, as a slot receiver, or in bunch formations. Frequently had to adjust to badly thrown balls, playing with below average QB play. A wide array of routes, showing an understanding of how to win in a variety of different ways. A red-zone nightmare due to his ability to be used in mismatch situations. Impressive hands, showing the ability to dig the ball off the ground.

Weaknesses: One of Fant's biggest knocks is his inconsistency throughout games, frequently going missing for big chunks of games. Lacks ideal size and frame to play in-line with regularity at the next level, failing to possess the adequate anchor and power.

Best Fit: All-around TE who should be used mostly as a receiver

Player Ranking (1-100): 87.4 – I love Fant and he's one of the best receiving TE prospects we've seen in years. I really hope he goes to a team that will utilize his athletic ability and not require him to do too much in-line or backfield stuff. He's a willing blocker, but certainly shouldn't be relied upon as such. Deserves to go very high in this draft class.

2. T.J. Hockenson TE Iowa 6'4 250 lbs

Strengths: Hockenson is a redshirt sophomore who has declared after a stellar season, totaling 49 catches, 760 yards, and 6 touchdowns. Hockenson is a compactly-built guy who possesses width and a power-packed frame with excellent overall weight distribution. Hockenson is everything you want in an inline tight end. Tremendous lower-body power and explosion to generate movement in the run game. A terrific run blocker who makes touch cut blocks at the 2nd level appear routine. Commits himself to win inside hand leverage and finishing blocks for the duration of a play. A fluid mover and sneaky good athlete who shows good acceleration out of his stance, quickly getting to the 2nd level. A nuanced route-runner who runs his routes with precision and sharpness, creating separation downfield. Really impressive ball tracking skills, showing the ability to adjust to the ball with a defender on his back. Really strong hands at the catch point, consistently winning the 50/50 balls in contested traffic. Impressive long-speed showing the ability in games to get behind safeties on vertical routes. Shows the innate ability to win jump ball situations, getting outstanding elevation over smaller defenders. A nimble open-field runner showing the ability to pick up additional yardage after the catch.

Weaknesses: Still has additional room in his core/lower body to put on more muscle and weight to help him anchor down better in pass sets. Can sometimes get too aggressive when pass protecting, getting overset and allowing defenders to win the edges. Would like to see him attack the football more, he tends to wait for the ball to arrive into his chest. Not a speed maven who is consistently going to separate like his teammate Fant.

Best Fit: In-line TE

Player Ranking (1-100): 85.9 – Hockenson is more of the blocking TE for Iowa who displays + receiving abilities as well. I was blown away by how effective in the run game he is, completely manhandling and mauling his assignment, rarely losing sustain. He showed his receiving upside this year as well, really understanding how to operate in space. Despite not being an elite athlete, he understands how to consistently get open, utilizing good footwork and always selling his routes. Late 1st round pick.

3. Dawson Knox TE Ole Miss 6'4 250 lbs

Strengths: Knox is a former walk-on for the Rebels who was a former high-school track athlete. Don't let that fool you though, he's not just a "hard worker." Knox is almost like a hybrid TE/WR who lines up both as a wide receiver and as a wingback. He's a rare athletic freak who shows tremendous movement skills and mobility down the field to stretch defenses. His lateral movement skills are outstanding, where he routinely looks more like a flexible wide receiver, showing the ability to flip his hips and cross-field with ease. While still a 'raw' blocker he does have some experience and physicality to not be a complete liability with more coaching/experience. I like the physicality he brings as a move-blocker, utilizing his hip torque and explosiveness to deliver some POP in the run game. Runs his routes with precision and sharpness, showing the ability to separate both at the line of scrimmage, in the stem and at the breakpoint. A good hands-catcher that shows the ability to catch the ball in contested situations and utilize his body control to adjust to the football.

Weaknesses: Very average production during his 2 years of starting experience, and has 0 career touchdowns. His 2nd level blocking needs serious work, as he routinely gets over his skis whiffing in space. In pass protection, he routinely over-extends, rather than anchoring and hunkering down. Despite his athleticism levels, he isn't much of a threat to do anything with the ball in his hands, lacking any kind of open-field ability.

Best Fit: Versatile TE receiving threat

Player Ranking (1-100): 84.2 – I really like Knox and I think he's going to be an outstanding receiving tight end at the next level. He's such a great athlete who has been effortless in his ability to learn the tight end position. He's going to get better and better with more time. While he isn't a great "yards after catch" guy or an overly physical plow-over tight end, he's a smooth route-runner who possesses a good frame with outstanding separation ability. 2nd round player.

4. Irv Smith Jr TE Alabama 6'3 241 lbs

Strengths: Smith is an athletically-built tight end who really came onto the scene this past season, breaking Alabama tight end receiving records, recording 44 catches, 710 yards, and 7 touchdowns. As a run blocker, Smith is physical and effective. He shows outstanding hand placement, usage, and strength to latch on and generate movement. Smith is a versatile joker TE who plays in the slot, as an h-back and in-line. As a receiver, Smith has a good understanding and awareness of zone-coverage, finding soft zones and sitting in. A fluid mover with loose hips and the ability to change directions without gearing down and losing built-up speed. Gets good extension with his arms, showcasing his full wing-span to snatch the ball away from his frame. Tremendous after the catch, showing excellent athleticism and open-field speed/shiftiness to create and run behind the defense. Smith is an outstanding athlete for the position and shows receiver-like traits, utilizing good body control and jumping ability to high-point the ball. A real red-zone threat who will routinely win in 1 vs 1 situations against defensive backs. Shows upside as a pass-protector, showing the toughness and 'want,' just needs additional timing and recognition work.

Weaknesses: Smith is prone to some poor concentration drops in open-field situations. Has a tendency to be a tick late off the snap of the ball. Did most of his damage against zone, where he knows how to operate in space, rarely having to beat man coverage. Lacks refinement or precision in his routes, tending to round off routes. Ran very simple routes that were mostly manufactured to get him in space. Little experience in contested situations. Can be a little careless with the ball in his hands, leaving the ball exposed to be knocked out.

Best Fit: Athletic mismatched slot TE

Player Ranking (1-100): 83.5 – Smith is one of the most athletic tight ends in this draft class. Surprisingly, he's a better blocker than I would have imagined with his frame. He's tough as nails and willing to do the dirty work. I would like to see him continue to utilize his athletic skill set and work on his footwork at all areas of his routes so that he can consistently separate against man coverage at the next level. 2nd round player.

5. Jace Sternberger TE Texas A&M 6'4 250 lbs

Strengths: Sternberger is a Kansas transfer who had to sit out his sophomore year. As a junior with the Aggies, Sternberger lit up the SEC with over 800 yards receiving and 10 touchdowns. Sternberger is an athletically-built tight end who carries nothing but muscle, displaying an excellent wingspan. A versatile threat, Sternberger lines up all over the line of scrimmage, including as an H-back, in-line and in the slot. Sternberger is a classic receiving tight end, displaying excellent speed and agility down the field. The thing that separates Sternberger is his "yards after catch" ability, routinely picking up additional yardage, showing good open-field shiftiness and strength. Completely comfortable in the middle of the field, showing strong hands to be able to fight contested catches. Knows how to use his body to consistently shield the ball from defenders in traffic. Utilizes his wingspan to routinely outstretch his arms and snag the ball away from his frame. A good move blocker who shows the ability to routinely hit moving targets at the 2nd level. Shows potential as a pass blocker, displaying both strength and nastiness. A feisty guy who plays to the echoes of the whistle.

Weaknesses: A 1-year wonder who has very little playing experience before his final (only) season with the Aggies. Needs to learn to consistently runs his routes with precision and sharpness, showing average footwork, preventing him from consistently creating spacing. Has potential with blocking, but far too often gets caught overextended, losing his assignment when pass protecting. Lacks great acceleration off the line of scrimmage, tending to be a build-up speed guy.

Best Fit: All-around TE

Player Ranking (1-100): 82.3 – Sternberger is another highly functional and talented tight end who absolutely has starter potential for the next level. I don't believe he's an immediate starter because he still needs to refine his route running and blocking abilities. But his upside and athleticism are outstanding, and I love the way he plays the game. To put up the numbers that he did this past season in the SEC is nothing short of outstanding. He's worth a 2nd round pick and could be a real steal in this class.

6. Caleb Wilson TE UCLA 6'4 235 lbs

Strengths: Wilson is a 3-year contributor for the Bruins with outstanding production his junior season. A good athlete who displays impressive quickness out of his stance and into the stem of his route, allowing him to break quickly and separate at the breakpoint. Understands how to use route deception and body lean to create at the top of routes to create separation. Aggressive and chippy guy who plays with a mean streak. Physical and powerful upper-body delivering nasty open field blows with his hands at the line of scrimmage and at the 2nd level. Has a good understanding of playing with leverage and utilizing good grip strength to latch on. Uses his explosive nature and forward lean to explode into defenders and generate a good initial push back. A bad ball catcher, Wilson shows the ability to fully extend and snatch balls off the ground or far away from his frame.

Weaknesses: An undersized blocking TE who lacks the ideal girth and anchor to be able to play in-line consistently at the next level. Had a bad foot injury his sophomore season causing him to miss most of the season. When asked to run more intricate routes or comeback type of routes, Wilson can look a bit clunky and round off his routes. Very few broken tackles at the college level, lacking any kind of production after the catch.

Best Fit: Receiving TE who can be used as a move blocker

Player Ranking (1-100): 80.2 – Wilson excelled with Chip Kelly this past season and showed what he is capable of as a receiver. He also showed glimpses as a sophomore before his injury. Wilson is a really good and refined receiving TE who is pro-ready. There are so many ways a team can utilize his receiving prowess. Love the player and think he's worth a 2nd round pick. He's an inconsistent blocker but there are traits to work with, and he certainly doesn't shy away from the physicality required. Not a liability by any stretch of the imagination.

7. Kaden Smith TE Stanford 6'6 252 lbs

Strengths: Smith is a 2-year starter for the Tigers, he had a tremendous final season as a junior with 47 receptions and 635 yards, including 2 touchdowns. A versatile threat who runs routes from in-line positions or in the slot. Smith runs like a wide receiver, showing excellent acceleration, easily running passed covering linebackers on vertical routes. Good vertical leaper coupled with his ball tracking ability to track the ball downfield. Displays excellent concentration to quickly locate the ball mid-flight, rarely losing a 50/50 ball. Uses his entire wingspan, easily outstretching his frame and catching the ball fully extended. Comfortable catching the ball in heavy traffic, showing fearlessness, reliability, and trustworthiness. Good point of attack blocker who engages his lower half and generates some solid movement in the run game. Good anticipatory skills while being used as a move-blocker, showing his ability to reach 2nd level blocks with ease, maintaining good cut-off angles.

Weaknesses: An upright runner who needs to do a better job of disguising his routes and selling fakes. Very raw route-runner who seemingly rounds off all his routes, rather than utilizing sharp footwork to create separation. Lacks any kind of nuance in his routes, seemingly running the same 2 or 3 routes on every snap. Would like to see him attack the football more often, can sometimes be too passive in waiting for it to arrive into his chest.

Best Fit: Receiving TE

Player Ranking (1-100): 79.8 – Kaden Smith is a joy to watch, he plays the tight end position like a wide receiver with his high-point/ball tracking abilities down the field. A fluid mover who shows down the field athleticism to be an added target in a pass-happy offense. Not a slouch when it comes to blocking either, showing good anchor ability and toughness as a finisher. The biggest knock on Smith is his route-running, it's poor. It prevents him from consistently separating at all levels of his routes. If he learns to use head/body manipulation and precise footwork, he can be a top tight end at the next level. But that's a 'BIG IF.' I would feel comfortable taking Smith in the 3rd round.

8. Thomas Sweeney TE Boston College 6'5 253 lbs

Strengths: Sweeney is a 3-year starter for BC who possesses a bulkier and compact frame. Solid career production and had his best year as a junior with over 500 yards receiving and 4 touchdowns. Sweeney's best attribute is his hands, showing sticky hands with the ability to make contested catches away from his body. Sweeney plays with natural leverage, showing the anchor and lower body power to anchor at the point of attack when in pass protection. Versatile and has experience playing in-line, as a receiver, or in an H-back role. Really like the way Sweeney runs routes, sinking his hips and utilizing body fakes to sell his routes. Uses his arms and hands well when blocking in the run game, quickly winning inside hands and sustaining and sealing edges. Keeps his legs driving and moving, getting some serious push in the run game.

Faster than you would think, showing smoothness in his ability to accelerate and run up the field. A bulldozer with the ball in his hands, with the ability to run over defenders.

Weaknesses: Very upright runner with the ball in his hands, keeping his frame far too exposed leading to some big hits down the field. Lacks the ideal frame, possessing a stockier and shorter frame. Needs technique and recognition work in run and pass blocking. A minimal straight-line athlete who lacks any kind of vertical threat down the seams.

Best Fit: All-around TE

Player Ranking (1-100): 77.3 – This kid is going to surprise a team. He's solid at both receiving and blocking. His physicality, strength, and toughness are going to make him a really good blocker with more coaching on the fundamentals. It's rare to see a TE be able to anchor against DE's, but you'll see it with Sweeney on multiple occasions. A better athlete than you would expect from his frame with an understanding of how to run routes and catch the ball cleanly. He's worthy of a 3rd round pick. I think he's going to be a starter in this league.

9. Dax Raymond TE Utah State 6'5 249 lbs

Strengths: Raymond is a big, tough and physical TE who displays all-around TE traits. Raymond's most impressive trait is his ability to utilize his wingspan to pluck out the ball in the air. It doesn't matter if it's with 2 guys on his back or on an up-the-field route in traffic. He's an impressive receiver, showing really good concentration and a large catch radius. An incredibly hard worker, he will battle on every snap on the field. Effective when used to block on the move, showcasing impressive skills while on the run. Shows the ability to alter his speed and use route deception to create for himself in-and-out of breaks. Understands how to utilize his body effectively to shield and box out smaller defenders. Plays with physicality and toughness in all areas of the game, showing bulldozer characteristics with the ball in his hands.

Weaknesses: Raymond competed in the Mountain West conference where he had very average production, with only 3 career touchdowns. He's not a great athlete and is a bit of a clunky runner, taking a while to build up speed. His routes lack precision, often times rounding them off rather than running with sharpness. Not a guy who is going to get separation down the field, reliant on his ability to utilize his wingspan and hands to catch in contested situations. Lacks a great anchor to sustain when playing head-on as an in-line blocker.

Best Fit: # 2 TE

Player Ranking (1-100): 72.2 – I really like Raymond and I think he has a chance to be a solid # 2 TE at the next level. He's a solid blocker who shows toughness and reliability in the receiving game with outstanding hands. In addition, he shows the willingness to be effective in the blocking game as well. 4th round player.

10. Alize Mack TE Notre Dame 6'4 247 lbs

Strengths: Mack is a senior TE who was a former 5-star recruit coming out of high school. Mack finally began to show signs of his potential as a senior for the Fighting Irish, posting 36 receptions, 360 yards, and

3 touchdowns. Possesses a good next-level physique with good height, girth, and wingspan. Mack is a tremendous athlete for the tight end position, showing smooth acceleration out of his stance, quickly getting to the 2nd level. A versatile option who often lines up as an h-back, an outside receiver, slot receiver or in-line. Good deep-speed with the ability to separate on vertical plains against defensive backs. An effective move-blocker, he shows the ability to consistently reach 2nd level blocks. Good ball tracker who shows the ability to adjust his body to poorly thrown balls. Shows potential when asked to stay in and pass-protect, maintaining a wide stance, showing the anchoring ability to sustain.

Weaknesses: Has had a number of minor injuries and off-the-field incidents, including being suspended for his entire sophomore season due to academic issues. Then was suspended for the bowl game in his junior season for a 'violation of team rules.' Work ethic has been a constant problem with Mack, and he doesn't always appear to run routes with urgency. Not a finisher, fails to have any kind of ability to break tackles in space, almost always going down upon 1st contact. Not the most physical guy in many areas of the game. When asked to pass protect, Mack consistently overextends his arms, allowing guys to easily get around his frame. Lacks great agility or change of direction ability, allowing linebackers/safety to stay on his hip pocket on lateral crossing routes. Lacks precision in his routes, failing to consistently show separation quickness or sharpness at all areas of his routes.

Best Fit: Developmental guy

Player Ranking (1-100): 71.9 – A very average college football player who can likely be a better NFL player than college player. He certainly flashes good athleticism in spurts, but it's just far too inconsistent. The interview process is going to be huge for Mack, seeing if his off-field concerns and worries are behind him. I don't love the player, but his talent alone makes him worth a 4th round pick. He needs major work and refinement in the nuances of playing the position.

11. Keenen Brown TE Texas State 6'3 250 lbs

Strengths: Brown is a 5th year senior who transferred from Oklahoma State following his junior season. A former 4-star wide receiver recruit from Texas who transferred to TE. Had a great season this year at Texas State with almost 600 yards receiving and 5 touchdowns. A compactly-built guy, he displays the toughness and functional strength required for the next level. Don't let his size fool you though, he's a rare athlete who was even used on sweeps and running plays for Texas State this season to get his hands on the football. Shows open-field ability to create for himself and make the 1st defender routinely miss. Utilizes his natural width to box out smaller defensive backs in contested and red-zone situations. Shows impressive body control down the field, adjusting to the football and making 50/50 catches with ease. A beast after the catch showing open field explosiveness and toughness down the field, shrugging off arm tackles with ease.

Weaknesses: There were concerns at Oklahoma State about him picking up the offensive playbook and whether he can grasp a more complicated offense. Dominated against lesser competition where he was frequently the best athlete on the field. Rarely used in pass protection due to his athleticism and ability in the receiving game. When used he needs to better utilize his lower body anchor and leverage to sustain when playing in-line, far too often gets walked back to the QB.

Best Fit: Receiving TE

Player Ranking (1-100): 68.2 – I really like Brown but don't expect him to be used as a blocker. He has the size to do it but looks completely out of his element when asked to block in-line. He's a complete liability in pass protection, but a dynamic receiving option. You can tell he's a former wide receiver and it shows in the way in which he plays. I like this kid as a developmental receiving TE. A 5th round player.

12. Zach Gentry TE Michigan 6'7 262 lbs

Strengths: Gentry is a converted college QB who has transitioned to TE the last 3 seasons. He's been a major contributor for the Wolverines offense in each of the last 2 seasons, really coming on in his final season, with over 500 yards receiving. A versatile tight end, he lines up as an h-back, in-line or in the slot. A total size mismatch who possesses incredibly rare length and size. Shows the ability to extend and catch balls outside of his frame. Gentry is at his best on a vertical plain, running seam routes up the field, showing good long-speed to separate. Shows some good suddenness in his routes, utilizing clean footwork at the top of routes. Has a good feel in his routes, especially when working against zone, showing the ability to quickly locate a soft opening. Can win at the 2nd level run-blocking in space, utilizing his length to engage.

Weaknesses: Has had some drop concerns, most notably in the Ohio State game this year. A slight/leanly built guy who lacks the physicality and toughness to consistently outmuscle at the catch point. Lacks the hand usage/release to be able to disengage quickly when pressed at the line of scrimmage. Has struggles redirecting his frame or creating any kind of separation on lateral routes. Not a powerful guy at the point of attack. Has natural leverage concerns when asked to pass protect, always losing the leverage battle, getting easily bull-rushed backward. Leaves his frame very upright when running, failing to minimize his surface area in space. Has only had 2 touchdowns in each of his last 2 seasons despite his yardage.

Best Fit: Developmental receiving tight end

Player Ranking (1-100): 67.3 – Gentry shows some developmental upside as a tight end, but needs more experience. There's some nuance in the way he plays the position, having a good feel for working against a variety of different coverages. The issue with him is his size, it is going to create major concerns when asked to pass protect. A bit of a clunky runner who is an easy cover for safeties or linebackers on a lateral plain, and needs to be used vertically to have success.

13. Josh Oliver TE San Jose State 6'5 246 lbs

Strengths: Oliver is a good-sized TE prospect who displays the necessary length and frame of a next level TE. Had an outstanding senior season in the Mountain West with over 700 yards receiving. A versatile receiving threat, showing the ability to line up in-line, in the slot or even as an outside receiver. A tremendous athlete for his size, showing the leaping ability to go up and grab the football as well as the quickness and acceleration to test different levels of the field. A nightmare to match up to in the red-zone due to his size, physicality and leaping ability. A good contested catcher of the football, showing reliability in tight windows.

Weaknesses: Oliver is a raw athlete who shows blocking traits, but is still quite unrefined. Relying more on his physical traits than actual solid fundamentals. Relied on being the best athlete on the football field at all times rather than actually take the time to perfect his craft, and once he goes up against better athletes he won't be able to simply count on his athleticism anymore.

Best Fit: Developmental athlete

Player Ranking (1-100): 66.9 – Oliver is a raw athlete who displays the traits to be a good player but he's so raw in every possible way. He's going to need time but is worth a 5th round flyer due to his size and physical makeup.

14. Drew Sample TE Washington 6'5 250 lbs

Strengths: Sample is a 5th year senior with the necessary size, wingspan and compactness to play at the next level. A versatile prospect, he lines up in-line, as an outside receiver or in the backfield. Good and reliable soft hands to catch the ball in heavy traffic. A physical finisher with the ball in his hands, showing toughness and physicality, picking up additional yardage after contact. At his best against zone-coverage, when he can quickly locate soft zone openings. A wide-bodied guy, he maintains lower-body strength to anchor in pass protection, showing an impressive ability to win inside hand leverage, sustaining through the duration of plays. A technician when asked to block in the run game, understanding how to use angles/anticipation to clear running lanes at the line of scrimmage and at the 2nd level. Very good when asked to move block, showing the ability to hit moving targets in space and remain under control.

Weaknesses: A bit of an older prospect, he will be 23 on draft day. A very subpar receiving tight end who has lacked much production in college, never totaling more than 252 yards receiving in a season at Washington. A very marginal athlete, he is a limited receiving threat lacking the mobility or fluidity to create any kind of separation against man-coverage. Very limited route-tree as a receiver, lacking experience in running any kind of nuanced routes. An upright runner, limiting his ability to change direction.

Best Fit: Blocking TE

Player Ranking (1-100): 65.9 – Sample isn't truly a "powerful" move blocker but he understands how to utilize good angles/positioning/space and plays like a true technician. He shows the wide-bodied frame which will allow him to continue growing and developing more true strength to be a very good blocking TE at the next level. Will always be a very limited receiving TE, lacking any kind of athletic ability. 5th round player.

15. Isaac Nauta TE Georgia 6'4 240 lbs

Strengths: Nauta is a former 5-Star high school football player who hasn't quite lived up to his potential at Georgia. Built with a smaller, but tight and compact build. Had his best season as a junior (his final season) with 30 catches, 430 yards, and 3 touchdowns. Plays both in-line, as a fullback and as a slot receiver. Good overall hands, showing the ability to consistently make catches in highly contested situations. Also shows the ability to extend and make catches outside of his frame. A build-up speed guy, he flashes good down the field speed to separate against linebackers in man coverage. Really good move blocker in the run game who can be used as a fullback or a blocking tight end, showing tenacity and physicality at the point of attack. Engages his lower body and his hip torque to generate some POP at the point. Commits himself to win inside hand leverage. Shows tremendous strength in his lower body to handle pass rushers in 1 v 1 situations. Plays with a nasty chippiness who will finish plays.

Weaknesses: Nauta is prone to some poor concentration lapses, leading to poor drops from time to time. A very average route runner who takes far too many steps at the top of his stems, leading to poor separation. Ran very basic and redundant routes over and over again. Lacks the core flexibility and fluidity in his movements to consistently get any kind of separation down the field. A straight-line athlete who will struggle when asked to change directions or play laterally.

Best Fit: In-line blocking TE

Player Ranking (1-100): 65.0 – Nauta is a physical, blue chip, and a nasty tight end who will hit you in the mouth. He doesn't have great size or speed, but he's tough as nails. He will be a really good #2 tight end in this league who can be used in all blocking situations.

16. Donald Parham TE Stetson 6'8 243 lbs

Strengths: Parham is a 3-year contributor for FCS level Stetson. Parham had a tremendous senior year totaling over 1300 yards receiving and 13 touchdowns. Parham is basically a hybrid receiver/tight end who displays tremendous and rare size and wingspan. He's a complete size mismatch who takes advantage of smaller, slower athletes when lining up in the slot. A deceptively fast guy who moves much better than someone of his size should, both initially and down the field. An outstanding threat after the catch, displaying tremendous burst, shiftiness, and open field ability. Fearless playing across the middle of the field. Shows the ability to win against man coverage or find soft zones when playing against zone schemes. Utilizes his size in contested or jump ball situations, showing his length and high point ability. A natural hands catcher, he shows soft hands and reliability to catch the ball away from his frame.

Weaknesses: Parham is simply a receiving tight end at this point and will offer little in the way of functional strength and pass protection ability. Played against inferior competition in the FCS where he generally was the best athlete on the field. Doesn't possess much finesse, preferring to either bully or box out at the catch point. Needs refinement in the nuances of playing football, such as running clean routes. Needs to continue to add functional strength to his frame.

Best Fit: Developmental receiving tight end

Player Ranking (1-100): 64.2 – A small-school prospect who has loads of potential with his combination of size and speed. He's worth a 6th round pick who can be a developmental prospect at the next level but will need some time before he can be expected to contribute.

17. CJ Conrad TE Kentucky 6'5 252 lbs

Strengths: Conrad is a 4-year starter for the Wildcats and has been a mainstay for their offense. Displaying experience and toughness as an in-line blocker, Conrad displays tremendous potential as a blocking TE. Having the frame with the length and core strength, Conrad shows the ability to seal outside edges. Uses his upper-body power and strength to lock on and sustain at the point of attack. While pass protecting, he shows the ability and the strength to use angles and leverage to sustain for the necessary amount of time. Despite minimal production as a receiver, Conrad shows that he can make tough and difficult grabs in traffic. Versatile guy who plays in-line, as an H-back, in the backfield as a FB, or even as a slot receiver. As a receiver, Conrad knows how to box out and seal off defenders on shorter/intermediate routes. Good safety blanket who makes himself accessible as a secondary target. A smart, tough kid who coaches absolutely love.

Weaknesses: Conrad has athletic limitations as a receiver, he isn't a speed threat, nor will he ever really be a # 1 option as a receiver when lined up outside. He's a good blocker, but by no means is he a mauler in the run game. Lacks the hip flexibility to adequately cross field without losing significant speed. Not a guy who shows the body control to adjust to badly thrown balls. Cannot threaten or do much of anything with the ball in his hands, often goes down on first contact. Struggles to separate, lacking the explosiveness out of his cuts to sink his hips and work back to the ball. Missed last few weeks of the season due to a Lisfranc injury on his left foot.

Best Fit: In-line blocking TE who can be used as a FB too

Player Ranking (1-100): 62.3 – Conrad is a 6th round player. I would be shocked if he didn't get drafted because of his experience in blocking. His best quality is his ability to run block. He's a dominant, forceful blocker and therefore valuable since there are very few of them in college. His receiving and athletic abilities are marginal at best.

18. Kendall Blanton TE Missouri 6'5 265 lbs

Strengths: Blanton has the definition of an ideal build, with a long and athletic frame, possessing outstanding muscularity and power throughout his frame. Blanton is used on special teams' in college due to his physicality. Reliable and sticky hands to snatch and catch the ball away from his frame. Outstanding length, possessing the wingspan to outstretch smaller DBs. Shows nice body control and flexibility in his ability to adjust to badly thrown balls. Shows good initial quickness out of his stance, quickly getting to the 2nd level to block. Blanton is very physical, showing tremendous upper body power and strength. You can tell he takes blocking very seriously. A really good move blocker who shows an ability to get out in space and block downfield at all levels.

Weaknesses: Very limited production as a receiver, never having more than 160 yards in each of his 3 years playing for the Tigers. Strictly a blocking TE at the next level with limited growth as a receiver due to his lack of athletic ability and movement skills. Has some tightness in his core, failing to accurately shuffle his feet at times when in pass protection. Poses no threat as a "yards after the catch" guy, usually going down on 1st contact.

Best Fit: Blocking TE

Player Ranking (1-100): 60.2 – I really think a smart team is going to take a chance on Blanton due to his size and frame. He's an athletically-built guy who absolutely has potential. I don't think he's strictly a "blocking TE" because there are some movement skills to work with. But at the very least you'll have a really solid blocking TE. 6th round player.

19. Foster Moreau TE LSU 6'4 250 lbs

Strengths: Moreau is a well-built TE with a developed physique and a long wingspan. Shows some in-line prowess as a blocker. Impressive lower-body power and explosive characteristics with the ability to utilize his hips and get good torque to move people in the run game. Understands how to play with angles in the run game, sealing the edges on outside-zone rushes. Delivers some explosive pop-on contact at the 2nd level. Shows some anchor ability with the ability to widen his stance and sink his hips. An aware blocker, he sees 2nd level blitzers attacking the pocket and picks them up routinely. A physical guy who plays with violence and tenacity, working his butt off on every snap. Shows versatility playing as a flex back, in-line or in the backfield.

Weaknesses: Not a great receiving threat, has posted very little production as a pure receiver during his career. Poor punch technique at the line of scrimmage allowing him to miss far too frequently. Lacks the hand strength to latch on and sustain for the duration of a play, losing sustain on the counter. Doesn't appear to understand how to utilize his length to extend and utilize his full frame in the receiving game. A tight-hipped upright athlete who isn't going to separate at any level. A very limited athlete who fails to have any kind of separation quickness or a 2nd gear.

Best Fit: Blocking TE

Player Ranking (1-100): 58.2 – A really good blocking TE who displays the size and the physicality to be used at the next level. The problem is he offers very little in the receiving end of the spectrum. A 7th round pick who needs to fit a very specific need for a team looking for that kind of tight end.

20. Tyler Petite TE USC 6'3 250 lbs

Strengths: Petite is a compactly-built guy who displays the strength and lower body anchor to pass protect. He also shows the movement ability to be effective when used on the move as a run blocker. Versatile guy who lines up all over the line of scrimmage, including as an H-back, in-line and as a slot receiver. An aware blocker, showing an understanding of where he needs to be and will latch on and hook at the 2nd and 3rd levels of the field. Shows some athleticism in his movement skills, getting open down the field at times, just rarely was ever thrown to.

Weaknesses: Petite has battled nagging injuries during his career at USC, most of them of a minor nature. Has had minimal production during his career, with his best year being his junior season with 300 yards and 3 touchdowns. Really struggled as a senior without Darnold with practically 0 production in the receiving game. Loses sustain when blocking due to his lack of length and inability to win hand placement consistently. A clunky guy, he lacks great movement skills or any kind of recovery ability.

Best Fit: Blocking TE

Player Ranking (1-100): 53.4 – Petite is a UDFA. He likely won't get drafted due to his poor senior season and lack of production. He's a pretty good blocker and might have a chance to catch on in training camp with a team.

TE Top-10 Rankings

1. Noah Fant
2. T.J. Hockenson
3. Dawson Knox
4. Irv Smith Jr
5. Jace Sternberger
6. Caleb Wilson
7. Kaden Smith
8. Thomas Sweeney
9. Dax Raymond
10. Alize Mack

Chapter 7

OT's

1. Jonah Williams OT Alabama 6'5 301 lbs

Strengths: Williams is a 3-year starter for the Tide who played his freshman season as the right tackle before getting kicked out to left tackle for his final two seasons. Williams is a really good athlete who plays with good acceleration out of his stance, quickly getting to the 2nd level. A strong guy, he plays with good power at the point of attack, showing the ability to anchor upon contact. A technician in the way he plays, understanding how to utilize his hands to control a block, utilizing good hand placement. A quick-footed guy who shows good lateral mobility to mirror in pass sets. In run sets, he shows the fleet of foot to consistently reach and hook at all levels. Also shows the ability to climb the pocket and beat linebackers to the spot of the ball, utilizing impressive 2nd level angle blocks. Engages his lower half while pushing piles or getting movement in the run game. Very aware blocker who shows outstanding anticipation and mental processing ability in the passing game, frequently picking up and slowing down blitzers, in addition to his main assignment. Good recovery ability, making up any lost steps if initially beaten. Transfers weight smoothly, gaining good depth on his initial kick-step, sliding with bent legs, fluidly moving between his feet.

Weaknesses: Williams lacks ideal left tackle length that teams are looking for, and will struggle in longer pass sets against rushers who are possessed with good length. Not a finisher, fails to lock on and control after a counter move. Not a mauler-brawler type in the run game who blows people off the ball. Lacks a great initial punch to jolt defenders upon initial contact. Has a tendency to struggle against speed rushers, where he can get caught lunging upon the snap of the ball.

Best Fit: Tackle, but some see him playing guard similarly to Connor Williams

Player Ranking (1-100): 87.0 – Williams is the most talented overall offensive lineman in this class, and should be a Top-20 pick. He's not as sure a thing as Cody Ford but he possesses a higher ceiling. Whether he plays as a tackle or a guard, it doesn't really matter he has the strength and athleticism to exceed in either. He's not an elite left tackle talent, but he's a solid one with very few flaws.

2. Greg Little OT Ole Miss 6'6 325 lbs

Strengths: Little possesses an NFL physique with outstanding size and length, perfect for an NFL LT. He's built right with an athletic frame and little body fat. His movement skills are easy, easing off the snap of the ball, showing impressive movement skills and quick feet. Keeps a wide base, allowing him to sit down on power rushers, rarely allowing any movement against even the most powerful bull rushes. Appears to understand the mental parts of the game, confidently knowing which blitzers to pick up and which to pass on. Great athlete who shows the lateral movement skills, fluid hips, and agility to perfectly mirror pass rushers. A physical finisher who plays with fire and a competitive nature, playing to the echoes of the whistle. Is committed to winning the leverage battle, keeping his knees bent through contact, and maintaining a wide base. In the run game, he shows the ability to fire off the ball and clear running lanes. Disciplined with his hands, showing the commitment to quickly win inside hands. Utilizes his movement skills to win good angles in the run game, reaching and hooking with ease.

Weaknesses: Can struggle when he leaves his chest exposed, allowing guys with good technique to quickly win inside leverage. Needs to take wider initial kick steps against speed rushers who can bend, will get beat against flexible athletes. Upright when asked to move in the running game, allowing and exposing too much of his frame. Still raw when it comes to utilizing his hands properly down after down. Fails to latch on and control after a counter move. Inconsistent strike percentage when looking to make 2nd level contact on the move. Needs to learn to steer wider edge rushers away from the ball or force them to take wider angles.

Best Fit: Left or right tackle in any scheme

Player Ranking (1-100): 86.4 – Little is a really good and talented tackle who has competed against some of the best pass rushers in the country the last few years. He certainly needs to become more well-rounded in the technical aspects of playing tackle, but his movement skills and strength make him a Day 1 starter at either tackle spot at the next level. 1st round pick.

3. Bobby Evans OT Oklahoma 6'5 301 lbs

Strengths: Evans is a 3-year starter for the Sooners who has started in all 40 games of his career, playing both on the right and left sides. Evans is built with an athletic frame, showing good overall weight distribution and leanly-built limbs. Evans is a physical, downhill run blocker who hits the hole with nastiness. Excellent at hitting moving targets in space, utilizing his length to make contact and sustain. A space clearer in the run game, he consistently dominates his opponent with good leg drive. An excellent move blocker who shows terrific change of direction and anticipation in space. A really good overall athlete with quick feet showing the balance and agility to mirror in space. Stronger than his size would seem to indicate, showing the lower-body strength to sustain and anchor. Plays with excellent awareness and communication ability, rarely allowing a free rusher in blitzing situations. Lacks the latch on strength in his hands to sustain following a counter move. Possesses the recovery ability if he takes any false steps.

Weaknesses: Evans is prone to a really bad whiff at times, especially in pass protection, reacting slow off the snap of the ball. Played in a 2-point system for Oklahoma where he lacks experience playing with his hand in the dirt. A bit undersized, lacking necessary bulk and muscle to play in a power-blocking system, needs to continue to develop his frame. Rarely had to hold up in pass protection for more than 2 or 3 seconds at a time.

Best Fit: Zone-blocking tackle

Player Ranking (1-100): 85.5 – I really like Evans as a next-level blocker. I understand he didn't play in an NFL offense and will need time translating, especially in pass sets. But his overall athleticism is rare. He's probably the best zone-blocker in this entire draft class and is an absolute beast in the run game or on screens. Late 1st round player.

4. David Edwards OT Wisconsin 6'7 315 lbs

Strengths: Edwards is a long, stout offensive tackle with a very thick frame. A former tight end who has built himself into the prototypical NFL frame with outstanding length. Edwards is a 3-year starter for the Badgers who has played almost every game at right tackle. Edwards is a physical, no-nonsense finisher and is already an exceptional run-blocker. Firing off the snap of the ball, Edwards utilizes his lower-body explosiveness to generate serious levels of push, completely taking defenders out of the play. Excellent on the move, showing experience as a 2nd level blocker, with a good batting average in space. Commits himself to win inside hand leverage to control the blockers for the duration of the snap. As a pass protector, Edwards maintains a wide base with good hand technique to anchor and hunker down against rushers. Edwards rarely gives up any ground against power rushers and has excellent lower-body strength. He perfectly utilizes his long arms to walk defenders backwards behind the QB, taking them seemingly out of the play.

Weaknesses: Edwards has had a few nagging injuries during his career, including a knee and an arm injury in his final season causing him to miss the final 3 games of his career. Lacks elite foot quickness and attempts to take too far a kick-slide causing him to overset, where he gets caught off-balance. His lack of foot quickness and upright frame can prevent him from mirroring quicker, more explosive bend athletes who can get under his pad level.

Best Fit: Zone-tackle

Player Ranking (1-100): 85.2 – David Edwards is a really solid offensive tackle who has played against some of the premier pass rushers in the country. He also comes from a program that is known for their high-quality producing of offensive lineman. While Edwards is still a work in progress when it comes to pass protection, he's an outstanding run blocker. If he continues to tighten up his footwork and work on his pass sets, he can be a premier NFL right tackle at the next level. I would keep him on the right side where he has played. Late 1st round player.

5. Yodny Cajuste OT West Virginia 6'5 321 lbs

Strengths: Cajuste is a monstrous left tackle prospect who possesses an ideal wingspan and frame. Played in an air raid offensive system where he frequently was relied upon in pass sets. Strikes opponents off the snap of the ball with a powerful initial punch. Then his incredibly large mitts latch on and don't let go, showing iron-grip strength in his hands. Really impressive in pass protection, showing outstanding footwork and initial quickness. Shows balance, agility, and patience in pass protection, rarely getting beat off the snap of the ball. Possesses surprising movement skills in the run game, showing functional athleticism with the ability to get up the field and block on screens and reach 2nd level defenders. Good recognition and awareness pre and post snap, adjusting the line if needed. Understands how to utilize his length to push rushers past the pocket.

Weaknesses: Had 2 major injuries to the same knee, causing him to miss some game time early on in his career. Worked mostly in short pass sets where he didn't have to hold up for long periods of time. Needs more time and experience in running sets, showing some balance concerns when getting out in space, raising his pads and playing flat-footed. Lacks the ability to overwhelm, rarely driving guys off the ball in the running game.

Best Fit: Power-blocking scheme

Player Ranking (1-100): 81.2 – Cajuste is a really good tackle prospect who has tremendous footwork to hold up on the left side. Teams are going to fall in love with his length and athletic traits. He needs more experience playing out of running sets, and I would like to see more aggression levels when firing out of his stance in the run game. 2nd round player.

6. Andre Dillard OT Washington State 6'5 310 lbs

Strengths: Dillard is a 3-year starter for the Cougars at LT. He possesses good size and an NFL tackle wingspan. Really good initial quickness out of his stance, showing quick feet and lateral mobility. Offers the recovery quickness and ability to redirect after getting initially beaten. A solid overall athlete who certainly displays mirror ability in pass sets, utilizing good technique and knee bend. Good overall hand strength, when placed right, showing the ability to latch on and sustain. Has a good understanding of beating defenders to the spot, utilizing good angles to create rush lanes on the edges and at the 2nd level. Easy mover, showing good strike accuracy at all levels. Shows good coordination between his upper and lower body. Good move blocker who consistently shows the ability to hook and reach block. Plays with good awareness and communication abilities, knowing who to pick up and who to pass. Utilizes his length against speed rushers to force rushers into taking poor angles to the QB.

Weaknesses: Takes too many short, choppy steps out of his kick slide. Has serious lower-body power and anchor limitations, frequently getting walked back to the QB when in pass protection. Needs major hand technique work, failing to utilize good strike accuracy with his placement. Lacks much fire in his play, and is too reactive instead of proactive.

Best Fit: Zone-blocking system

Player Ranking (1-100): 80.8 – Dillard has had a really good career blocking against some quality defensive ends but there are serious point of attack power concerns for the next level. He lacks the adequate anchor and power to sit down on speed to power rushers. A 2nd round player who has a chance to be a starting RT as a rookie. He's going to need to spend some time in a NFL strength & conditioning program.

7. Jawaan Taylor OT Florida 6'5 328 lbs

Strengths: Taylor is a 3-year starter for the Gators who has almost exclusively played at right tackle, but has started a few games at left tackle due to injury. Taylor is a big guy with really good height, size, and weight distribution. Heavy hands in protection, frequently shocking defenders upon impact. Activates his lower body and hips when driving in the run game, getting some really good movement and push. Plays with outstanding physicality and a nasty demeanor and mean streak. Shows the looseness in his core to be able to redirect and recover if initially beaten. Above-average initial quickness off the line of scrimmage, easing off the snap of the ball with bent knees. Shows the lateral movement skills you want in a tackle, with good agility and balance. Good in space, showing the ability to quickly get out in front and reach at the 2nd level. Shows good lower body power and anchoring ability when in pass protection.

Weaknesses: Has a tendency to overset with his outside foot to account for speedier rushers, leaving the space between him and guard far too large against an inside move. Overaggressive in his punch, preventing him the opportunity to latch on and sustain through the duration of a play. Very inconsistent in pass protection, at times he plays with perfect technique and mirror ability. Other times, his technique looks terrible and he gets beat easily on the snap of the ball. Can sometimes have slow reaction times/reflexes upon snap of the ball allowing guys an easy pressure. Struggles against the speedier rushers who can bend and grab the edges. Inconsistent pad level leaving his pads far too exposed causing him to get moved around too much.

Best Fit: Can play in either but looked a bit lost in Florida's zone-scheme. Would prefer in man-blocking system

Player Ranking (1-100): 80.2 – A good prospect, but not a great prospect. I have serious question marks about his ability to hold up in pass protection. Between his pad level, lack of sustaining blocks and slow reflexes, he gives up a lot of pressures. He has good overall movement skills and strength, which will cause him to get drafted likely higher than he should have based on 'potential.' I wouldn't take him until the 2nd round.

8. Tytus Howard OT Alabama State 6'5 322 lbs

Strengths: Howard is a converted TE who moved to tackle early on in his college career. Possesses an ideal tackle physique with long limbs and little body fat. His background experience as a TE is evident in the way he moves. He's an outstanding athlete who shows fluid and easy movement skills. Displays impressive coordination between his upper and lower body, maintaining good distance and spacing from rushers. Despite his TE background, he's not just an 'ATHLETE,' he actually possesses really good strength in his lower half. Eases off the snap of the ball with terrific initial quickness getting to the 2nd level in an instant. An agile athlete showing the ability to recover and redirect upon any lost steps. Shows really good lateral agility, balance, and movement skills to mirror pass rushers. Has done well when playing against big-time college programs, including Auburn.

Weaknesses: There will be questions about his competition levels in college, despite some big-time college games against good programs. Most of his concerns are with his footwork. He either takes short, choppy steps in his kick-slide or he oversets to his right leaving far too much room between him and the guard. Needs to learn to utilize all his length and not let guys into his frame, he turns too many pass sets into wrestling matches.

Best Fit: Scheme-versatile tackle

Player Ranking (1-100): 79.2 – I really like Howard and I think he is going to be a really good player at the next level. He might need some time to continue refining his footwork having to play against NFL competition, but he's a good player. 3rd round player. NFL starter and quality athlete.

9. Chuma Edoga OT USC 6'4 303 lbs

Strengths: Edoga has played on the right side of the USC offensive line the past 2 seasons and has greatly impressed. An outstanding athlete, he shows fluid footwork out of his stance. Tremendous initial quickness showing an explosive kick-slide which allows him to perfectly mirror even the speediest edge defenders. Plays with a fire and toughness, showing physicality and aggression in all areas. Has above-average length which he utilizes to force defenders to take wide pursuit angles to the QB. Does a nice job firing off the ball in the run game, rolling his hips and driving his legs to steer opponents away from the ball carrier. Impressive when used as the move blocker on zone-style runs, getting out in front and making good contact with the 1st defender. A real finisher who takes his job seriously, and fights to the echoes of the whistle. Utilizes his natural leverage ability to sustain and anchor.

Weaknesses: Edoga had a disappointing senior season after a really good junior year. Battled some injuries causing him to miss some game time in his senior and junior seasons. A little bit undersized, I would like to see him gain additional muscle for the next level. His lack of size is evident when defenders have additional space to utilize speed to power on him to drive him backward. His overaggressive nature allows him to over/under set his feet, which can cause him to quickly get beat inside on rushes.

Best Fit: Zone-blocking scheme tackle

Player Ranking (1-100): 79.0 – I really like Edoga and I think he has the right combination of athletic traits and strength. He's not a bulldozer, but he's physical and fearless in his style of play. His movement skills make me confident he can play on the outside at the next level. Some teams might like him better as an interior player, but I think his length allows him to be versatile. 3rd round player.

10. Kaleb McGary OT Washington 6'7 321 lbs

Strengths: McGary is a 3-year starter for the Huskies who has started exclusively at right tackle every game since the beginning of his sophomore season. Possesses an NFL physique, with tremendous overall size and wingspan. McGary is outstanding in fully utilizing his length, maintaining good hand placement to control defenders and keep them at arms' length. Does a nice job of corralling and latching on, rarely losing sustain on the counter move. A finisher who routinely brings his opponent down to the ground, playing to the echoes of the whistle. Really good athlete who shows quick feet and balance, perfectly mirroring defenders in loads of space. Shows the recovery footwork to quickly regain lost steps. Powerful upper body with a great initial punch to offset rushers. Overall, he possesses really good functional strength, engaging his lower body to generate movement and push in the run game. His lower body power is manifest when taking on bull rushers who show some explosiveness, McGary rarely loses any ground, sitting on rushers for several seconds at a time.

Weaknesses: McGary can be prone to get overset to his outside, giving up the inside rush lane. Despite his athleticism, McGary really struggled when going up against wide rushers who take wide rush stances. Little experience in move blocking, rarely getting to the 2nd level. Needs to more consistently play with a lower pad level, keeping his frame and chest plate far too exposed. Has had 3 different heart procedures stemming from his heart arrhythmia. A bit of a stiff-hipped lineman who struggles to change direction.

Best Fit: Man-blocking RT

Player Ranking (1-100): 78.6 – McGary is the definition of reliable and consistent. He's played a major role for the Huskies offense for the last 3 seasons and even played some as a rookie as well. He's a better athlete than one would expect with his size, but he's also a tremendously powerful guy. He has some stiffness to his lower body, but overall he's a very solid prospect who should be a 3rd round player. Absolutely an NFL starter.

11. Dennis Daley OT South Carolina 6'5 304 lbs

Strengths: Daley is a JUCO transfer who played his last 2 seasons for the Gamecocks. Possessed with a great frame, showing excellent length and next-level size. An aggressive blocker, Daley plays with a mean streak and a toughness playing to the echoes of the whistle on every snap. He extends his arms and strikes opponents with a powerful initial punch completely offsetting and displacing rushers. Possesses the lower body power and anchor to sustain against bull rushes. Really good initial acceleration off the line of scrimmage quickly getting to the 2nd level, showing power at the point of attack. Has the ability to locate and lock onto defenders at the 2nd level when used as a move blocker. A mauler in the run game, he consistently clears running lanes and will push piles forward.

Weaknesses: Came off a disappointing senior season after a really good junior campaign. In pass protection, he continually fails to latch on to the rusher, losing sustain on the counter move. Has some awareness concerns, failing to pick up oncoming blitzers or know who his assignment is on occasion. A classic waist bender who plays with a really narrow base exposing his frame and chest. Consistently struggles to play with leverage, allowing his knees to rise through contact. A slow-footed athlete who fails to accurately mirror or stay in front of athletic edge rushers. Shows some stiffness in his core and lacks the lateral movement ability or redirect ability.

Best Fit: Developmental upside, swing tackle immediately

Player Ranking (1-100): 77.7 – A developmental prospect who possesses some awesome physicality and toughness as a blocker. Intriguing size and traits, but still needs developing especially when it comes to his footwork and technique in pass protection. Has a lower ceiling due to average athletic ability. Not a huge fan of the player because there is a limited ceiling but he's not a bad player. 3rd round.

12. Isaiah Prince OT Ohio State 6'7 310 lbs

Strengths: Prince is a 3-year starter at RT for the Buckeyes. Displaying outstanding size and length for the position, Prince is a player who has improved in each of his campaigns. Physical finisher in the run game, showcasing outstanding lower body power and explosion. Looks to quickly latch on and roll his hips. Displays necessary power in his upper body and hands to latch on and control defenders. Old-school RT who plays with a mean streak and with a real mauler- brawler mindset. A bulldozer in the run game, Prince will wash out the line of scrimmage and crash down or combo block effectively at the 2nd level. An above-average athlete who shows functional athleticism utilizing quick and light feet when reaching or hooking. Fluid mover in his hips, showing the ability to re-direct and recover any lost steps. Impressive in his ability to fight through counters and stay locked in, rarely losing sustain.

Weaknesses: Still doesn't quite know how to fully utilize his length, preferring to play belly-to-belly against smaller defenders, and letting defenders into his chest too easily. Plays with far too narrow a stance, overextending himself and getting caught leaning. Doesn't always "SEE" things pre-snap failing to always know his assignment on crucial 3rd downs. Overaggressive in pass-sets, frequently getting overexposed and overextended, rather than letting guys into him and maintaining distance. Not the most competitive guy, he can at times look disengaged and disinterested.

Best Fit: RT

Player Ranking (1-100): 77.4 – The physical traits are there, but are the mental? The sky is truly the limit as far as strength and functional mobility. Truly one of the most talented offensive lineman in this class from a purely physical standpoint. The question is, does he want to be great? The good news is; he has improved tremendously over the years. I would take a chance on him in the 3rd round.

13. Mitch Hyatt OT Clemson 6'5 310 lbs

Strengths: Hyatt is a true 4-year starter at LT for Clemson displaying plenty of experience in big-time games for the Tigers against elite defensive fronts. Hyatt is an athletic tackle, showing smoothness and quickness upon each snap of the ball. Has a nice understanding of fluid footwork when in pass protection, maintaining and getting good depth on his kick-step sliding easily. Really good snap awareness and anticipation, quickly winning inside hands and getting into the frame of defenders to control the line of scrimmage. Aggressive tackle who utilizes his aggression and low pad level to control the point of attack. Shows the recovery ability to quickly regain any lost steps. Good awareness and instincts to take on stunts, easily passing guys. Keeps his head on a swivel always looking and locating.

Weaknesses: Hyatt is an undersized tackle who lacks the necessary power and anchor to sustain at the next level. He needs to continue to add strength and weight to his frame. Played with athletic quarterbacks where he didn't have to sustain pass blocks for long periods of time. Tends to be a bit of a waist bender. Will get overpowered by quick-twitch speed-to-power rushers.

Best Fit: Zone-Tackle

Player Ranking (1-100): 76.3 – I think Hyatt can be a starter in this league. I love that he's played in so many big-time games and he's played for 4 straight years. He just needs to work with the strength and conditioning coaches to add additional lower body power and weight to better anchor and sustain. 3rd round player.

14. Paul Adams OT Missouri 6'6 315 lbs

Strengths: Adams possesses a prototypical offensive tackle build with long limbs and a lean physique. A team captain who has played at both right and left tackle. Maintains outstanding technique, keeping his base wide showing the ability to absorb and anchor down. A really powerful guy who displays upper and lower body power and rarely grants any movement against even the strongest defenders. A real finisher showing a relentless style, battling and fighting through the whistle. Has SEC experience and has had some of his best games against SEC fronts, including Alabama's this past season. Strikes opponents with a really powerful initial punch, then latches on with his iron-grip strength rarely losing sustain. Fires off the snap when in run sets, rolling his hips and utilizes his powerful leg drive to get movement.

Weaknesses: Keeps too much of his frame exposed at times, allowing guys into his frame, relying on his anchor to hunker and hold on for dear life. Rarely was asked to do too much in space and is strictly a fit in a power-blocking scheme. Very average foot quickness and can get exposed when playing in too much space in pass sets.

Best Fit: RT in a power-blocking scheme

Player Ranking (1-100): 74.9 – Adams is a good player who possesses impressive power and strength. He can be a starting RT or a swing tackle for a team immediately. His level of experience makes him have very little bust potential. 4th round player.

15. Tariq Cole OT Rutgers 6'6 320 lbs

Strengths: Cole is an impressively-built tackle for the Scarlett Knights who has played both on the right and left sides of the line. A powerful, powerful guy who has the ability to sit down on rushers and anchor. Understands how to utilize his length to extend and push rushers away and behind his QB. Shows some recoverability when losing any steps. Strong upper-power in his arms and hands to corral, latch and jolt defenders with his initial punch. A real finisher, he works well with his teammates in utilizing combo blocks to open running lanes. Shows the ability to fire off the ball in the running game, clearing out running lanes and steering defenders away from the ball carrier. Bows his back and utilizes his lower body power to move piles forward on short-yardage plays. Rarely allows any movement in the passing game against bull rushes.

Weaknesses: Struggles when playing laterally, which affects his ability to consistently reach and hook in space. Has some tightness in his core and hips. Lacks the adequate foot quickness to mirror and get out in front of speedier rushers. Some inconsistencies in his footwork, lacking the necessary depth needed to maintain distance and to control rushers. Lacks great reflexes to quickly react off the snap of the ball, allowing him to get beat initially. Not a guy who is going to be used on much 2nd level stuff, strictly a power-blocking scheme fit.

Best Fit: Power-blocking scheme

Player Ranking (1-100): 74.2 – I like Cole and the physicality and toughness he brings to an offensive line. Although he's not a great athlete, he isn't awful. He can sometimes be a tick late off the snap of the ball, but generally, he recovers. He's an ideal RT in a power-blocking scheme. Might need another year or two of development but I think there's a starter in there somewhere.

16. Max Scharping OT Northern Illinois 6'6 320 lbs

Strengths: Scharping is one of the most impressive MAC conference players in this draft. Built with an impressive frame, Scharping displays outstanding length and size. He's the definition of reliable having started every game the last 4 seasons, at both right and left tackle. Scharping has a good understanding of solid fundamentals and angles to create running lanes and engage defenders at all levels. Impressed with his ability to sit down on rushers and maintain a solid anchor for the duration of a play. Understands how to use his length to stay square and maintain hands. Utilizes his upper-body power to sustain blocks and lock defenders in. Frequently stuck on an island in the passing game, showing the ability to settle in and finish blocks. Gives very little movement against bull rushes.

Weaknesses: Despite his size, Scharping isn't an overpowering tackle who simply moves and plows in the run game, and is reliant on angle blocks. Lacks great lateral movement ability to redirect or recover any lost steps. Needs to understand how to better utilize his hips and leverage to maximize his movement in the run game. Very average and choppy footwork which needs to get cleaned up taking too many steps on his kick slide. Can get beat initially off the line of scrimmage against MAC levels of competition. Lacks great athletic ability to be a 2nd level player consistently and can be a tick late off the snap of the ball.

Best Fit: Man-blocking scheme tackle. Might be kicked out to guard by some teams.

Player Ranking (1-100): 71.3 – While not an overpowering blocker, Scharping is still better suited in a man-blocking scheme where he isn't required to play in too much space and can worry about his assignment. He is a 4-year starter but the transition will be great at the NFL level for him coming from the MAC conference. He is a likely a swing tackle from day 1 and can possibly develop into a starter in a year or two.

17. William Sweet OT North Carolina 6'6 300 lbs

Strengths: Sweet is a well-built and incredibly lean offensive tackle for the Tar Heels with an impressive overall physique. Sweet is a finisher who routinely brings guys to the ground. Possesses above average length and perfectly utilizes it to keep defenders off his frame. Plays in a zone-blocking system where he is usually the move blocker for the offensive line. Has a good understanding for playing in space, showing a good batting average connecting with his blows at the 2nd level. Plays with really good anticipation and awareness at the line of scrimmage, understanding where he needs to be and assists teammates if he doesn't have an assignment. Good overall upper-body power and strength. Understands how to play with solid angles and technique, frequently utilizing cut blocks and hook blocks on zone-style runs.

Weaknesses: Missed most of 2017 after a season-ending knee injury. Can get too aggressive in pass sets, getting caught over his skis. Not a smooth mover, takes far too many short and choppy steps in his initial kick-slide. Oversets to his left to account for his lack of foot quickness, leaving the inside counter wide open. Fails to have the recovery ability if he loses any ground. Lacks a great anchor to sustain and sit down on rushers, almost always loses ground against bull rushes. Fails to have the latch-on strength in his hands to sustain blocks on the counter.

Best Fit: Zone-developmental tackle

Player Ranking (1-100): 66.2 – Sweet is a developmental player who shows some positive traits. But his lack of foot quickness can be exposed against speedier rushers on far too many occasions. He usually utilizes his anticipation and pre-snap awareness to help offset it, but it doesn't always work. A combination of lacking great lower-body strength and foot quickness isn't a good sign. 5th round player.

18. Oli (Olisaemeka) Udoh OT Elon 6'6 327 lbs

Strengths: Udoh is a 4-year starter for FCS program Elon and is built with a massive frame. Udoh is a mountain of a man, he is built with tremendous thickness throughout his frame. Displays a tremendous wingspan with 85 inch arms, showing the ability to keep the spacing between him and defenders. Known on campus for his weight-room strength, Udoh is a powerful man who displays tremendous lower body strength and anchoring ability. Despite his size, he shows surprisingly good agility and lateral mobility when in pass sets to mirror. Can beat power with power, rarely getting beat against powerful, bigger rushers. Strikes opponents with a powerful initial punch to offset rushers.

Weaknesses: Takes too many short, choppy steps in his kick-slide, lacking great athleticism to mirror against better athletes. His lack of foot quickness and speed is evident against counters or bendable athletes who can grab the edges. Despite his strength, Udoh fails to latch on and sustain, lacking great hand strength. Gets caught playing on his toes, getting caught overreaching in the run game, giving guys free access at the 2nd level. Can struggle to redirect his frame if initially beaten on the snap of the ball. Struggles against inside pass rush moves, getting caught flat-footed. FCS competition, he hasn't competed against top tier athletes in college.

Best Fit: Developmental tackle in a man-blocking system. Some teams, I would imagine will kick him inside to guard.

Player Ranking (1-100): 65.9 – I really like Udoh as a developmental tackle. His strength and size are impressive and if he were to lose 15-20 lbs he could be a better athlete, to mirror better in pass sets. He could be effective as a guard, despite never having played there. He certainly displayed the wide-bodied frame that teams desire. He is worth a pick in the 5th round.

19. Derwin Gray OT Maryland 6'5 330 lbs

Strengths: Gray is a 2-year starter at left tackle for the Terrapins and greatly impressed during his time. Built with a power-packed frame, posing a gigantic frame with big mitts and long arms. The first thing you'll notice about Gray is the power in his hands to jolt and strike defenders with a powerful initial punch. He possesses the iron-grip strength in his hands to lock on and rarely lose sustain. A good straight-line athlete, he shows some 2nd level ability to quickly erase defenders in space. Gray shows tremendous power at the point of attack, mauling and clearing large rush lanes. Plays in a pro-style offense.

Weaknesses: Gray is a bit slow to react at the line of scrimmage, showing some hesitancy. Struggles when playing against angled-fronts, lacking the necessary lateral mobility and initial quickness to get in front. Lacks any kind of recovery ability if initially beaten off the snap. Below average athlete who plays with some stiffness in his core, struggling to re-direct. Unnatural in the way he moves, oversetting his feet, taking far too many short choppy steps. Lacks the agility and balance to be able to mirror athletic edge rushers. Doesn't always finish plays.

Best Fit: RT or might have to move inside to guard

Player Ranking (1-100): 65.5 – Gray is a big-bodied mauler who is impressive in the way he plays in the run game. Not a great pass protector and lacks the natural footwork or the quick feet to do it consistently. 5th round player.

20. Andre James OT UCLA 6'5 305 lbs

Strengths: James is an experienced man-blocking LT for the Bruins. A violent and physical guy, he is a real finisher in the run game, consistently playing until the final whistle, driving his man into the ground. He's an outstanding run-blocker who understands how to seal the edge, routinely capping off the edges maintaining good angles/depth at all times. Bows his back and shows the leg drive to move the pile forward. Good initial anticipation and quickness out of his stance on run sets.

Weaknesses: James really struggles in pass protection. Lacks the lower-body strength and anchoring ability to sit on blocks. He consistently has timing issues with his hands, causing him to easily give up swim/rip moves. Plays with a narrow stance, causing him to have some hand placement issues at the line of scrimmage, getting too high. Lacks the iron-grip strength in his hands to latch on and sustain blocks. Has some stiffness in his core, fails to recover or redirect if he has any lost or misplaced steps. Lacks the foot quickness to mirror and stay in front of edge rushers.

Best Fit: Power-blocking system

Player Ranking (1-100): 61.3 – James is very unrefined when it comes to pass protection. He's a major liability who will need serious technique and recognition work when it comes to pass sets. It's a shame because he's one of the best run-blocking tackles in this class. He really is the tale of two players.

21. Daniel Cooney OT San Diego 6'8 315 lbs

Strengths: Cooney possesses rare size and wingspan, allowing him to completely engulf smaller defenders. Cooney is a finisher who fights to the end on every snap. Some really impressive quickness off the line of scrimmage allowing him to easily and smoothly get to the 2nd level. Good success rate at the 2nd level showing an ability to locate and latch onto defenders. Alert and aware, always locating and assisting his teammates when possible. Easy movement, showing the ability to recover.

Weaknesses: Competed against FCS level of competition. Really struggles with pad level and leverage concerns due to his statue and upright nature. A tick late off the snap of the ball, failing to react and show necessary snap awareness. Gets caught on skates far too often overextending and allowing guys to get under him. Straight ahead athlete, but really struggles with the lateral movement stuff. Lacks the necessary hand and upper-body power to latch on, almost always gives up sustain on the 2nd move. Fails to keep his feet shuffling upon contact.

Best Fit: Developmental zone-scheme

Player Ranking (1-100): 54.3 – Undrafted free agent. Cooney is a developmental tackle who shows some traits and has great length but will need major time. It's rare that many 6'8 tackles succeed at the next level. Worth a 7th round flyer.

22. Jackson Barton OT Utah 6'7 303 lbs

Strengths: Barton is a 2-year starter and 4-year contributor for Utah who has played on both the right and left sides of the offensive line. Barton is a long, rangy tackle, he possesses an athletically-built frame. Barton is a technician in the way he plays, playing with good technique and angles. A smart and disciplined blocker who utilizes good body positioning and fundamentals to give away little movement. Shows a secondary burst to recover if he's a tick late off the snap of the ball or if he gets initially beaten. When used as a reach blocker at the 2nd level, he shows good initial acceleration with good overall strike accuracy.

Weaknesses: An older prospect who will be 24 during his rookie season. Has a bad habit of allowing his pads to rise mid-play, losing the leverage battle. A slow-footed athlete who lacks the necessary depth on his initial kick-slide to sufficiently mirror and get out in front of speedier rushers. Doesn't sufficiently utilize his length, allowing defenders to easily get into his chest plate. Has serious power and anchor limitations, lacking the ability to sit down against speed to power rushers.

Best Fit: Zone-blocking tackle

Player Ranking (1-100): 54.0 – Barton lacks much upside as a blocker, and is more of a technician than a talented athlete. Nor does he possess the power required to play at the next level. An undrafted free agent.

OT Top-10 Rankings

1. Jonah Williams
2. Greg Little
3. Bobby Evans
4. David Edwards
5. Yodny Cajuste
6. Andre Dillard
7. Jawaan Taylor
8. Tytus Howard
9. Chuma Edoga
10. Kaleb McGary

Chapter 8

Interior Offensive Lineman (Guards or Centers)

1. Cody Ford OG/OT Oklahoma 6'3 338 lbs

Strengths: Ford has started in all 3 seasons for the Sooners, but didn't become a mainstay of their offensive line until his final season. Ford has moved from guard to right tackle prior to this season, but best projects as a guard at the next level. An incredibly compactly-built guy with thickness and strength. Ford is a massive man with tremendous strength in his upper body and hands, securely holding on, and rarely losing sustain. A patient blocker who rarely overextends, keeping his arms out, and quickly committing himself to win inside hand leverage. Delivers forceful initial blows with his hands at the line of scrimmage and generally, it's over if he gets his hands on you. An immovable force due to his width and lower-body strength, rarely losing any ground when he takes on speed-to-power rushers. An impressive straight-line mover for a guy as large as he is, showing the ability to get to the 2nd level in a flash. Ford is a complete mauler who never gives up on a play, and plays to the echoes of the whistle. In the run game, he engages his lower half, showing the ability to get serious push and movement from his hips/legs.

Weaknesses: Broke his fibula his sophomore season, causing him to miss the first several games of the season. Can overcompensate with his footwork in two primary ways. First, he has a tendency to take too many short and choppy steps at times, attempting to overcompensate for his lack of great foot quickness. Second, the depths of his kick-slide are inconsistent, tending to take too wide a 1st step, leaving him exposed on inside moves. Plays in that Oklahoma 2-point stance offensive system, where he didn't have to put his hand in the dirt. Very limited game experience, as he has only started a few games prior to his final season.

Best Fit: Man or Power-Blocking offensive scheme. I honestly feel he can play guard or RT at the next level. Most teams will prefer him at guard, where he likely has higher upside and can play immediately.

Player Ranking (1-100): 88.4 – Not a lot of negatives on the player at all! An outstanding athlete for his size, he just needs to refine his footwork, especially in pass protection. But he's a massive man with incredible power, a perfect fit for an offensive line that runs a man blocking offensive system. This kid has tremendous upside and might have some growing pains in pass protection, but he certainly has the NFL size/strength already. Late 1st round player.

2. Chris Lindstrom OG Boston College 6'4 303 lbs

Strengths: Lindstrom is a 4-year starter for the Eagles and has played both outside and inside, but best projects inside at the next level. Plays with natural leverage ability, widening his stance and sinking his hips to power down and anchor against power. In the run game, he utilizes his leverage to keep his body low and deliver powerful torque and move defenders out of the way. Completely comfortable playing on an island, Lindstrom utilizes his balance, lateral agility and technique to perfectly mirror. As a run blocker, Lindstrom fires off the ball showing good 2nd level skills finding targets and generally possessing a good batting average in space. Possesses the upper-body strength and hand power to latch on and sustain for the duration of a play. Shows an impressive secondary burst to recover if he is ever late off the snap of the ball. Understands hand placement and commits himself to win inside hands to control through the duration of the ball. Shows really impressive anticipatory and change of direction while on the move.

Weaknesses: Plays in a very run-heavy offense where he wasn't relied upon in too many pass sets. Not a mauler type who is going to frequently clear large running lanes or blow people off the ball in the run game. A bit undersized to play as a tackle at the next level. Lacks prototypical length. Good athlete but isn't an elite athlete.

Best Fit: Any scheme

Player Ranking (1-100): 83.2 – Lindstrom is one of the least talked about guys who NEEDS to be talked about. He's a smart, aware, athletic, and powerful prospect. Not to mention, he has experience playing both outside and inside, and I wouldn't hesitate for one second utilizing him at tackle in a pinch. This kid is a Day 1 starter. REALLY good player. I believe he should be a 2nd round player.

3. Elgton Jenkins C/G Mississippi State 6'4 314 lbs

Strengths: Jenkins is a 2-year starter at Mississippi State at center and has previously played both tackle spots and at guard. Built with an outstanding frame, displaying the length and wingspan to play inside or outside, but is probably best suited as a guard. Powerful anchor who shows the lower body strength even when losing the hand battle at the line of scrimmage. Utilizes his anticipation skills to put his feet into good position, maintaining disciplined angles and leverage throughout running plays. Powerful upper body with outstanding iron-grip strength, rarely letting guys off on counter moves. An absolute beast in pass protection, Jenkins rarely gives up a pressure. Engages his hips in the run game delivering powerful torque and push in the run game. A smart kid who is loved by the coaches at Mississippi State. Reads things well pre-snap, and quickly processes things post-snap. A smooth athlete, he shows suitable lateral mobility to mirror and an ability to get to the 2nd level with ease. Good success rate in space, utilizing his long arms and big mitts to consistently reach block. Has 4 years of experience in the SEC against the best interior defenders in the country.

Weaknesses: Little bit of an older prospect who will be 24 during his rookie season. Doesn't always finish running plays, allowing guys off, and then they end up making the play 10-15 yards down the field. Good athlete but isn't a great athlete and has fairly slow feet in space. Lacks the mean streak or aggression levels that you typically want in an inside blocker.

Best Fit: Power-blocking scheme

Player Ranking (1-100): 80.3 – Jenkins to me is a borderline 2nd/3rd round pick. He's an outstanding pass protector who rarely will give anything away. He's not a great athlete that you want playing in loads of space in a zone-based system, but in the right fit Jenkins to me is a Day 1 starter. This kid dominated in the SEC, and I feel confident he's going to be a fairly good starter at the next level.

4. Erik McCoy C/G Texas A&M 6'4 310 lbs

Strengths: McCoy is a 3-year starter and team captain for the Aggies who has played almost every game at center, except for a few at guard. McCoy has a really impressive frame for a center, showing width, length and compactness throughout his frame. McCoy is a perfect zone-blocking center who displays really good acceleration off the snap of the ball, getting to the 2nd level in a flash. Excellent understanding of how to play as a move blocker, generally used as the lead blocker for screens and misdirection style runs. Great in space, showing good 2nd level batting average to consistently latch on and sustain. Strong punch out of his stance, frequently displacing defenders at the line of scrimmage. Keeps his head on a swivel, always looking to assist when he's left without an assignment. Good football IQ and intelligence, showing a good understanding pre-snap of what the defense is doing. Shows good anticipation and change of direction while on the move. A powerful guy who has the anchoring ability to sit down against bull rushers.

Weaknesses: A belly to belly blocker who doesn't consistently utilize his entire wingspan to keep defenders off his frame. Can allow his pads to rise mid-play, minimizing his effectiveness to sustain and control blockers. Not a finisher who always finishes off his blocks. Not a dominant forceful blocker who shows the ability to move people in the run game, reliant on angles and technique to win against bigger rushers in the run game.

Best Fit: Zone-blocking center, can play as a guard if needed

Player Ranking (1-100): 79.9 – McCoy is a good athlete who has above-average power and strength as well. He's an ideal zone-blocking center who will make any teams' offensive line a more effective and athletic one. He plays with good fundamentals and awareness, seeing and reacting to things that are developing quickly. A 3rd round player.

5. Dru Samia OG Oklahoma 6'5 304 lbs

Strengths: Samia is a 4-year starter for the Sooners who started as a tackle his freshman season but then kicked inside to guard before his sophomore year. Samia is a rare athlete for the guard position showing outstanding initial quickness out of his stance to reach the 2nd level with relative ease. Offers the lateral mobility to consistently reach and hook with accuracy. His movement skills allow him to beat blockers to the spot and help him take on excellent angles and body positioning in the run game, sealing 2nd level openings. Good batting average when reaching the 2nd level, almost always striking a defender in space. Eases off the snap, utilizing outstanding knee bend sliding between his left and right foot. Maintains good technique with good knee bend and good initial strike placement. Utilizes his long arms to keep rushers off his frame. An aware blocker who keeps his head on a swivel with very active eyes when he doesn't have an assignment.

Weaknesses: A smaller-framed guy who could have some leverage and power concerns at the next level. Has a tendency to allow his pads to rise mid-play allowing quicker-twitch rushers the opportunity to get under him. More of an angle/seal blocker than a mauler- brawler type who will clear running lanes or get much push in the run game. Appears he has some tightness in his core preventing him for routinely redirecting and controlling after a counter move. Overall a good anchor, but I do see him lose some ground against speed-to-power rushers. Can overset to his right on occasion giving up the inside gap.

Best Fit: Zone-blocking guard

Player Ranking (1-100): 79.6 – Samia is one of the best athletes out of the interior lineman in this draft class. His movement skills, agility, and fluidity are probably 2nd to none. I have some concerns about his lankier build playing inside at the next level. It wasn't exposed tremendously in college, but I have a feeling it will if he doesn't put on additional strength and weight in his lower body. 3rd round player.

6. Ben Powers OG Oklahoma 6'4 310 lbs

Strengths: Powers has been a mainstay on the Sooners offensive line the past few seasons. Powers possesses a developed physique with good length and size. Has loads of experience and looks comfortable playing in space, showing good initial quickness getting out into space routinely. Was frequently the pulling or the moving guard for the Sooners, showing the ability to get out to the perimeter. A finisher who plays with power at the point of attack. Good pass protector, he shows the ability to hold up and really utilize his lower body strength and anchor to sit down on rushers, rarely allowing any movement. Understands how to use and place his hands on the snap of the football, utilizing good strike placement and controlling and latching on for the duration of plays. Maintains a good pad level, keeping his stance low and maximizing his ability to seal edges or get torque movement in the run game.

Weaknesses: Plays out of a 2-point stance in Oklahoma's spread offense and will have to get used to playing with his hand in the dirt. Above-average at everything, not great at any 1 quality. Not an overly dominant guy who plays with tremendous power, nor is he a great athlete per se. Not a drive athlete at the 2nd level, preferring to reach as opposed to clearing lanes.

Best Fit: Zone-blocking guard

Player Ranking (1-100): 79.2 – Powers is a good player who lacks a defining characteristic. He wasn't tested very often against outstanding quick-twitch rushers who could frequently challenge him horizontally. He generally played against lesser competition where he was more than sufficient to hold up. I like him and think he can absolutely be a starter at the next level, just not an upper-echelon one. 3rd round player.

7. Dalton Risner C/OT Kansas State 6'5 308 lbs

Strengths: Risner is a versatile pass protector who has played mostly at RT, but early on as a center at Kansas State. Risner is a smart kid who will impress coaches with his understanding of the game. He's a solid athlete who eases off the snap of the ball, maintaining bent knees and light feet. Really impressive in his ability to quickly and smoothly get to the 2nd level. Does a nice job of utilizing angles and length to maintain gaps and separation. Plays with solid fundamentals rolling his hips and driving his legs to steer opponents away from the ball. Really good awareness to easily pass stunts and inside blitzes. Impressive mobility and initial quickness in his kick slide to mirror defenders. Fluid mover showing the ability to loosen his hips to redirect and properly position his frame. Solid anchor who will give minimal movement against even the more powerful edge rushers. Strong hands with iron-grip strength showcasing the power in his hands to latch and lock. A really powerful upper body who strikes opponents with a powerful initial punch.

Weaknesses: Older prospect who will be 24 years old during his 1st training camp. Risner is a good athlete but I'm not sure he's an elite LT type of athlete, most likely will have to stay on the right side as he did in college. Didn't compete against many top-level pass rushers in college. Can struggle some and get overset by speed rushers when the QB holds onto the ball. Generates very average leg drive in the run game, failing to consistently move people. More of an athlete than a mauler- brawler type. Has some concentration concerns and will lose sustain and let guys off after initially blocking them.

Best Fit: Zone-blocking tackle or center. I like better at center

Player Ranking (1-100): 78.5 – Risner is a solid athlete who can be a plug and play center or tackle. He hasn't gone up against elite level edge rushers, so his transition might be difficult but he shows the fundamentals to be able to do it. His versatility is certainly an intriguing trait for coaches. A 3rd round player.

8. Terronne Prescod OG North Carolina State 6'5 338 lbs

Strengths: Prescod is a 3-year starter for the Wolfpack who has played mostly at guard, but has played some at right tackle as well. Prescod is a powerfully-built man who displays tremendous power at the point of attack to move people in the run game. Rolls his hips and drives his legs to steer opponents away from the ball. He's aggressive to winning inside positioning, beating defenders with good angles then walking them completely out of plays. Tremendous power in his hands to offset and displace defenders with a good initial punch. Commits himself to win inside hand placement, rarely allowing defenders to displace his hands in pass sets. Rarely loses sustain, showing tremendous strength to latch on and never let go. Excellent lower body anchor ability, rarely granting any movement against speed to power rushers that attempt to bull rush. Above average mobility, showing good footwork and mirror ability.

Weaknesses: Prescod's huge frame isn't without its downsides, and has some sloppy weight minimizing his ability to always mirror against more explosive rushers. Plays on his toes, getting over his skis getting caught off-balance. Average lateral mobility, and can struggle against speedier rushers on an island. Not a great move blocker and is better in a man-blocking scheme. Has had some awareness concerns, failing to always keep himself busy when lacking an assignment.

Best Fit: Man-blocking scheme guard

Player Ranking (1-100): 78.0 – Prescod is one of those guys that really surprised me on film. He's got very few downsides and is an absolute load to handle in the running game. If he loses a few sloppy pounds, he has serious potential. He's no slouch in pass protection either, showing outstanding lower-body anchor ability as well as the hand strength to latch on. He's a Day 1 starter for me, who will be an outstanding and effective run blocker in the right system. He reminds me a bit of Will Hernandez from last year, although not quite as talented. Prescod deserves to be a 3rd round player.

9. Damian Prince OG Maryland 6'6 320 lbs

Strengths: Prince is a 4-year starter for the Terrapins, he started his career as a RT before moving to RG the last couple of seasons. Prince is a powerful wide-bodied man who plays with an incredible anchor to sit on even the most powerful rushers. A feisty guy who plays with a mean streak and will battle to the very end. Strong upper body with a really good initial punch to slow and erase opponents. Once he locks on, it's over, displaying iron-grip strength in his hands. Prince utilizes impressive technique and fundamentals, maintaining a good, wide base. Commits himself to win the hand battle on the snap of the ball, maintaining a healthy distance between him and the rusher. Good functional athleticism with the ability to recover any lost steps and climb to the 2nd level. Good lateral mobility to be able to consistently reach and hook block. Plays with aggressiveness in the run game showing the ability to drive and create movement at the 1st and 2nd levels.

Weaknesses: Lacks the footwork and foot speed to play on the outside at the next level. Frequently plays too far over his toes getting caught lunging in pass sets. Has an aggressive nature which can cause him to underset his feet and get exposed on his outside shoulder. A little bit of a clunky mover when playing in too much space, failing to maintain proper balance in space. Could have some leverage issues playing inside at the next level against speed to power guys who can get under him.

Best Fit: Man-blocking scheme

Player Ranking (1-100): 77.7 – Really physical guy who can be an absolute load to handle in the run game. Doesn't have the greatest feet, but even when he gets beat he can recover quickly. He's a quality starting guard in this league and his tackle experience will make him even more attractive. 3rd round player.

10. Connor McGovern OG Penn State 6'5 326 lbs

Strengths: McGovern is a 3-year starter who has played all 3 interior positions on the offensive line. A well-built prospect with outstanding size, length, and girth. A smart guy who shows good initial footwork quickly getting set. Utilizes his length effectively, keeping defenders off his frame, keeping them at arm's length. Commits himself to win inside hand leverage, showing good placement and strength to control defenders. Despite his long frame, rarely loses the leverage battle, keeping his knees bent through contact to absorb. Good upper-body and hand strength to latch on, rarely losing sustain after a counter move. A finisher who plays to the echoes of the whistle. A technician in his style of play, rarely allowing a mistake, committing himself to play with good angles. Will fight power with power, showing excellent core strength, rarely losing any ground against speed to power rushers.

Weaknesses: McGovern is an average athlete who lacks the lateral mobility to consistently reach/hook block in space. Lacks a lot of fire in his play. More of a technician than a move blocker, and lacks great power at the point of attack. Fails to engage his lower body to move people in the run game. When playing as a center, I noticed he has the tendency to overextend in pass sets, getting caught off-balanced, giving up the inside counter. Not a great space player that can consistently locate and lock onto defenders at the 2nd level. Has some core stiffness, struggling to re-direct and recover.

Best Fit: Should play in a man-blocking scheme as a center or guard

Player Ranking (1-100): 77.3 – I like McGovern but not as much as most do. He's a solid starting interior player who won't blow anyone away. He doesn't have a truly defining characteristic and isn't great at any 1 thing. But he's either above-average or good at every single aspect of playing offensive line. A smart, disciplined guy who plays like a technician and will absolutely make an offensive line stronger. 3rd round player.

11. Ross Pierschbacher C/G Alabama 6'3 306 lbs

Strengths: Pierschbacher is a prototypical sized athlete who has played LG for the Crimson Tide. A positionally-versatile guy that has experience playing both at LG and center for Alabama, and can likely play either at the next level. He displays a really nice length for the position, showing the ability to control blockers at the line of scrimmage, keeping them off his frame. He's got a powerful anchor, showing outstanding lower body power and strength to sit on rushers. He's generally Alabama's move blocker, and is used to leading the way on most screens, zone runs or trap blocks. Understands how to play with angles, utilizing good awareness and anticipation to seal edges for his backs. He has really helped the Crimson Tide to consistently have one of the best running games in college football the last few seasons, and he's a major reason for it. Creates drive and push in the run game, opening up holes and pushing the pile forward.

Weaknesses: Had a high ankle sprain his junior season causing him to miss some game time. Doesn't have a great batting average in space, missing and whiffing on too many 2nd level blocks getting caught flailing. Has the tendency to overextend himself in pass protection, causing him to lose balance against more athletic defensive lineman to get around him. Needs to more consistently play with a good pad level, especially in pass protection where he needlessly allows his pads to rise mid-play. Possesses very limited athleticism, and isn't a great side to side athlete, he will get exposed against more athletic rushers who challenge him, at the next level.

Best Fit: Center or guard

Player Ranking (1-100): 77.0 – Good player who should be a starter in this league. Is already a very good run blocker, but will be overset and get exposed some in pass protection, especially early on. He's worth a 3rd round pick.

12. Michael Deiter C/G Wisconsin 6'5 304 lbs

Strengths: Deiter has rare length and size for the inside positions. Deiter played as a left tackle at times for Wisconsin but played earlier seasons as a center and guard. Best used as an interior guy at the next level. Versatile guy who has played every position on the offensive line, showing to be a jack of all trades. Deiter does an outstanding job of keeping his tall frame low and compact, keeping his pads low so that he can consistently win the leverage battle. Deiter is a powerful guy who displays iron-grip strength in his ability to lock on guys and never lose sustain. Good initial quickness out of his stance, showing the ability to get to the 2nd level in the blink of an eye. Really good awareness, always looking for someone he can block. Saw a few plays where he blocked multiple guys in 1 play. Really impressive power at the point of attack. Smart kid who really understands the mental side of the game with good instincts and football IQ.

Weaknesses: Has a bad habit of stopping his feet upon contact, which causes him some trouble when trying to win the leverage battle. Not the greatest athlete and struggles with the side to side movements, lacking great agility. Doesn't always show impressive contact balance, whiffing in space frequently. Needs to do a better job of keeping guys off his frame, tending to leave himself too exposed. Shows limited recovery ability if initially beaten.

Best Fit: Center or guard

Player Ranking (1-100): 76.5 – Deiter is a 3rd round pick at the next level. Isn't a great athlete, but has the football IQ, instincts, and versatility teams are looking for to play across multiple fronts and be a Day 1 starter.

13. Beau Benzschawel OG Wisconsin 6'6 307 lbs

Strengths: Benzschawel is a 4-year starter who has played almost every game as the RG for the Badgers. Large man displaying an impressive wingspan and the frame to put on additional weight at the next level. Due to his larger frame, he can envelop smaller rushers, knowing how to utilize his length. A real mauler-brawler type in the run game, he fires off the ball really quick. Really understands playing with sound fundamentals and utilizing his hands committing himself to win the hand battle immediately upon snap of the ball. Powerful anchor and lower body strength, utilizing it to sit down on rushers and anchor at the point of attack. Strong upper body and a good initial punch to set defenders back. Utilizes good knee bend with a wide base allowing him to lose little ground against power rushers. Does a nice job of rolling his hips and driving his legs to get movement and push in the run game. An aware guy who is always looking to assist teammates if he doesn't have an assignment on any given snap.

Weaknesses: His weaknesses were not highlighted due to the fact that he played on one of best offensive lines in the country. Due to his physique and size, he has a very difficult time playing with any sort of leverage. This will affect him against squattier, shorter defenders who can get under his pads in the passing game. Struggles with any kind of side-to-side movements due to his height and stiffness in his hips. Can really struggle if asked to pass protect in 1 v 1 situations on an island.

Best Fit: Man-blocking guard

Player Ranking (1-100): 76.2 – Really good run blocker but can really struggle in the passing game. His lack of leverage, agility, and side-to-side movement skills make me worried that he's always going to struggle in pass protection. A 3rd round player.

14. Garrett Bradbury C North Carolina State 6'3 304 lbs

Strengths: Bradbury is a compactly-built center who was originally recruited by the Wolfpack as a tight end. His former tight end movement skills are evidenced by his quickness and lateral mobility. A true technician of the game, he plays with excellent leverage and technique. He utilizes his natural leverage skills to sink down into his stance, maintain good knee bend and a wide stance to perfectly mirror in pass protection. Possesses above-average lower body strength to anchor in pass sets for the most part. An excellent help blocker who is always keeping his head on a swivel looking to assist and help out his teammates. A really good athlete who maintains an understanding of angles and leverage when run blocking. Smart guy who quickly locates and responds to pre-snap defensive reads.

Weaknesses: An older prospect who will be 24 during his rookie season in the NFL. Has a bad habit of locking his elbows out and allowing guys to disengage on the counter move? Lacks elite and prototypical size and length. Not a power blocker who can consistently move guys in the run game, reliant on technique and angles. Can get caught off-balance when on the move and far too often finds himself on the ground. Generally, a good anchor, but can have issues with guys who play with speed or blitzers who come in fast. Struggles against rushers that have length. Despite his movement skills, he misses far too often in space failing to stay on the balls of his feet.

Best Fit: Zone-blocking center

Player Ranking (1-100): 74.9 – Overall a good blocker who displays good quickness and athletic traits. I have serious concerns about his playing strength as to how it will translate at the next level. Despite his athleticism, far too often he whiffs in space which is also troubling. He could potentially be a starter at the next level but will need some time in an NFL strength and conditioning program. Still relatively new to the position and needs seasoning. 4th round player.

15. Nate Davis OG/C Charlotte 6'3 317 lbs

Strengths: Davis is a 4-year starter for Conference USA Charlotte who has played mostly inside at RG. Davis is a former defensive lineman who transitioned as a freshman. Responsible for one of the best rushing attacks during his career in college football. Davis is a really good athlete who fires off the ball in the running game, rolling his hips and driving his legs through contact. Does a nice job of showing good anticipation and change of direction while on the move. Impressive in his ability to reach 2nd level blocks and sustain and latch on. Offers the lateral mobility to consistently reach and hook. Commits himself to play with technique, maintaining a wide stance and quickly winning inside hands. Possesses the power and lower body to sustain and anchor down against bull rushes.

Weaknesses: Was suspended for a violation of team rules this past season. A smaller, compact built guard who lacks elite length and wingspan to keep defenders off his frame. Played in Conference USA where he didn't compete against many upper-tier defensive linemen.

Best Fit: Zone-blocking system

Player Ranking (1-100): 74.8 – A really good player who will need to greatly impress in all the pre-draft workouts for teams to draft him early on Day 3. From his film alone, he's a 4th round player. Has a chance to be an early starter.

16. Michael Jordan OG/C Ohio State 6'7 312 lbs

Strengths: Jordan possesses a long-levered frame with the necessary build to continue adding additional muscle mass. Jordan moved from guard to center prior to his final season, showing position versatility. Jordan has started every game the last 2 seasons, showing consistency and reliability. A good athlete, he displays easy movement skills with good initial quickness out of his stance. Jordan understands how to utilize his long arms to keep defenders off his frame. Despite his height and leverage concerns, Jordan shows a surprising amount of lower-body anchoring ability, showing the ability to sit down against rushers. Really good against power, showing the ability to fight power with power. Has the frame and length to smoothly absorb speed-to-power. Good recovery skills if he is a tick late off the snap of the ball. Impressive upper-body and hand-strength showing the ability to latch on and sustain. Fires off the ball in the run game, showing the ability to move the pile and engage his lower body explosiveness. Generally, is used as the move blocker for the Ohio State offensive line, showing good lateral movement, balance, and awareness to hit accurately on the move.

Weaknesses: Jordan is still very raw at the center position, finally starting to look comfortable towards the end of the season. Due to his height, his hand placement and leverage issues are going to be a constant battle. He usually can offset these deficiencies but sometimes they manifest. Good quickness and movement skills, but has a tendency to get over his skis in space, flailing and losing balance at the 2nd level. Has some difficulties redirecting his frame on counter moves, especially noticeable when competing against 1-gap quicker-twitch interior rushers. Needs to be more patient when playing in pass sets, far too often getting over aggressive getting caught off-balance.

Best Fit: Zone-blocking guard

Player Ranking (1-100): 74.4 – I really like Jordan and while he is still raw, he shows impressive traits. He's a really good athlete who shows the ability to move well in space. I do worry that he's going to have similar issues to Cam Irving, due to his height, but there are absolutely traits to work with. He's very good in the running game already, and above-average in pass protection. He will never be the mauler type, but he can be a really solid cog in the wheel for an athletic offensive line. 4th round player.

17. Martez Ivey G Florida 6'5 305 lbs

Strengths: Ivey is a 4-year starter for the Gators who has played both tackle and guard during his career, after being one of the highest graded high school football players. Scouts are torn whether Ivey is best served moving inside or to keep him at tackle. To start with, Ivey possesses a massive frame which will have coaches drooling. An outstanding wing-span and a powerful upper-body make rushing against Ivey quite difficult. He utilizes his long arms to maintain a healthy distance between defenders in the passing game. Ivey excels in the run game, showcasing his ability to use his aggression and mean streak to bully defenders. He commits himself to win inside hand leverage immediately on the snap of the ball. When Ivey gets his hands on defenders who attempt to bull rush him, he rarely grants them any movement due to his powerful anchor and good leverage ability. He keeps his base wide and anchors down, showing his lower body power and strength. He's a mauler and a brawler who will tire defenders out by the end of games.

Weaknesses: Ivey is an older prospect who will be 24 his rookie season. Ivey really struggles in pass sets, getting exposed quite a bit in his career. A slow-footed guy who struggles to move laterally to be able to consistently stay in front of his assignment. Struggles against speed rushers who can win the outside edge. This lack of quickness affects his ability to reach and hook block in space. His batting average at the 2nd level is low due to his continual overextension and lack of coordination between his upper and lower body. Shows loads of stiffness in his core, struggling to re-direct and recover after any lost steps. Loses sustain far too frequently letting his defender off after the counter move. Has battled knee, ankle and shoulder concerns throughout his college career.

Best Fit: Inside at guard in power blocking scheme. Can play tackle in a pinch if needed.

Player Ranking (1-100): 73.6 – Ivey never quite lived up to his potential coming out of high school, but he has made strides throughout his career. At the end of his senior season, he had some of the best games of his career, prompting some to think he should stay at tackle. I would rather see him use his physicality and mean streak inside in a power-blocking system. Ivey is a high upside player who will continue to get better at the next level. You take a chance on a kid with this level of talent. 4th round player.

18. Jesse Burkett C Stanford 6'4 300 lbs

Strengths: Burkett is a smaller, but a compactly-built guy playing with a low center of gravity. He shows really impressive initial quickness off the snap, getting to the 2nd level in a flash. Good athlete who moves with smoothness, can get in front of screens in a flash. Smart guy who keeps his head on a swivel and assists whenever he doesn't have an assignment. Does a nice job of playing with leverage, utilizing his natural leverage to sustain and get under blockers. He can anchor and sustain in the passing game due to his leverage ability. Has impressive strength in his hands with the ability to latch on and prevent defenders from disengaging. Shows the lateral movement skills to be able to reach and hook. Has a good understanding of how to utilize cut-off and angle blocks in the run game. Keeps a wide base perfectly, utilizing his length to keep defenders from getting inside his frame.

Weaknesses: Noticeable strength concerns in both the passing and in the running game. In the run game, he fails to generate any type of movement from his lower half. A smaller-framed guy who could stand to put on some additional muscle to sustain better. He gets to the 2nd level so quickly but fails to adequately locate and lock on at the 2nd level. Has some balance concerns at the line of scrimmage. Can play a bit too far over his toes, getting caught lunging.

Best Fit: Zone-blocking system

Player Ranking (1-100): 73.0 – Burkett needs to go to a zone-blocking system that can utilize his athleticism and movement skills. He's not blessed with great size, but he can get stronger with time in an NFL Strength & Conditioning program. Solid center who can be a really good starter. 4th round player.

19. Garrett Brumfield OG LSU 6'4 303 lbs

Strengths: Brumfield is a 4-year contributor and leader for the Tigers who has started exclusively at left guard. A compactly-built blocker, Brumfield is an absolute beast, showing incredible strength and power throughout his frame. Brumfield plays with a mean streak, showing toughness and an aggressive nature. Physical in his upper-body showing good hand strength and an initial punch to reset defenders. Brumfield always keeps his legs moving through contact, never stopping his feet. An athletic move blocker who shows good 2nd level contact ability when playing with good leverage. An easy mover, he shows good balance and fluidity in his movements. A good communicator who always assists when he fails to have an assignment.

Weaknesses: A classic waist bender who overextends in space, lacking the necessary coordination between upper and lower body. Widens his stance far too much in pass protection, limiting his lateral movement ability to mirror. Appears to have some core stiffness preventing him from redirecting his frame if initially beaten. Overaggressive in space, leading to some poor whiffs at the 2nd level. Needs to learn to better time his attacks with his hands.

Best Fit: Zone-blocking guard

Player Ranking (1-100): 72.4 – Brumfield is a really good athlete who plays with a nasty mean streak. His zone-blocking ability is certainly going to be appealing for zone-style offensive schemes. He gets exposed quite a bit in pass sets, failing to play laterally and mirror when his stance is off. 4th round player.

20. Javon Patterson OG Ole Miss 6'3 306 lbs

Strengths: Patterson is a 4-year starter for the Rebels who has played all 3 interior positions in college. A smart kid, both on and off the field and is beloved by his coaches. Patterson is built with a compact and low center of gravity frame, utilizing his natural leverage ability to rarely get moved off his spot against bull rushers. Strong and powerful blocker who shows really good power at the point of attack to fight power with power. Patterson keeps his head on a swivel at all times when he doesn't have an assignment and assists his teammates. Makes 2nd level cut blocks look routine. Has experience in space, showing the ability to locate and lock onto defenders at the 2nd level. Utilizes good fundamentals and technique, maintaining a wide base and squaring his frame up in pass protection.

Weaknesses: Patterson can be a tick late off the snap of the ball. Overextends his arms, failing to always keep his frame squared, causing him to have some balance concerns. Slow footed athlete who struggles mirroring and moving laterally in too much space. Shows limited recovery ability if initially beaten off the snap of the ball. Square-built guy that lacks ideal length for the next level. Doesn't always engage his lower body in the run game, despite his size, failing to get any kind of movement or push.

Best Fit: Man-blocking system

Player Ranking (1-100): 71.2 – Patterson is a strong guy who possesses a good natural base to be an effective pass protector. My concern with Patterson is that he possesses very little length to be an effective move blocker at the 2nd level. He isn't the best athlete either. Good in pass protection, just OK when run blocking. 4th round player.

21. B.J. Autry OG Jacksonville State 6'3 351 lbs

Strengths: Autry was a former Baylor Bear and JUCO transfer before transferring to Jacksonville State. Autry is a massive, massive man with a tremendously powerful physique with good arm length. A finisher who fights to the echoes of the whistle on every snap. Has the power throughout his frame to sit down against even the more powerful DTs in college football. A bully who displays tremendous upper-body power frequently throwing defenders to the ground and striking them with a powerful initial punch. A space clearer in the run game, bowing his back and showing the leg drive to move the pile backward in the run game.

Weaknesses: Violated team rules at Baylor getting him dismissed from the team. Has some stiffness in his core preventing him from recovering or redirecting after a lost step. Has some lateral mobility deficiencies causing him to get beat off the initial snap of the ball if he misses with his hands. Lacks the elite quickness off the snap of the ball to be used effectively in a move or zonal situations at the next level. Shows some awareness issues, very late to react to oncoming blitzes and stunts. Frequently locks his elbows out, allowing rushers to beat him on the counter. Frequently gets too high with his hands affecting his ability to latch on.

Best Fit: Power-blocking scheme

Player Ranking (1-100): 68.3 – A powerful, mauler in the run game, Autry is a scheme-fit in a power-blocking offensive system where he can focus on staying on the line of scrimmage and blocking his assignment. He's a physical, mauler type who loves the physical aspects of the game. He shows effectiveness as a run blocker but lacks the athleticism and quick feet to be a great pass protector. A 5th round player.

22. Nate Herbig OG Stanford 6'3 336 lbs

Strengths: Herbig is a mountain of a man who has been a 3-year starter at both guard spots for the Tigers. A surprisingly fluid mover with good initial quickness out of his stance for a man so big. Excellent in the Stanford zone-system showing the ability to be the lead blocker and frequently get out in front in space. Shows good lateral mobility to consistently hook/reach block at the 2nd level. Rolls his hips and drives his legs to steer opponents away from the ball. Understands how to utilize his hands maintaining a safe healthy distance from his opponent. Shows a powerful initial punch to slow opponents down. Possesses a good overall anchor, maintaining good leverage and a wide base to hunker down and barely lose any ground. Shows good awareness and communication at the line of scrimmage, always recognizing what is coming.

Weaknesses: Far too passive for a man as big as Herbig. A very inconsistent player who looks great at times, and terrible in other situations. Seems to have some concentration lapses, most notably in pass protection, playing with poor technique and allowing guys to get free rushes at the QB. Fails to latch on after the counter move, and lacks the hand strength. Concerns about the players lack of effort, looking like he's disengaged on the field at times. Herbig has a tendency to play on his toes, getting overset and easily beaten on either side.

Best Fit: Zone-blocking guard

Player Ranking (1-100): 67.4 – Herbig is a really big, strong man but needs to play more like it. He's a solid athlete for a guy as big as he is, which makes me think there's something to work with there. I just feel that his concerns in pass protection are quite troubling. He could be worth the pick if he's committed to continuing to refine his craft and get better. He's worth a 5th round pick.

23. Hjalte Froholdt G Arkansas 6'4 311 lbs

Strengths: Froholdt is a compactly-built prospect for the Razorbacks who transitioned from the defensive line after his freshman season. He has been a mainstay of their offensive line the last 3 seasons starting practically every game at LG. Good initial quickness out of his stance, quickly getting to the 2nd level. Fires off the ball in the run game, rolling his hips forward and getting excellent leg drive to push the pile forward. Smart kid who is very often the 'move' blocker and used on pulls and reach blocks in the run game. Always keeps his head up, consistently aware of what is going on around him. Really good athlete, he excels getting out on the perimeter to latch onto defenders with a really good success rate in reaching a linebacker in space. Maintains good technique keeping a wide base and knees bent.

Weaknesses: Noticed some issues when moving laterally, failing to keep his feet shuffling at all times. Can get overwhelmed with power in pass sets, conceding some movement and push. Lacks a lot of fire in his play, almost always appears passive. Loses sustain on counters by defenders who play with length. Can be a bit slow to get his hands-on rushers, allowing defenders to dictate the terms. Not an overly physical guy who always finishes plays. It appears that he lacks ideal length. Lacks a powerful punch to slow defenders down at all.

Best Fit: Zone-blocking guard or center

Player Ranking (1-100): 64.3 – A good athlete who seems to be at his best when on the move. Some teams might want him as a center because of his lack of power. 6th round player.

24. Alex Bars OG Notre Dame 6'6 315 lbs

Strengths: Bars is an impressive and incredibly versatile guy having played 3 different positions on the Irish's offensive line. (RG, LG, RT) Has almost started every single game during his college career minus his sophomore year after an ankle injury. The definition of reliability and consistency. Bars is a team captain, showing outstanding intangibles and leadership skills. Smart kid who comes from a football family with a father and brothers who all played college football. Possesses the necessary length to kick out and play RT if needed to at the next level. Shows fluidity and smoothness in his ability to play in space and locate linebackers at the 2nd level. Commits himself to the technical and fundamentals of playing offensive line, with good hand placement, contact balance, and bent knees.

Weaknesses: Plays far too upright when coming out of his stance negating his power and strength to anchor. Lacks the lower body power and explosiveness to generate much movement in the run game. Lacks necessary upper body power to lock onto defenders and utilize his hand strength to sustain. Is he too big to play inside? His height and lack of natural leverage prevent him for sitting and anchoring against shorter/squattier built defenders. A bit of a clunky athlete who struggles to play laterally or in too much space. Lacks punch at the line of scrimmage to throw defenders off.

Best Fit: Developmental inside guy

Player Ranking (1-100): 63.2 – Not a bad player but lacks a GREAT quality. Not a very good athlete, nor is he a dominant physical guy who can clear run lanes. 6th round player.

25. Venzell Boulware OG Miami 6'3 306 lbs

Strengths: Boulware, who was a Tennessee graduate transfer, started 6 games for the Hurricanes this year. Boulware is built like a phone-booth with stout and compact limbs. A belly-to-belly blocker who utilizes his natural leverage ability to sit down and absorb. Excellent lower-body strength and explosion to generate serious push and movement skills in the running game. A physical guy who plays with a nasty mean streak, fighting until the whistle. If initially beaten, Boulware shows the strength and recovery ability to regain lost steps. Very aware blocker, always looking to assist his teammates when he doesn't have an assignment. Shows good ability to locate and lock onto defenders at the 2nd level.

Weaknesses: Boulware had some academic issues at Tennessee, ruling him academically ineligible to play in their bowl game. Very limited experience, starting a handful of games for the Vols and only 6 for the Hurricanes. Has a tendency to play on his toes, getting caught off-balance, frequently reaching in pass protection. Has some coordination concerns between his upper and lower body, not always playing balanced. A stubby guy who lacks the length to be able to sustain blocks on the counter move.

Best Fit: Developmental guard, can play in either scheme

Player Ranking (1-100): 61.5 – There's absolutely something to work with, but he's a developmental guy with very limited game experience. He possesses the strength, anchor ability, and some athletic movement skills. 6th round player.

26. Ryan Bates OG/T Penn State 6'4 305 lbs

Strengths: Bates is a 3-year starter who has started almost every game of his college career, splitting time between playing left tackle, left guard and right tackle. Despite playing most games at left tackle, Bates has the traits to best translate as a guard at the next level. Shows some secondary burst to recover if he's a bit late off the snap of the ball. Plays with good natural leverage, maintaining bent knees and a wide stance. A technician in his ability to utilize his hands to displace and win inside hand leverage. Has the footwork to get out in front of outside zone runs or crack tosses. Keeps his legs moving and churning throw contact, getting some good movement in the run game.

Weaknesses: Bates lacks ideal length, especially notable when he is playing on the outside as a tackle. Fails to have an overly powerful initial punch to disrupt defenders. He lacks the latch on strength in his hands to sustain blocks on the counter move. Lacks great lateral mobility and can struggle when asked to play on an island in too much space in pass sets. Needs to gain additional functional strength in his lower half, lacks sufficient anchor ability when in pass protection.

Best Fit: Guard. But also offers value as a backup tackle or center on an NFL roster.

Player Ranking (1-100): 60.3 – Bates best attribute is his versatility. He's a serious liability in pass protection and struggled both as a guard and as a tackle against better defensive fronts. He demonstrates above average functional athleticism with good footwork and good overall hand usage. As a run blocker, he shows the ability to utilize his natural leverage and momentum to get some good push. He is a 6th round player.

27. Alec Eberle C Florida State 6'3 295 lbs

Strengths: Eberle is a 3+ year starter and team captain for the Seminoles who has started in 44 straight games at center. Eberle plays the position like a wrestler, grappling and fighting until the end of the whistle. Understands how to utilize proper positioning and angles to force wide rush lanes. An aggressive blocker who plays with really good upper-body power, latching on and bringing defenders down to their knees. Plays with natural leverage ability, when keeping his pads down, he's a difficult guy to move.

Weaknesses: Played on an offensive line that really struggled this year, both in pass protection and opening up holes in the run game. Gets into too many personal battles, failing to always keep his eyes scanning to his teammates. Eberle is a limited athlete who lacks any kind of zone ability to play in space or be utilized as a move blocker. Lacks next-level length and fails to utilize full-arm extension, allowing defenders to quickly get inside his chest plate and control the line of scrimmage. Has serious anchoring and lower-body power to sit down against more powerful interior defenders, frequently gets walked back to the quarterback.

Best Fit: Man-blocking center

Player Ranking (1-100): 58.3 – Eberle is a limited player who will need to impress in training camp. His longevity and durability certainly are traits which will make him attractive. He had his best year as a sophomore when he was opening up run lanes for Dalvin Cook. Since then, his draft stock has regressed quite a bit. 7th round player.

Interior Lineman Top-10 Rankings

1. Cody Ford
2. Chris Lindstrom
3. Elgton Jenkins
4. Erik McCoy
5. Dru Samia
6. Ben Powers
7. Dalton Risner
8. Terronne Prescod
9. Damian Prince
10. Connor McGovern

Chapter 9

Edge Players (4-3 DE's and 3-4 OLB's)

1. Nick Bosa EDGE Ohio State 6'4 263 lbs

Strengths: Bosa, like his brother who plays for the Chargers, is just a flat-out football player. Possessing prototypical size and length with physicality and muscular definition throughout. He has been dominant since he's been a rotational freshman with the Buckeyes. As a sophomore, he was at his best, with 16 tackles for loss and 8.5 sacks. Bosa is a complete player who shows proficiency in all areas of the game. He's an outstanding athlete, showing excellent get-off at the line of scrimmage. Plays like a technician, knowing exactly how he's going to attack the offensive tackle on every snap. Utilizes violent hands to maintain separation between himself and the blocker, as well as a diverse set of hand tactics to attack in different ways. He's a relentless player who refuses to be blocked by 1, 2 or even 3 guys. Shows the strength and physicality to hold up at the point of attack and close running lanes in the run game. Uses a powerful over-under swipe move which is almost impossible to stop. Bosa has experience rushing on both sides of the line and will even kick inside at times. Does a nice job of being effective with his counter moves, showing to be a slippery guy to sustain. Plays with a wide variety of pass-rush moves.

Weaknesses: Bosa missed most of his junior season with a core muscle injury needing surgery, only playing in 3 games. Has a bit of an overaggressive style of play especially on misdirection's, bootlegs or waggles where he can take himself out of the play. Some NFL evaluators were upset he decided to forego the rest of his senior season when he might have been healthy enough to return in December. Overruns passing plays far too often getting behind the QB. Lacks position flexibility, truly only a 4-3 defensive fit as a straight DE. Can be a tick slow in his reaction time at the snap of the ball, often times he's the last one to move on the line of scrimmage. A bit tip-hipped lacking the elastic flexibility to bend and consistently capture the edge.

Best Fit: Bosa is a 4-3 DE that can play on either side of the line.

Player Ranking (1-100): 95.3 – Bosa is truly a speed-to-power maven! It's hard to find a truly 'WEAK' part of his game. He's a 10+ sack a year defender. Strong, long and absolutely dominant. I think he's a better player than his brother was in college. My only slight concern is his families injury history. But if he lives up to his potential, he could easily be one of the best defensive linemen in the NFL.

2. Clelin Ferrell EDGE Clemson 6'5 260 lbs

Strengths: Ferrell displays the prototypical height, length and size for an edge rusher at the next level. Ferrell has gotten better and better in every season for Clemson, totaling 11.5 sacks, 20 tackles for loss and 3 forced fumbles his senior season. Displays terrific snap anticipation and timing, quickly getting a jump on the snap of the ball. Shows good initial quickness out of his stance, and is capable of shooting gaps quickly. Quick twitch guy with the ability to win the outside edge on tackles. Plays in a variety of different positions along the defensive front, but mostly plays as right side end. Plays with a wiggle in his hips making it difficult to sustain him for the duration of a play. Shows a wide variety of pass rush moves, including a nice spin move. Violent hands to maintain separation between him and blockers. Shows the strength and the lower body anchor to hold up at the point of attack and maintain the edges. So disruptive and has led his team to pressures in each of the last 3 seasons. Has experience being used in space, showing smoothness and balance when asked to drop in coverage. Converts speed to power by utilizing natural momentum to barrel through bodies. Plays with a terrific motor, accelerating fluidly to chase ball carriers from the back side.

Weaknesses: A close but no cigar player who is disruptive but doesn't finish enough plays consistently. Shows the speed to turn the edge, but lacks the elastic flexibility to consistently sink his hips and grab the edge. Needs to do a better job of keeping his pad level down and not leaving his chest exposed.

Best Fit: Think he's best as a 4-3 DE

Player Ranking (1-100): 94.5 – Absolutely love Ferrell and I think he's the best defensive lineman Clemson has had these last few years. Is outstanding in both the run game and shows serious pass rush potential. It's really impressive the number of pressures and sacks he generates despite playing mostly in a 3-man front. He's a top 10 player.

3. Montez Sweat EDGE Mississippi State 6'6 252 lbs

Strengths: Sweat absolutely looks the part with ideal height and an incredible wingspan. Sweat is a really good athlete who shows the athleticism and fluidity in movements that teams covet. Has played in both 4-3 and 3-4 defensive systems, showing he can play standing up or with his hand in the dirt. Despite his wiry build, Sweat has better than anticipated upper-body strength and power. 2 seasons in a row with 10+ sacks against the best offensive lines in college football. Uses his long arms to control blockers in the run game, keeping them off of his frame. Impressive in his ability to utilize his outside arm to corral running backs while engaging with the other arm. Utilizes relentless hands in his ability to disengage and quickly swipe defenders off of him. Cuts off running lanes and edges due to his length.

Weaknesses: Was suspended at Michigan State for the entire season for a "violation of team rules" and then transferred to Mississippi State for his final 2 seasons. Sweat lacks ideal power and lower-body anchoring ability and will struggle to maintain the edges at the next level in the run game. Experience in coverage, but has some core and hip stiffness that prevents him from opening his hips to play in too much space. A straight-line athlete who struggles to redirect and play laterally when initially blocked, lacking great counter ability. Fails to generate torque in his lower half to generate much of a bull rush.

Best Fit: 4-3 RDE

Player Ranking (1-100): 88.2 – Sweat is a really good athlete with prototypical next-level size, he shows a variety of different ways to attack the pocket. He's a 1st round player who will be a really great sub-package player early on as he continues to add strength to his lower half. I don't think he'll ever be an elite pass rusher due to his lack of lateral mobility and core stiffness, but he'll be a very solid 3-down player and will be a 6-9 sack a year guy.

4. Zach Allen EDGE Boston College 6'4 280 lbs

Strengths: Allen is a 3-year starter for BC who has shown really solid production all 3 seasons. He's a long, stout and strong kid who shows outstanding muscular girth and strength throughout his frame. Allen possesses the perfect length to be an ideal 3-4 DE or an oversized 4-3 DE. He's a schematically versatile guy who knows exactly how to use his size and length to close down running lanes and control gaps. Despite his size, Allen shows surprisingly good lateral agility to play sideline to sideline. On the snap of the ball, Allen is committed to winning inside hands, controlling the point of attack. Allen shows an ability to kick inside and generate a pass rush from interior positions in sub-packages. Uses his length to disrupt passing lanes and get in QB's line of sight. Allen is so strong in his upper body, rarely getting stuck on blocks. A relentless motor that goes 110% on every snap of the ball. Really impressive initial quickness coupled with good snap anticipation that allows him to get a really good jump on the ball. Always around the football, had over 100 tackles as a junior, which is unheard of for a defensive lineman.

Weaknesses: Allen is a bit of an upright rusher who plays with inconsistent pad level when rushing the passer. I've noticed that Allen has some mental lapses in concentration causing him to slowly diagnose and process things in front of him. Good athlete, but not an ideal athlete who can consistently chase down plays backside or consistently win the edge. Lacks a great pass rushing array, relying on his strength and bull rush too often.

Best Fit: Schematically versatile, might be more attractive to 3-4 defensive teams with his length. Can even play as a 3-tech DT as well in a 4-3.

Player Ranking (1-100): 86.1 – I don't care that I love Allen more than most. He's a flat-out football player who plays every snap and NEVER gets hurt. He makes so many plays and disrupts so many more that aren't on the stat sheet. He'll likely never be a 10+ a year sack guy but he'll be a really good player on a defense. Late 1st round player.

5. Josh Allen EDGE Kentucky 6'4 260 lbs

Strengths: Allen possesses a long and rangy build with good height and length for a defense. Has increased his girth and size between his junior and senior seasons, adding necessary strength and muscle. Allen had a good sophomore and junior season but really has raised his draft stock tremendously after an awesome senior season. Shows the versatility that very few guys possess at the college level, Allen can be used in so many different ways. Allen has experience all over the field for Kentucky, even playing some inside linebacker. He shows good ability and fluidity when playing in space, showing an ability to cover slot receivers and TEs. A really good athlete who has quick-twitch ability to get off the edge. Shows elastic flexibility with the ability to dip his shoulder and get around the outside edges. Plays with a good pad level, keeping his body low to the ground and with good contact balance. Does a nice job of utilizing his length to control the line of scrimmage and set the edge. Comfortable on both the right and left sides of the defense.

Weaknesses: A bit of a tweener who lacks a true position for the next level. Doesn't always appear to have a plan when trying to win, running out of options quickly and looking disengaged. I don't see him get his sacks with pure pass rush ability, but rather as a result of good coverage by his defensive backs. Wins mostly with motor and being at the right place at the right time. Plays a little too passive, lacks the mean streak or the fire in his belly. Has the tools to be a great pass rusher, but lacks the experience and pass rushing arsenal to consistently threaten. Good athleticism, but isn't an elite athlete who is consistently going to put pressure on the QB at the next level. Tends to be overaggressive against RPOs, quickly attacking the 1st option rather than staying disciplined and patient.

Best Fit: Scheme versatile but probably best as a 3-4 OLB

Player Ranking (1-100): 85.2 – I don't like Josh Allen as much as others. I respect his size and his versatility, but I don't see a true game-changer at the next level. His best position is probably a 3-4 OLB. In order to be an elite edge player, he needs to learn how to utilize his skill set to be an effective pass rusher. Late 1st round player.

6. Jachai Polite DE Florida 6'2 242 lbs

Strengths: Polite is a shorter, but compactly-built edge defender for the Gators who impressed greatly this season with 11 sacks, 19.5 tackles for loss and 6 forced fumbles. Strong hands, showing the awareness to always rip at the ball upon contact. Has played on both sides of the line. An excellent motor that runs hot, showing the ability to make a lot of plays chasing down backside. Polite's best attribute is his bendability. He shows great ankle and hip flexibility to be able to turn the corner and grab the outside edges. He combines his bend, snap anticipation/awareness and excellent 1st step quickness to routinely beat the tackle off the snap of the ball. Plays with natural leverage ability, limiting his contact points, preserving his frame small, frequently getting through tight windows. A hustle player who will make a lot of plays due to never giving up on the play. Good in the running game, showing the ability to set the edge effectively and routinely make tackles, rarely missing one.

Weaknesses: Polite is a bit of a 1-year wonder who kind of came out of nowhere this year, with minimal production levels before this season. Lacks ideal size to be a systematic-versatile guy, and will likely be only a fit in a 3-4 defense as an outside linebacker. Despite his stand-up experience as a linebacker for the Gators, he possesses very little experience in coverage. A bit of a splash player who will impress for a couple of snaps and then disappear for large chunks at a time. Adequate length, but not great, and will get enveloped by larger tackles who can control his chest plate. Lacks a counter plan. If he doesn't win with speed at 1st attempt, he fails to be able to utilize his hands effectively to win on the counter move. Quick but not especially fast, he lacks true 'make-up' speed to make up lost ground.

Best Fit: 3-4 OLB

Player Ranking (1-100): 84.9 – I like Polite but I don't believe he's a 1st round player. He has good explosion, bend, and physicality for his size. His lack of height/length to play as a 4-3 DE will limit his appeal for teams. I worry that he's a bit of a 1-year wonder and he fails to have any kind of counter ability if initially blocked at the line of scrimmage. But overall, he's a solid prospect who shows the athleticism to continue to refine and improve.

7. Brian Burns EDGE Florida State 6'5 235 lbs

Strengths: Burns is a 3-year contributor for the Seminoles who has started almost every game since he arrived. Had a tremendous final season as a junior, totaling 52 tackles, 15.5 tackles for loss, 10 sacks and 3 forced fumbles. Burns is an athletic rusher who shows above-average burst at the line of scrimmage. He combines his athleticism with his good snap anticipation to beat tackles immediately. He's anything but a 1-trick pony, utilizing a variety of different maneuvers in his arsenal to beat a blocker. Possesses quick hands, showing the ability to quickly stack and shed. Attacks with a plan, showing the ability to utilize his feet to set up tackles, both with inside and outside moves. A slippery rusher, he makes it very difficult for blockers to sustain him on the counter move, seemingly knowing what he is going to do ahead of time. Plays with a relentless motor and brings it on every snap, always in pursuit. Plays bigger than his size indicates, most notably in the run game. Utilizes his length effectively when working back towards the football, securely wrapping up ball carriers from behind. Outstanding at ripping at the football, without sacrificing solid tackling fundamentals, causing 6 forced fumbles the last 2 seasons. A flexible and bendable athlete who shows elasticity throughout his frame, just needs to learn how to maximize it when going through contact.

Weaknesses: A very slightly-built guy who will need to maximize his frame and gain additional muscle mass to play as a 4-3 defensive end with his hand in the dirt. Has trouble converting speed to power, rarely getting any movement on a power rush. Despite Burns athletically-built physique and little body fat, he isn't an exceptional athlete. The fear is, should he gain too much more muscle or bulk he will be a slow-footed player. He needs to learn how to bend his hips to consistently grab the outside edges, takes too wide a rush lane, washing him completely out of too many plays. A high-torso build, which prevents him from moving great laterally, due to his long legs.

Best Fit: 4-3 DE

Player Ranking (1-100): 84.5 – Burns reminds me a bit of Randy Gregory as a player. He's an undersized 4-3 defensive end who is a lot stronger than his frame suggests. Both bendy athletes who play with outstanding pass rush arsenals. Burns is going to need more time in an NFL strength and conditioning program to continue to gain strength and muscle. But his pass rush upside is outstanding. And he's no slouch in the run game either. Teams are going to be in love with his length and athletic physique. 2nd round player. He should win snaps immediately in passing situations as a rookie.

8. Charles Omenihu EDGE Texas 6'6 274 lbs

Strengths: Omenihu is a long and well-built DE who is built like an NBA power forward with excellent length. Has had a really great senior season with 9.5 sacks and 16 tackles for loss really coming onto the scene. A versatile defender who can be moved to all 4 defensive line positions, and be successful at each one of them. Understands how to utilize his length to keep blockers off his frame, controlling them throughout the duration of a play. A flexible rusher who displays 0 tightness, showing the ability to get skinny through narrowing gaps or bend around the edge. Omenihu possesses outstanding get-off with explosiveness in his first few steps and then combines that with his long strides to close quickly. A technician who displays outstanding hand usage and technique, delivering accurate blows at the line of scrimmage and possesses the upper-body power to violently shed blocks.

Weaknesses: Has had some conditioning issues during his college career, needing to take plays off. Needs to strengthen his lower-body so he can sufficiently anchor in the run game, especially if he's kicked inside at all. Despite his burst, he lacks the speed-to-power to generate any kind of push when taking on lineman head on. Lacks a consistent plan when rushing, relying far too often on just a bull rush. A little late to utilize his counter moves, allowing valuable seconds to pass by. Due to his frame and size, he's going to have some pad level concerns, and he does allow his pads to rise mid-play far too often.

Best Fit: DE or 3-tech DT

Player Ranking (1-100): 83.5 – Some have him graded as a DT and some have him graded as a DE. I'll keep him as a DE, but honestly, his grade wouldn't change at all for me. Part of the package with the player is that he can do both REALLY, REALLY well. Rare to see a guy who can rush from 4 positions successfully. A 2nd round player that I absolutely love.

9. Austin Bryant EDGE Clemson 6'6 265 lbs

Strengths: The first thing you'll notice about Bryant is his size and length. Displays prototypical NFL size and physique, perfectly capable of holding up in the trenches for all 4 downs. Bryant is a raw athlete who has barely touched the surface of his ability going forward. Already a really good run defender, he shows the stoutness in his lower half to hold up against double teams. Also shows the awareness to quickly locate the ball and the discipline to shut down gaps and running lanes. Good motor with a relentless work ethic to work back towards the ball. Impressive closing speed and can close in a burst. Two straight years of solid production at Clemson. Schematically versatile guy who can play in a 3 or 4-man front. Keeps himself in QB's line of vision to disrupt passes and get his hands in the way.

Weaknesses: Bryant is a bit of a flash player who shows up in spurts then disappears for long stretches of games. Lacks a definitive plan when attacking the QB, seemingly running out of ideas. Doesn't know how to utilize his hands to control the point of attack, allowing blockers to control and win inside hands by keeping himself too exposed. Not a twitchy or a bendy athlete, relying mostly on his power and motor to get after the QB. Upright rusher who lacks the flexibility to capture the edge causing him to overrun tight windows. Played on a stacked defensive line which consistently gave him 1 on 1 situations where he wasn't the focal point of an offensive game plan. Broke his foot during his sophomore season causing him to miss a number of games.

> **Best Fit:** LDE in a 4-3

Player Ranking (1-100): 83.3 – Bryant is a really good player who would be ideally suited in a 4-3 defense where he can play as the LDE and take on double teams consistently in the run game. As he continues to learn how to utilize his size and strength, he will be a shutdown run defender and occasionally offer some pass rush as well. 2nd round player.

10. Jalen Jelks EDGE Oregon 6'5 250 lbs

Strengths: Jelks possesses an athletic and lean frame displaying outstanding size and length to play in either a 4-3 or a 3-4. Jelks possesses outstanding quick-twitch ability, getting a good jump off the line of scrimmage. Shows some speed-to-power ability by effectively utilizing his bull rush to walk lineman back to the QB. Fluid accelerator showing the long speed to chase ball carriers backside. Understands how to cut-off running lanes and set the edge by getting extension with his arms. Utilizes his length to knock down the football at the line of scrimmage. Outstanding hustle, always working and finding a way to the ball. Possesses powerful upper body strength and hands to be able to rip and disengage, as well as bringing down ball carriers. While limited experience in doing so, displays the fluid movement skills to be able to drop and handle space when asked.

Weaknesses: Long and rangy frame, he lacks adequate girth and power to anchor as a 3-down DE at the next level, might be limited to sub-package snaps early on. A liability at this point against the run. Overruns far too many plays rushing the QB, taking wide pursuit angles to the football. It appears on film that he lacks the flexibility and bend to turn the corner routinely. Very average production as a sack artist in college.

> **Best Fit:** 4-3 DE or 3-4 OLB

Player Ranking (1-100): 81.2 – Jelks reminds me a bit of Leonard Floyd a few years ago. A rare athlete who possesses the length and athleticism to develop. His film is good, but his upside is better. You should take a chance on this kind of athlete. 2nd round player.

11. Oshane Ximines EDGE Old Dominion 6'3 241 lbs

Strengths: Ximines is a 5th year senior for Conference USA program Old Dominion. He's really had an incredible career with 32.5 sacks, 51 tackles for loss and 11 forced fumbles. The most impressive part of Ximines game is his ability to utilize his quick, active hands. It's rare for a college player to know how to utilize his hands in so many diverse ways and win effectively from each. Ximines is a smart guy who plays with a rush plan on every snap, knowing how to set up offensive tackles. His quick and sharp reflexes allow him to get a good pre-snap jump on the ball. Hard worker who is relentless is the way he pursues the ball, showing effective ability on the counter. Good upper-body power with excellent grip strength to quickly shed. A very slippery guy, he rarely stays on blocks, showing the lateral quickness, body control, and motor. When he fails to get home or the ball comes out quickly, he does a really nice job of always getting his hands up quickly to disrupt the QB's vision or knock the ball away. Turnover conscious, always looking to strip the ball carrier and it shows with his 11 forced fumbles. Was used both as a RDE, LDE, and a stand-up linebacker. Shows some speed-to-power with an effective bull rush walking lineman back to the QB.

Weaknesses: Has lacked great opposition during his career and will need to really impress during all pre-draft festivities. Might be limited to a 3-4 defensive system due to his lack of run support ability. He's frequently bullied and washed out of too many running plays, due to his lack of lower power anchor. Not a real flexible guy who can effectively bend and get under the pads on rushes.

Best Fit: 3-4 OLB

Player Ranking (1-100): 79.2 – I really like Ximines and think he's a really outstanding rusher. Not sure he possesses the strength and the power to play with his hands on the ground at the next level. If he can be used early on as a sub-package rusher, maybe with some training and time with an NFL strength and conditioning program he can gain additional strength and play all 3 downs. 3rd round player.

12. Chase Winovich EDGE Michigan 6'3 255 lbs

Strengths: Winovich is a 5th year senior who is a converted TE. Winovich has shown really solid production his last 3 seasons at Michigan as a DE. He's the definition of a warrior, battling and winning with hustle and a never-say-die approach. He never takes plays off nor does he ever give up on a play showing an ability to chase plays down the field 40 or 50+ yards. A very disciplined guy who reads the game well, showing outstanding instincts and awareness on run-pass-option plays. (RPOs) Big hitter who isn't afraid of laying the wood or delivering a knock out blow. Aggressive makeup showing fearlessness and toughness that can't be coached. His attitude is infectious with his teammates. Strong hands with a devastating punch which allows him to disengage quickly at the line of scrimmage.

Weaknesses: Lacks ideal mass, length or size to consistently play on the line of scrimmage at the next level. Lacks the necessary frame to put much more muscle on his frame, has already gained 20+ pounds since his freshman season. Good athlete, but isn't an elite change of direction athlete who can play in space as a 3-4 OLB. Not ideal explosive twitch off the line of scrimmage to convert speed-to-power on his bull rush, or win the outside edge with pure speed. His overaggressive style of play can lead to some poor rushing angles and pursuit lanes.

Best Fit: 4-3 DE

Player Ranking (1-100): 78.4 – Really good player who will likely be an exceptional special teams' player immediately and a rotational pass rusher in sub-packages. I would never write this player off! He made himself a lot of money in the Notre Dame game this year. He was consistently in the backfield rushing from all sides of the field. I want this guy on my team. 3rd round player.

13. Jaylon Ferguson EDGE Louisiana Tech 6'4 256 lbs

Strengths: Ferguson is a prototypical RDE in a 4-3 system with outstanding size, length, and weight distribution. A 4-year starter who has had tremendous production in each season at LA Tech, especially his senior season with 15 sacks and 23.5 tackles for loss. Ferguson offers special teams' value as well with multiple blocked kicks in his career. Ferguson is a quick-twitch rusher with outstanding get-off and 1st step quickness. He utilizes his first step in conjunction with his outstanding snap awareness and instincts to create mismatches against slower-footed tackles. Ferguson has the great straight-line speed to quickly close on QB's and finish plays in the backfield. Impressive ability to convert speed to power and put bigger tackles on skates by driving them back with his bull rush. Plays with a plan, using a diverse set of hand tactics to attack in different ways.

Weaknesses: Lacks repertoire in his pass-rushing arsenal, tending to rely solely on his speed rush. Needs to work on developing a counter plan, as he gets stuck on blocks and lacks the ability to disengage. Overaggressive at times, needing to do a better job of maintaining proper positioning to set the edge in the run game. Gets washed out of too many run plays, having little impact on the run game.

Best Fit: 4-3 RDE

Player Ranking (1-100): 78.0 – Ferguson is an upside player who shows good pass rush ability and explosive-twitch which teams are looking for. He also displays outstanding size and length for 4-3 teams. I like him, but wished he showed more transferrable traits for the next level. 3rd round player.

14. Ben Banogu EDGE TCU 6'3 247 lbs

Strengths: Banogu is a talented rusher who transferred from Louisiana Monroe after his freshman season. Has had 16 sacks the last 2 seasons for TCU with 5 forced fumbles and 34 tackles for loss. Loose-hipped rusher with elastic flexibility to bend and grab the edge. Does a nice job of reading plays pre-snap at the line of scrimmage, showing good snap awareness and anticipatory skills. Excellent athlete showing the quick-twitch to get-off quickly as well as the long-speed to be able to run plays from behind backside. Possesses good length, understanding how to maintain the distance between himself and the offensive tackle on rushes. Really impressive spin move which he frequently uses to win. Active hands at the line of scrimmage, utilizing an array of tactics to shed/disengage. Shows a relentless nature doing a nice job of countering and getting off after initially blocked.

Weaknesses: Pass rushing repertoire is devoid of variety, tends to utilize the same 1 or 2 moves on every snap. Lacks much of a plan when attacking an offensive tackle. Far too often overruns plays and gets beyond the QB, leaving gaps exposed. At this point, he's a liability in the running game. Lacks the necessary lower body anchor to be able to hunker down. Also lacks the upper body strength to fight through blocks, and shed and stack quickly in the run game. A raw athlete who needs technique work in the finer parts of playing at the next level. Doubts about whether he can handle a 4-3 defense system with his hand on the ground at the next level.

Best Fit: 3-4 OLB

Player Ranking (1-100): 77.2 – Banogu is a talented rusher who possesses good athleticism but is likely limited to a 3-4 OLB role. Shows the movement skills to be able to drop and handle coverage despite limited experience. Good player. A 3rd round player who will contribute as a rusher early on for an NFL defense.

15. Shareef Miller EDGE Penn State 6'5 260 lbs

Strengths: Miller is a 2-year starter who really came onto the scene following his impressive sophomore season. Miller possesses an outstanding and prototypical 4-3 defensive end frame, with great length and overall girth. Had a really impressive final campaign as a junior with 16 tackles for loss and 8 sacks. Miller is a physical guy who understands how to play the run, coming across the face and making stops in the backfield. Rushes from a wide angle on passing situations, showing the desired bend and twitch ability to grab the outside edge. Good snap anticipation and awareness, getting an outstanding jump at the snap of the ball. Disciplined against option-plays and running QB's, maintaining disciplined eyes and setting the edge. Outstanding motor and hustle, routinely making plays down the field and running plays down from 20-30 yards downfield. A powerful finisher who displays good upper-body strength to be able to finish and forcefully bring ball carriers to the ground.

Weaknesses: Miller fails to consistently engage his hands and utilize his length, preferring to play belly-to-belly, keeping his chest pad far too exposed. A 1-dimensional pass rusher who attempts to win with speed only. Strictly has played on the left side of the defensive line only. A bit tight-hipped in space, failing to redirect his frame if initially blocked. Despite his size, Miller lacks the adequate anchor strength in his lower-body to effectively hunker down and take on double teams.

Best Fit: 4-3 defensive end

Player Ranking (1-100): 76.8 – Miller is a good developmental prospect who will be attractive to teams with his blend of size, length, and speed. He's really improved this season as a pass rusher, as evidenced by his production. He's still a bit too much of a 1-trick pony and needs to develop more of a pass rush arsenal. He's competed against some outstanding offensive tackles who now play in the NFL, and had some success against them. I believe he's worth taking in the 3rd round. He's not a complete liability against the run either, just needs to gain a bit more strength in his lower body.

16. Christian Miller EDGE Alabama 6'4 255 lbs

Strengths: Miller is a 3-year contributor for the Tide and had an outstanding senior season, finally staying healthy. A team leader who is beloved by the coaches for his attitude and hardworking nature. A versatile defender, he has shown an ability to drop into coverage at times this year. Shows fluid movement to drop and handle space, and will get better and better with more experience. Miller's a good athlete who accelerates fluidly to chase ball carriers down from behind. Outstanding and violent hand usage, displaying a diverse set of hand tactics to beat blockers. Utilizes his full length to maintain a healthy distance between blockers. A loose-hipped athlete who shows the ability to bend and grab the edges. A slippery rusher, he plays with good leverage and counter ability, always a threat to disengage and rarely gets hung up on a block. His best move is his rip move, showing the ability to quickly swipe hands and grab the edge. Disrupted a lot of plays this year that weren't on the stat sheet.

Weaknesses: Missed most of his junior season after tearing his bicep, and dealt with a few other nagging injuries during his career as well. A lankier-framed guy who still lacks ideal bulk and anchor to hold up as a 4-3 hand in the dirt defender. Fails to show adequate leg explosion by utilizing speed to power to barrel through bodies. A good athlete, but lacks the explosive twitch to win the corner on athleticism alone.

| Best Fit: 3-4 OLB |

Player Ranking (1-100): 76.2 – A good athlete who really impressed this year. I worry about his injury history and whether he can stay healthy long-term but he's a good player. He's really done a nice job of adding muscle mass to his body and retooling his frame during his 5 years at Alabama. He's truly NFL ready and will absolutely play a roll on passing downs immediately. A 3rd round player.

17. Maxx Crosby DE Eastern Michigan 6'5 255 lbs

Strengths: Crosby is a long, rangy-built defensive end for MAC conference Eastern Michigan. He's really had some outstanding production in the last 2 seasons, combining for 35.5 tackles for loss, 8 forced fumbles, and 18.5 sacks. Crosby is a loose-hipped athlete who shows terrific elastic flexibility to grab the edge and get underneath tackles. Crosby brings a diverse skill-set with a variety of pass rush moves including an effective swim move. A relentless motor which he brings on every snap. A slippery rusher, he always keeps himself moving and active, making it very difficult for a lineman to latch on. Quick, explosive hands to knock away would be blockers. Outstanding awareness who quickly locates the football post-snap, and if he can't make the play he makes sure he gets his hands up to disrupt the pass. Possesses twitchy reflexes with the ability to quickly diagnose. Shows the upper-body strength to be relied upon in tackling situations.

Weaknesses: Needs to gain additional functional strength to play as a 3-down player at the next level, especially if teams want to use him with his hand in the dirt. His over-aggressiveness causes him to overrun a lot of plays and take himself out of run plays, where he fails to set the edge. Fails to convert speed to power, lacking the ability to engage his lower half and generate any kind of forward push on his bull rushes. Lacks the anchoring ability to hunker down in the run game.

| Best Fit: Situational pass-rusher early on in either 4-3 or 3-4 |

Player Ranking (1-100): 75.8 – Crosby was an impressive guy to watch on film. He completely tore up the MAC conference the last 2 years. He still needs to gain serious functional strength, but his quickness/explosiveness is really impressive. I love how elusive he is at the line of scrimmage, rarely getting stuck on blocks. Until he shows he can play in running situations, he's a 3rd down rusher only. I would take him in the 3rd round.

18. Porter Gustin EDGE USC 6'5 260 lbs

Strengths: Gustin has rare size and prototypical NFL length, certainly passing the eyeball test for the next level. Gustin really understands how to use his hands and arms through the course of a rush, winning the hand battle on the snap of the ball. Maintains discipline in gap control, always being at the right place at the right time when asked to set the edge. He plays with violent hands and a nasty punch, showing the ability to control the point of attack. Wins with motor, constantly battling and fighting on every snap. Always in pursuit, displaying the ability to run down plays backside and showing good long speed to make plays. Aggressive in run support, showing the anchor and the strength to sustain the edges.

Weaknesses: Very average pass rush production, despite being used to attack the pocket on almost every snap. Misses too many 1 on 1 opportunities where he struggles beating tackles. Lacks the great 1st step, preventing him from winning with speed. Doesn't have the great elastic flexibility to grab the edges or dip his shoulder. Has some stiffness in his core to be able to recover or redirect. Missed a lot of tackles in each season, missing some big stops in the backfield. Lacks much of a pass rush arsenal to win in different ways.

Best Fit: Scheme versatile but probably best used a 4-3 DE because of his size and length

Player Ranking (1-100): 73.5 – Gustin displays the size and the motor that teams covet. He's a good athlete but isn't a great athlete. I don't see him ever being a top-notch pass rusher. Will be solid and consistent and a force in the run game. 4th round player.

19. Joe Jackson EDGE Miami 6'5 258 lbs

Strengths: Jackson is a 3-year contributor for the Hurricanes who has shown solid production in all 3 seasons. Built with prototypical NFL defensive end size, showing good thickness and muscle tone throughout his frame. Jackson possesses a nonstop motor, bringing it on every snap. A powerful guy at the point of attack who consistently takes on double teams, showing good leg drive and anchoring ability in the run game. In the passing game, Jackson converts speed to power and natural momentum to barrel through bodies and get a serious push with his bull rush. Has a large arsenal when it comes to his pass rush repertoire, utilizing a number of different moves. Effective utilizing his length to cut off plays, and chase down backside. Jackson is used to drop a bit in coverage, showing experience, and solid movement skills. Above-average 1st step coupled with good snap awareness to get some good initial penetration.

Weaknesses: Lacks the lateral movement ability to get off blocks on the counter, sits on blocks for far too long. Allows his pads to consistently rise mid-play, keeping his chest plate far too exposed. Gets good initial penetration, but then gets stuck, failing to know how to utilize his hands to shed. Too many times on tape where he's easily blocked by the tight end in the passing game. Doesn't always play with great play awareness, missing great opportunities because he fails to locate the ball post-snap. Has trouble redirecting his frame if he takes any false steps. Struggles with discipline against running quarterbacks, failing to read keys and set the edge properly, crashing far too hard inside time after time. Had an outstanding freshman season, and hasn't shown significant improvement on his weaknesses.

Best Fit: 4-3 DE but shows some coverage ability to play as a 3-4 OLB

Player Ranking (1-100): 72.9 – There are certainly traits and upside to work with in the player, but the concern is he's had 3 years with good coaching and hasn't improved much. He's a good athlete but isn't a great one on tape. He certainly has the size and motor that you want to see in a defensive line prospect. If he can consistently keep his pads down, he can win with power as well. There are just too many "IF's" with the player and I'm not sure he has starter ability at the next level. 4th round player.

20. D'Andre Walker EDGE Georgia 6'3 245 lbs

Strengths: Walker is a 4-year contributor but only started his senior season on an every-down basis. Well-built with outstanding size and length, possessing the frame to continue to add muscle mass and strength. Utilizes his long arms effectively, keeping blockers off his frame and allowing him to take inside or outside pathways to the ball. An athletic rusher, he shows some quick-twitch ability and the ability to dip his shoulder and grab the edge routinely. Possesses a variety of different hand tactics to knock away would-be blockers at the line of scrimmage. Shows some physicality and toughness at the point of attack, remaining square. A slippery rusher, doing a good job of utilizing his hands and motor to consistently get off blocks. Possesses an effective club hand in the run game, showing strength and the ability to slow running backs with his other hand. A large variety of pass rushing moves, including an effective spin to beat double teams.

Weaknesses: Takes overly aggressive paths to the football, leading to some poor pursuit angles which resulted in many missed tackling opportunities in space. Despite being a standup linebacker, Walker has very limited experience in coverage situations. A tweener who lacks a true position and will likely need to play as a 3-4 OLB at the next level, lacking the systematic and schematic versatility. Questions will be asked why he didn't get more snaps early on in his career. Had some struggles with terrible undisciplined penalties his first couple of seasons at Georgia. Fails to always have a direct plan when attacking the pocket. Much of his production was on stunts, designed to get him in space.

Best Fit: 3-4 OLB

Player Ranking (1-100): 72.4 – An upside player who showed impressive production despite limited snaps his first 3 years at Georgia, before blowing it up his senior year as a starter. I like his pass rush variety and his overall physique to play at the next level. He needs to continue to refine his technique, and will likely need to prove he can consistently cover effectively to play in a 3-4 system. A 4th round player.

21. Jordan Brailford EDGE Oklahoma State 6'3 250 lbs

Strengths: A 2-year starter for the Cowboys who had a tremendous junior season with 10 sacks, 2 forced fumbles and 17 tackles for loss. Brailford plays a unique position for the Cowboys who mostly plays as a standup linebacker in base situations then blitzes or plays as a rush linebacker in passing situations. A schematically versatile guy who has experience playing practically every position on the front 7. Outstanding read/react awareness and anticipatory skills, utilizing his instincts and vision to shoot gaps and make plays in the backfield. Good 1st step quickness, showing the ability to get a really good jump at the line of scrimmage. Active in pursuit at all times, always finding a way to work back towards the ball.

Weaknesses: Not a bend rusher who has elastic flexibility to turn the corner. The majority of his production comes on manufactured plays, generally either a blitz or a stunt. A liability in run support, completely washed out and easily sustained by tight ends and running backs. Lacks much of a pass-rushing arsenal, reliant on a spin move or a speed rush on every snap. Has some balance concerns, and is on the ground frequently. Far too often he gets close but fails to make the play.

Best Fit: 3-4 OLB

Player Ranking (1-100): 71.8 – A talented and versatile rusher who lacks any 'ELITE' traits. He's a quick-footed guy who understands how to utilize his anticipation to shoot gaps and get after the QB but he isn't a 'pass-rusher' per se. Have to find a role for him at the next level. 4th round player. Is best suited in a 3-4 defense due to his stand up experience and lack of power to hold up against the run.

22. Anthony Nelson EDGE Iowa 6'7 271 lbs

Strengths: Nelson is a 3-year starter who has really impressed in his levels of production in each season, increasing his sack and tackle for loss counts each year. As a senior, Nelson had 9.5 sacks and 13.5 tackles for loss. Nelson possesses a rare frame, with excellent height and length. Nelson plays on the left side of a 4-man front but possesses the size/length to play in multiple different schemes. Utilizes his length intelligently, keeping his frame clean in pursuit. A hustle player who plays with a HOT motor, always in pursuit, never giving up on a play. When firing low out of his stance, Nelson shows impressive speed to power driving linemen backward. Violent upper body showing the ability to shed quickly with a snatch move. A very aware player, he has a good grasp and feel for the game. Utilizes his long arms in the run game to cut off run lanes and take on double teams. A high character prospect that coaches will rave about.

Weaknesses: Nelson is an upright rusher who is going to constantly battle with his pad level. An average athlete lacks the speed to threaten or win the edges. Not a natural rusher that plays with any kind of elasticity or bend in his frame. Lacks a consistent plan of attack when attacking the edges, attempting the same move over and over again. Lacks the agility or the change of direction ability to consistently win on a counter move. A rangy built guy who needs to continue to add bulk and strength to his frame.

Best Fit: LDE in a 4-3. Can play in a 3-4 but will need to gain additional strength/muscle

Player Ranking (1-100): 71.5 – Nelson is a left defensive end who has limited pass rushing upside at the next level. But he's a solid overall player who has 2-down ability and can provide a nice change of rotation for your defensive line. He has the ability to potentially start immediately in base situations for a defense. Coaches and scouts LOVE his size and length combination.

23. Justin Hollins EDGE Oregon 6'5 242 lbs

Strengths: Hollins is a 3-year contributor for the Ducks defense who came onto the scene after a stellar senior season in which he totaled 6.5 sacks, 64 tackles, 5 forced fumbles and 14.5 tackles for loss. Hollins possesses violent hands and upper body, showing the ability to fight through blocks and stack/shed quickly in the running game. Very good athlete who shows upside with more pass-rush coaching. Speed is evident in his ability to chase plays backside. Good start/stop move when pass rushing to freeze offensive tackles and utilize his quick-twitch ability to win on the 2nd move. Aggressive hands, always swiping and ripping at the ball, as was evidenced in his 5 forced fumbles. A nonstop motor, he brings it on every snap of the ball. Does a nice job of utilizing his length to disrupt the quarterback and knock down passes at the line of scrimmage. Has experience playing in space and was utilized in quite a few zone drops for the Oregon defense.

Weaknesses: Hollins is an upright-framed player who fails to play with any kind of bend or elastic flexibility in his frame. Continuously takes on blockers head-on, failing to dip his shoulder or utilize any kind of bend. Very limited pass rush arsenal, and tends to fail over and over again without any kind of counter or plan B. Limited to strictly a speed rush or a bull rush. Doesn't engage his lower body on his bull rushes to get any kind of movement or penetration. Erratic tackler, because of his poor pad level tends to be a drag down tackler which allows additional yardage.

Best Fit: Developmental outside linebacker

Player Ranking (1-100): 70.1 – Had a really good pre-draft campaign and has certainly upped his stock. I just don't see a great or effective rusher at this point. Nor is he a reliable tackler or physical presence for a defense. He has the athletic ability that needs to be maximized with additional coaching, but I don't think he's ready to play valuable snaps as a rookie. 4th round player.

24. Jonathan Ledbetter EDGE Georgia 6'3 271 lbs

Strengths: Ledbetter is an intriguing defensive end for the Bulldogs with a power-packed frame. Despite his large physique, Ledbetter carries very little body fat and is mostly lean, certainly passing the eyeball test. His strength is evidenced in the way he holds down the point of attack, maintaining a solid anchor in the run game, setting the edges. Does a nice job of playing with leverage, keeping his pad level down and fighting through blocks. Good get-off at the line of scrimmage. A relentless rusher, he shows a nonstop motor with the ability to work through blocks, winning quite a bit on effort alone. Bulldogs coaches moved him inside quite a bit as well, showing his versatility. Powerful upper-body with the ability to shed and violently rip defenders off his frame.

Weaknesses: Ledbetter is an average athlete who lacks the ability to win with speed or quick-twitch ability alone. Was arrested twice for DUI and drinking-related charges, but appears to have grown past that. Has had some really stupid undisciplined penalties as a result of his stirred-up emotion levels. Fails to have ideal height and length to play outside at the next level. Gets stuck on blocks far too often when pass rushing, lacking the length to disengage quickly.

Best Fit: 4-3 LDE or 3-tech DT

Player Ranking (1-100): 67.2 – A stout and compactly-built guy who can have a role at the next level. Not going to offer much as a pass rusher, but can be a solid rotational guy who will flash here and there and contribute in the running game. 5th round player.

25. Sutton Smith EDGE Northern Illinois 6'0 234 lbs

Strengths: Smith is a former running back at the school before transitioning to a 3-4 linebacker. Smith is an undersized production machine at MAC Conference Northern Illinois the past 2 seasons. With 7 forced fumbles, 56.5 tackles for loss and 29 sacks, Smith has certainly proved his worth. To say Smith is a high-motor guy is doing him a disservice, he BRINGS it on every snap. Good initial quickness out of his stance, showing some quick-twitch ability. A slippery rusher, Smith uses outstanding footwork at the line of scrimmage to alter his rush. His natural leverage abilities generally win the leverage battle for him, getting some good push on his bull rushes. Features the upper-body to finish plays and deliver some big blows. A loose-hipped guy who shows some bend frequently grabbing the edges.

Weaknesses: Smith has clear and obvious size/length concerns for the next level. He will likely only be able to play as a 3-4 OLB or a SAM linebacker in a 4-3 but can occasionally be used in rushing situations. Not a great athlete per se, and lacks much in the way of dominant physical characteristics. Rarely can take a blocker on head-on, will get completely engulfed. Fails to have any kind of stack/shed ability with his lack of length, making him a win on the 1st move only kind of rusher. A liability in the run game, failing to have the anchor to sustain the edges. Strictly a pass-rusher who wants 0 assignments in gap-control or in the running game.

Best Fit: 3-4 OLB

Player Ranking (1-100): 66.3 – A really good college player who reminds me a bit of Michael Sam a few years ago with his production levels. Unfortunately, he doesn't really have a lot of suitors because of his lack of size. His rush traits and skills should merit him a chance. I like him a lot. I would take him in the 5th round despite the size. Can't deny the production he's had.

26. Cece Jefferson EDGE Florida 6'1 252 lbs

Strengths: Undersized edge rusher who utilizes his smaller stature to win upon the snap of the ball and win the leverage battle. Jefferson utilizes his outstanding 1st step and explosiveness to capture the edges. Has played in different defensive systems, both in 2-point and 3-point stances. One of top-rated 5 Star recruits coming out of high school who still has huge untapped upside. Does a nice job of chasing down plays backside, utilizing good closing speed and pursuit. Impressive in his ability to sort through the garbage in the run game, almost like a linebacker. Understands how to convert speed-to-power in his bull rush to put an offensive lineman on skates. Plays well with loads of space or in slanted fronts where he doesn't have to take on offensive tackles head-on.

Weaknesses: A hybrid player who lacks the ideal size to take on offensive tackles consistently at the next level. Has had some minor disciplinary related issues due to poor academics in college causing him to get suspended and miss a couple of games. If he doesn't win immediately, Jefferson will sit on a block for the duration of the play. Had significant shoulder surgery before his senior season. Has lacked great pass rush production through his career. Will get engulfed by bigger players who can easily control him.

Best Fit: 3-4 OLB

Player Ranking (1-100): 63.2 – Jefferson is a developmental type of prospect who needs to be situated in the right defensive system that is willing to use him to the best of his abilities. He's a long shot to make an NFL roster. He's a 6th round player.

27. L.J. Collier EDGE TCU 6'2 280 lbs

Strengths: Collier is a big-bodied versatile presence from the Horned Frogs defense who has been a valuable contributor for 3 seasons. He's moved all over the front showing his power-packed frame and versatility as he transitions to the NFL. When playing as a 3-technique DT, Collier displays the ability to shoot gaps and utilize his functional athleticism to be a mismatch. Appears to have good length, fully utilizing his wingspan by getting extended and cutting off running lanes. A reliable tackler, showing the upper-body power and driving ability from his hips to forcefully bring down opponents. A physical player with a relentless motor, he tirelessly fights through blocks. Accelerates fluidly from behind showing the ability to chase ball carriers down from behind. Strong and stout, possessing the anchor ability to fight through combination blocks in the run game.

Weaknesses: Collier is a very subpar athlete who lacks much explosiveness to be an effective pass rusher and would be limited to mostly a LDE with gap-control assignments in the run game. Collier is a naturally strong guy but his frame and body need serious refinement. Possessing far too many soft pounds, Collier needs to tighten up and reshape his body.

Best Fit: 4-3 LDE

Player Ranking (1-100): 62.2 – Collier is a really good player against the run but needs to retool his frame to impress coaches in training camp and show he can hold up and take valuable NFL snaps. Will battle in camp for a spot. Worth taking in the 6th round.

28. Carl Granderson EDGE Wyoming 6'5 246 lbs

Strengths: Granderson possesses a prototypical NFL physique with a great wingspan with the necessary size/girth. A converted skilled position player after only weighing 185 pounds as a freshman. A raw athlete who has barely touched the surface of his potential. Rushes both from a 2-point and 3-point stance. Does a really nice job when rushing from a slanted front in getting skinny and fighting through tight windows to make a play in the backfield. Really effective and strong hand usage, especially when attempting to win the outside shoulder, showing an effective swipe move. Surprisingly effective when asked to kick inside showing an ability to win on the snap against a less athletic interior lineman.

Weaknesses: Granderson missed half his sophomore season after tearing his ACL 6 games into the season. Disappointing senior campaign after a really stellar junior season where he won many Mountain West awards after he led the conference with 16 tackles for a loss. Tends to be too reliant on running gains and stunts than taking on blockers straight up. Lacks elite quick-twitch to consistently win the edge or be effective on speed rushes. Lacks a great motor and frequently has to leave the field. Needs to develop a plan B, far too often if he doesn't win immediately, lacks an effective counter.

Best Fit: 4-3 DE

Player Ranking (1-100): 61.2 – Granderson is a good player who lacks great production in a less competitive conference. He's raw and will continue to get better considering he's a converted defensive player and is still growing into his frame. He's a 6th round player who is worth the gamble, due to his size/length.

29. Gerri Green EDGE Mississippi State 6'4 255 lbs

Strengths: Green is a 4-year contributor for the Bulldogs who had his best season as a junior with 5 sacks, 11 tackles for loss and 3 forced fumbles. The definition of reliable, having never missed a game in his 4-year career. Green is built tough, with a power-packed frame and excellent overall weight distribution. He's an ideal candidate for a 3-4 defense, having played mostly as a standup linebacker. Shows fluidity in his drops, with good overall movement skills. Really good length, with a tremendous wingspan showing the ability to keep his frame clean at the point of attack. A really good motor, he will frequently run down plays 20 or 30 yards downfield. Violent in his style of play, utilizing a powerful club hand, delivering powerful knocks at the line of scrimmage. Shows the ability to shed on the counter with a relentless style.

Weaknesses: Green is a limited athlete who lacks any kind of consistent penetration as a pass rusher. He lacks the lateral mobility and short-area bursts to attack the pocket. Fails to keep his pads down, and doesn't appear to play with the bend in his frame. Wins mostly with effort, lacking the athleticism to grow and develop into a pass rush threat. Lacks any kind of pass rush arsenal, tending to rush straight up with power on every snap. Too many times he's sustained and blocked by tight ends on tape.

Best Fit: 3-4 OLB, can also play as a 4-3 strong-side linebacker

Player Ranking (1-100): 57.2 – Green is a productive player who has a chance to be a bottom of the roster rotational defender for a team. He will WOW teams with his impressive physique and overall size. But he's not going to blow anyone away with his ability to consistently make plays in the run or passing game. But he's the definition of reliable, with his hot motor being his best characteristic. 7th round player.

30. John Cominsky EDGE Charleston 6'5 286 lbs

Strengths: Cominsky is a prototypically-built NFL DL who shows a muscled up physique with great length and wingspan. Playing for Division-2 Charleston, Cominsky showed some impressive traits to transition to the next level. Charleston moved him all over the defensive front, utilizing his strength and mismatch ability to be effective from different points. A powerful guy, he utilizes his violent hands and upper-body to fight through blocks and get into the backfield. In the passing game, he shows a good swim move and rotates it with his rip. A relentless motor who works tirelessly to work towards the football. Possesses the upper-body strength and power to be able to finish as a tackler. When playing on the outside, he remains disciplined in option-style runs, sealing edges and taking sharp angles. Long-strider who shows some comeback speed ability to chase plays backside as well as chase down running quarterbacks.

Weaknesses: Lacks great foot-speed, appears to be a bit heavy-footed. Despite Division-2 competition, he only had 3 sacks his senior season. A tight-hipped guy in space who lacks the fluidity and movement skills to be able to change direction and redirect. Has some leverage concerns due to his frame and makeup especially when having to take on combination blocks or play inside at all. Lacks much of a pass-rushing arsenal.

Best Fit: Developmental 3-4 DE

Player Ranking (1-100): 55.2 – Cominsky should be a 7th round pick that you take a chance on due to his frame and size. I like him best as a 3-4 DE because he possesses the power to play 2-gap and set the edge. And it allows him to focus on the running game and playing disciplined as opposed to having to get after the QB in a traditional 4-3 defense.

31. Corbin Kaufusi EDGE BYU 6'9 275 lbs

Strengths: Kaufusi comes from a football family with good football lineage. You can't ignore Kaufusi on film, he possesses rare size and length for the position. He's a tough guy who is known to fight through all kinds of injuries. A high-effort guy who plays with a relentless motor. Good upper-body strength to be able to finish as a tackler. Knows how to utilize his length to seal the edges in the run game through contact. Violent hands to maintain separation between him and blockers.

Weaknesses: Older prospect who will be 26 years old on the day of the draft. Had a season-ending knee injury causing him to miss the end of the season. Not an instinctual guy, a tick late off the snap of the ball. Will struggle with pad level due to his height, practically losing the leverage battle on every snap of the ball. High-torso built guy with skinnier legs, lacks the ability to hunker down and anchor in the run game. Cannot take sharp angles to the football due to his lumbering physique, overrunning and pursuing the football. Despite his size, Kaufusi is strictly a 4-3 DE at this point, failing to have the power/leverage to kick inside.

Best Fit: 4-3 LDE

Player Ranking (1-100): 53.4 – Kaufusi will likely be an undrafted free agent who will need to impress in training camp. His size makes it really difficult for him. He's a hard worker and absolutely deserves a chance, but his lack of athletic ability and lower body anchor make his chances slim.

Edge Rushers Top-10 Rankings

1. Nick Bosa
2. Clelin Ferrell
3. Montez Sweat
4. Zach Allen
5. Josh Allen
6. Jachai Polite
7. Brian Burns
8. Charles Omenihu
9. Austin Bryant
10. Jalen Jelks

Chapter 10

Defense Tackles (Includes 3-4 DE's)

1. Ed Oliver DT Houston 6'3 280 lbs

Strengths: Oliver is a 3-year starter for the Cougars who possesses a power-packed frame and excellent overall weight distribution. Oliver plays with a nonstop motor, battling and giving it 110% on every snap. Really impressive read/react ability combined with short-area quickness to explode out of his stance and make plays in the backfield. Good ball awareness and reactionary skills to quickly process things. Explosive quick-twitch rusher who showcases the quickness and the closing speed to make plays. Really impressive snap awareness and instincts to get a great jump on the ball. Good functional upper-body strength and power, showing the ability to utilize his hands and also disengage himself from blockers. Rare that you see a nose tackle dominant a game like Oliver does, he completely takes over games. Launches himself into ball carriers and delivers powerful aggressive tackles. Tremendous anchor and lower-body strength to convert speed-to-power and walk centers/guards back into the QB. Understands leverages and utilizes it to his advantage to put blockers on skates.

Weaknesses: Suffered a knee injury this past season causing him to miss 4 straight games. Some concerns about his attitude, whether he loves football, and had an intense dustup with his coach on the sideline in 1 game this past season. Smaller than ideal, lacking the necessary height and length to consistently control interior lineman and affect throwing lanes for QBs. Lacks an adequate plan when rushing the passer. Far too often relies on his quickness and motor to consistently win rather than utilizing an arsenal of moves. When double teamed consistently, Oliver failed to show he can sufficiently overcome it.

Best Fit: 4-3 (Can play either a 0, 1 or a 3 technique)

Player Ranking (1-100): 92.4 – Oliver is such a talented interior player that can completely dominate from all DT positions. I would be tempted to use him as a 3-technique because of his quickness and ability to shoot and penetrate. But he possesses the power and strength to play the other defensive tackle positions as well. Love this kid as a football player. One of my favorites in the class. I hope he does well in the interview process and doesn't raise any additional concerns.

2. Quinnen Williams DT Alabama 6'4 290 lbs

Strengths: Williams is a redshirt sophomore who only has 1 full year of starting experience. Williams had an outstanding sophomore (final) season at Alabama with 71 tackles, 19.5 tackles for loss and 8 sacks. Williams possesses outstanding snap anticipation coupled with a great 1st step, almost always the 1st one to get a jump at the line of scrimmage. Has experience and versatility, having moved all over Alabama's front, including even playing as a defensive end. Tremendous upper-body power, he can quickly shed blockers with a violent rip move. Twitchy reflexes showing the ability to quickly diagnose pre and post snap. Superb ball awareness, always aware of the ball carrier even when his back is towards the ball. Consistently anchors against double-teams, rarely getting moved off his spot. In passing situations, he shows the quickness and counter ability to beat double teams. A violent finisher who doesn't simply bring down quarterbacks or backs, he completely blows up plays and lays the wood from powerful hip torque. Almost impossible to block on an island or 1 v 1. Possesses a wide array of pass rush moves, most of them stemming from his active, violent hands. Good core-flexibility and strength to get skinny and fight through tight spaces. Quick-footed athlete who shows the ability to alter speeds and catch offensive lineman off guard on the counter.

Weaknesses: Will lose the leverage battle on occasion due to his height. Lacks ideal arm length, allowing longer-armed blockers to win inside hand placement. Despite his ability to play all over Alabama's front, his lack of ideal size/length will make him primarily only a scheme fit in a 4-3 defense or as a nose tackle in either scheme. Overly reliant on winning on the 1st move and if he doesn't win, he gets stuck on blocks, lacking elite agility and looseness in his hips to win on the counter. Generally, his motor runs hot, but there are times when he looks completely gassed and he looks complacent. Some have been concerned about maturity levels, questioning his 'heart' or his 'desire' about how much he really loves football.

Best Fit: 4-3 DT (Can play either 1 or 3 technique)

Player Ranking (1-100): 92.1 – Williams will and should be a top-10 pick. I really like the player and his level of production this year against top offensive lines was outstanding. There are too many times in games though where he goes missing and can't get off blocks. I didn't see that nearly as much with Ed Oliver. Both are absolute studs, but also at the same time have some off the field concerns. Williams is a Day 1 starter who will immediately upgrade any defensive line in football. His ball awareness, play recognition and hand usage are the best in the class. Whoever gets Williams is going to get a heckuva player. Top-10 player.

3. Jeffrey Simmons DT Mississippi State 6'4 300 lbs

Strengths: Simmons possesses a powerful and thick frame with excellent strength throughout. Simmons is an impressive 1st step athlete, showing good 0-10-yard explosion at the snap of the football. This allows him to get serious movement from the inside of the pocket. Very active hands that are relentlessly in attack mode, showing a powerful punch upon impact as well. A scheme-versatile defender, he shows the ability to play in either a 3-4 or 4-3 system. Has success playing all over the defensive front, showing the power and strength to consistently take on double teams and still make plays. An aware player who shows good play-recognition to force a lot of stops in the backfield or sniff out screens. When he isn't close to the football, shows the awareness to get his hands up and either knock down the pass or disrupt the QB's vision. Tremendous lower-body push showing speed-to-power ability to walk lineman into the quarterback. Does a nice job of utilizing his length in the run game to seal lanes. His upper-body power is manifest in his ability to drive runners to the ground, delivering powerful blows. A high-motor player who is loved by his teammates and coaching staff for his leadership qualities.

Weaknesses: A much-maligned prospect who might be completely removed from some draft boards due to his 2016 assault incident where he hit a woman. Fails to finish enough plays as a pass rusher, only had 1 sack his last season with the Bulldogs. Has a tendency to get into too many personal battles causing him to miss the ball carrier, failing to accurately locate the ball. Has some struggles when it comes to redirecting his frame after initially sustained. A bit of an inconsistent tackler who struggles when asked to tackle with arms outside of frame.

Best Fit: Can play anywhere but is probably best suited as a 3-technique in a 4-3 due to his gap-penetrating quickness

Player Ranking (1-100): 91.1 – Simmons really was a pleasant surprise to watch on film. He's an absolute load to have to handle at all areas of the game. Despite his lack of sack production his junior year, his tackles for loss numbers were still outstanding. I really like Simmons as a prospect and I think he's deserving of a top-15 pick. He's going to make someone's defensive line infinitely better.

4. Rashan Gary DT Michigan 6'5 285 lbs

Strengths: Gary is a 3-year starter for the Wolverines who has moved all over the line of scrimmage. Equipped with a long and powerful frame, Gary possesses the prototypical size/length to play for any defensive team at the next level no matter the scheme or system. Gary is a rare athlete who showcases the movement skills to even play as a RDE on a 4-man front. When playing on the outside, his ability to convert speed to power is impressive. Excellent ability to chase plays down backside and utilize his length to make up ground quickly. Possesses the power in his frame to stack with 1 arm and utilize the other arm to cut off running lanes or close off the outside edges. Understands how to utilize his length to engage contact 1st and control their chest plates. Has been praised for his leadership ability by his coaches. A relentless motor who gives it 100% on every snap. A smooth accelerator who also displays impressive short-area quickness.

Weaknesses: A bit of a 1-trick pony as a pass rusher, he fails to have a variety of weapons in his arsenal. A little bit of a close but no cigar player in that he gets CLOSE a lot but fails to consistently make the play. Doesn't fully understand how to utilize his hands when pass rushing. Relies a bit too much on his raw size and athleticism as opposed to winning with proper technique and fundamentals. Can be run at in the run game, failing to adequately anchor and hunker down when plays are coming towards him. A bit of an upright player which will hurt him in the run game. Needs to continue adding strength to his lower body. Overruns a lot of snaps as a pass rusher when playing on the outside, failing to adequately get his pad level down and bend the edge. Plays mostly on the outside in college and will likely need to transition to inside for most teams at the next level.

Best Fit: 4-3 DT (3-technique) or a 3-4 DE (5-technique)

Player Ranking (1-100): 89.7 – Gary is a really good player who hasn't really scratched the surface of his ability as an athlete. He's a rare physical specimen who is raw and needs additional time. He's going to be a nightmare matchup for an offensive lineman due to his athleticism, size, length, and ability to play with power. Give him time, but he's going to be a good player. 1st round player.

5. Christian Wilkins DT Clemson 6'3 300 lbs

Strengths: Wilkins possesses the prototypical build with long limbs and a huge wingspan. Does a nice job of utilizing his length to get his hands on the football or disrupt the pass. Possesses positional and schematic versatility with the ability to play in any defensive system. Has experience playing as a nose tackle, 5-technique 3-4 DE, or a 3-tech DT. Does a tremendous job of disengaging and winning the leverage battle on the snap. Sets the edge, maintaining good technique and balance. Understands how to properly play with good angles. Wilkins is a very good athlete with good short area quickness. Displays the fluidity and flexibility to quickly change direction. Shows good core flexibility and the strength to get skinny and fight through tight spaces. Plays with good natural instincts, quickly reacting and attacking the ball carrier. Tremendous at utilizing his club hand to control the blocker, while utilizing his other hand to contain the run. Shows the ability to take on multiple blocks and allow his linebackers to run free. Plays with really good snap awareness, getting a good jump on the snap of the ball. Is an absolute beast in the run game, making a ton of stops in the backfield.

Weaknesses: Wilkins lacks elite athleticism, and doesn't have the closing burst to finish plays consistently. Has some awareness issues and doesn't locate the ball quickly. Not a great pass rusher, and lacks much of a pass rush arsenal to attack blockers in different ways each snap.

Best Fit: Scheme versatile but best in a 3-4 defense as a 5-technique

Player Ranking (1-100): 86.9 – Wilkins is a supremely talented kid who displays tremendous versatility and talent. He's going to be overvalued by 3-4 teams because of his experience. Won't be surprised if he goes top-10 but I wouldn't take him until the end of the 1st because he simply isn't an effective 3-down player at this time.

6. Dexter Lawrence DT Clemson 6'4 340 lbs

Strengths: Lawrence is a 3-year starter for the Tigers who came onto the scene following a stellar freshman season in which he had 62 tackles and 6.5 sacks. Lawrence is a mountain of a man who possesses a gigantic frame with thick limbs throughout. Lawrence possesses the power and length to consistently make tackles outside of his frame, and routinely bring opponents down with his powerful hands and upper body. Tremendous point of attack power who regularly wins with strength/power. Quick, active hands showing the ability to quickly stack/shed. Generates excellent movement with his initial punch, then maintains movement with his leg drive, generating excellent speed to power. Impressive ball awareness to quickly locate and find the ball, even with his back to the ball. Lawrence is best when playing with an angled-front, utilizing his length to close down running plays backside. A disciplined player, he shows good play-recognition, constantly sniffing out screens. Shows the anchoring ability to take on double-teams in the run game.

Weaknesses: Lawrence has too much sloppy weight on his frame, preventing him from having great movement skills. Always a tick late off the snap of the ball, preventing him from getting great initial penetration. Stiff in his hips and core, preventing him from redirecting his frame and changing direction effectively. A marginal athlete when he has to chase down plays or when attempting to pursue an athletic, running quarterback. His additional weight affects his ability to consistently play with a HOT motor. Due to his height, he struggles consistently keeping his pad level down, leaving his chest plate far too exposed. His production decreased each season in college and he never quite lived up to his freshman showcase. Was suspended for his teams' final two games, in the playoff and championship for testing positive for a banned substance. Teams will likely look into that.

Best Fit: Nose tackle. Can play as a 1-technique if he loses some weight

Player Ranking (1-100): 85.9 – I really like Lawrence as a player. He was a 5-star recruit out of high school for a reason, and there are a lot of traits there. His tape against Lamar Jackson/Louisville as a sophomore was one of the most impressive tapes I've watched during this pre-draft process. He was absolutely dominant and took over the game, dominating both the center and the guards. If he can lose 15-20 pounds and gain some additional movement ability, he would be a 1st round player. He's impossible to block 1 on 1 because of his power and strength. I would take him in the late 1st round.

7. Daniel Wise DT Kansas 6'3 290 lbs

Strengths: Wise is a 4-year starter for the Jayhawks who has quietly had a tremendous career, totaling 17 sacks and 43 tackles for loss despite playing in a 3-man base defensive front. Built with an impressive lower half, Wise shows strength and girth in his frame. Wise is a positionally and schematically-versatile defender who can play as an inside 3-technique in a 4-3 or as a 5-technique in a 3-4 defense. The definition of a constant, Wise hasn't missed a game since his freshman season. A bull in the run game, frequently taking on double teams, showing the ability to anchor down. Gets great initial penetration firing off the snap of the ball and keeping his pads low throughout. No slouch while rushing the passer, Wise shows good hand usage and a variety of different ways to attack the pocket while rushing. Impressive flexibility and bend in his frame for a defensive tackle, frequently dropping his shoulder and getting good ankle bend to turn the corner. Plays with a hot motor and nonstop pursuit, almost always staying in the TV frame. Has the upper-body strength to consistently finish tackles when he gets his hands on a ball carrier.

Weaknesses: Situational awareness and ball location need to improve, failing to always identify and find the ball carrier in the run game. Has a maximized frame with little room to gain additional size without sacrificing athleticism. Reliant on winning on the 1st move, lacking the lateral mobility to offer anything on the counter consistently.

Best Fit: Can play anywhere along the defensive front, but I would love seeing his quickness and bend as a 3-technique DT

Player Ranking (1-100): 83.3 – One of my favorite under the radar players in this entire draft class. Not sure why he isn't getting more publicity but he's a Day 1 starter for practically any defensive front in this league. He's a versatile guy who will absolutely play all 3 downs at the next level. 2nd round player.

8. Marquise Copeland DT Cincinnati 6'2 287 lbs

Strengths: Copeland is a 4-year starter for the Bearcats who has played both DE and DT during his career. Built with a physical and wide frame, Copeland shows the girth to play inside at the next level. Situates his frame low to maintain his center of gravity at all times, holding the point of attack in the run game. Impressive athlete showing good explosion out of his stance when rushing the passer. Also shows the closing speed and burst to close running lanes and cut off the edges. Versatile defender, he has both the athleticism and the strength to play in any defensive system, inside or outside. Was even used some in coverage in zone situations early in his career. Tremendous awareness always quickly locating the football and working back towards the ball. A hard-working guy that is relentless in his pursuit to the ball. Slippery rusher, rarely getting hung up on blocks, utilizing his active hands to shed quickly.

Weaknesses: Has lacked great pass rush productivity every year in college, with only 3.5 sacks each of his last 2 seasons. Lacks ideal length for some teams to be able to play as a DE at the next level. A close but no cigar player who gets close on so many snaps, but fails to consistently make the play. Can struggle when trying to redirect/change direction. Stiff hips and lower body who needs to keep things in front of him.

Best Fit: Very few guys I've ever evaluated on the defensive line that I thought could play any position along the line, but Copeland is one of those guys. Ideally, he should play as a 1-gap player to maximize his read/react ability and not force him to think which would limit his athleticism. Ideally a 3-technique or a 4-3 LDE.

Player Ranking (1-100): 82.2 – Copeland is one of my favorite players in the draft. I genuinely believe he is going to be a really solid DT at the next level. Despite his lack of production, you'll notice on every game tape you turn on, his disruption is there. A 2nd round player who is going to be a better NFL player than college.

9. Dre'Mont Jones DT Ohio State 6'3 295 lbs

Strengths: Jones is a well-built and prototypically built 3-technique for the Buckeyes. Jones had a monster final season, as a junior, with 8.5 sacks, 13 tackles for loss, 1 interception and 1 forced fumble. He's ideal where he can be a 1-gap player and utilize his outstanding 1st step quickness with his snap anticipation and instincts. Consistently takes on double teams and occupies multiple blockers when rushing the passer. Shows really good pursuit speed and will constantly chase down ball carriers, showing good athleticism and recovery speed. Fluid mover, showing great change of direction and agility to cross the field. Displays really good contact balance, staying on his feet despite taking on multiple blocks. Relentless hands, frequently fighting and battling through blocks. Shows really nice counter ability to work through and make plays even after initially blocked. Plays with a really solid anchor, maintaining a good wide base, rarely getting moved off his spot.

Weaknesses: Has been mostly a rotational player for the Buckeyes, he has lacked great production prior to his senior season. A very raw player who is still growing into his frame, and has limited experience playing inside on the defensive line. Lacks much of a pass rush arsenal and needs to continue to develop his moves. Has a tendency to be a close but no cigar player, getting close on many occasions but not finishing plays. Needs to consistently keep his pads down in the run game, allowing them to raise as the play progresses, and he gets washed out.

Best Fit: 4-3 DT (3-tech)

Player Ranking (1-100): 80.3 – An explosive athlete who is just beginning to reach his potential as a player. One of the best, most explosive 1-gap penetrators in this entire draft class and will be a hot commodity for a 4-3 defense. Has a chance to really up his stock even more during this pre-draft process with his levels of athleticism. I would feel more comfortable with him as a 2nd round pick. I have concerns that he posted little production his first two seasons, despite significant snaps.

10. Khalen Saunders DT Western Illinois 6'1 320 lbs

Strengths: Saunders is a compactly-built DT who played for Western Illinois in the Missouri Valley Conference. Saunders is a 4-year starter who completely dominated his level of competition. Tremendous athlete, he shows rare fluidity and loose hips to be able to change direction and fit through narrow gaps. Quick, explosive hands to disengage and knock away would-be blockers. Plays with a natural leverage advantage, utilizing his pad level to control the line of scrimmage. Shows good initial quickness to slip gaps quickly, and also the snap awareness and get-off to get in the backfield in a snap. Shows the ability to play in a 2-gap defense, frequently taking on double teams and still being disruptive. Powerful upper body to be able to quickly shed and finish plays. A reliable tackler who drives and brings down ball carriers with ease. Displays the athleticism and explosive characteristics to play in a 1-gap system. Completely dominated during the Senior Bowl practices, showing his explosive characteristics.

Weaknesses: Lacks ideal height to disrupt throwing lanes routinely. Possesses some sloppy weight in his core and midsection. Didn't compete against top-tier competition on a week-in week-out basis. Lacks the schematic versatility to play in a 3-4 system, simply a 4-3 DT at this point.

Best Fit: 4-3 DT (Can play either 1 or 3-tech)

Player Ranking (1-100): 79.6 – Good prospect who will get better with more experience and playing against elite levels of competition. He showed he can do it at the Senior Bowl and was one of the best players there. He's a really good athlete for his size, and as he drops pounds, he will be even better and more explosive. 3rd round player.

11. Kingsley Keke DT Texas A&M 6'3 286 lbs

Strengths: Keke is a 3-year contributor and team leader for the Aggies who had a really impressive final season with 7.5 sacks and 51 tackles. The first thing that jumps off the film for Keke is his athletic ability, showing the long-speed to chase down plays outside the hashes as well as the impressive 1st step to quickly generate penetration into the backfield. Tremendous wingspan with over 82" arms, showing the ability to extend and close gaps. Utilizes his length to make tackles outside of his frame. Commits himself to win inside hand leverage. Keke is a slippery rusher that limits his surface area and has the agility and loose hips to play laterally. This allows him to always be effective on the counter, rarely getting stuck on blocks. Impressive core flexibility to get skinny through tight windows. Rare bend for a guy of his size, showing the ability to dip his upper-body as well as bend his lower body to grab the edges on interior blockers. Good ball awareness, quickly locating and working toward the ball. A wide variety of pass rush moves allows him to attack in several different ways.

Weaknesses: Inconsistent reaction time, lacking great reflexes off the snap of the ball limiting his explosive traits off the snap. Fails to always wrap up reliably, allowing runners to gain additional yardage. Allows his pads to rise mid-play leading to poor hand placement on occasion. Not always a finisher, puts himself in a good position but fails to always make the play. A bit of a tweener who lacks a true position at the next level.

Best Fit: Can play in any scheme, but in my opinion, he would best be used as a 3-technique in a 4-3 to maximize his athleticism and bend

Player Ranking (1-100): 78.9 – Really impressive player who shows impressive size, wingspan, and athleticism. Keke lost 20-30 pounds following the season in an attempt to be more attractive to all defensive systems. He was already explosive, his explosiveness now will be even greater with less weight. The question will be, does he have the strength to hold up now with the lost weight? It's a bit of a question mark since he hasn't played at this new weight before. His versatility and size will create intrigue and interest from every team. I wouldn't hesitate to play him even as an end on occasion. 3rd round player.

12. Gerald Willis DT Miami 6'3 300 lbs

Strengths: Willis is a former Florida Gator who transferred back in 2014. Willis finally lived up to his billing and potential this season with outstanding production. Shows tremendous natural talent levels, when combined with good fundamentals and technique are really hard to stop. Possessing a rare 1st step, Willis can reach the backfield in a flash, noticeable in his 18 tackles for loss this past season. Plays with really good hand technique, utilizing an array of violent hand tactics to beat blockers. A powerful-framed guy who shows the anchor ability in his lower half and also the upper-body strength to disengage and shed. Routinely takes on double teams in the run game, showing the ability to fight through and still make plays. A really good athlete, he shows fluidity and change of directional abilities to redirect his frame without losing much build-up speed. Also shows the long-speed to chase plays down backside.

Weaknesses: Older prospect who will be 24 his rookie season. Has had a number of off-the-field concerns at Florida, having issues with coaches and teammates. Then was suspended due to a violation of team rules. After transferring to Miami, decided he needed to take a year off in 2017. Partially tore his MCL which required surgery following the 2016 season. Reliant on his pure strength and athletic abilities, and can far too often play with poor technique and pad level. His poor pad level leaves his body exposed and easily sustained at the line of scrimmage. Very inconsistent player who 'flashes' brilliance and elite explosive qualities at times. Far too often lacks a direct plan pre-snap to attack blockers.

Best Fit: 4-3 DT (3-tech DT)

Player Ranking (1-100): 78.3 – As long as Willis checks out 'OK' in the interview and the pre-draft process, he's absolutely worth a Day 2 pick. I would take him in the 3rd. He's tremendously talented and might be the most talented 3-tech in this draft class. He also possesses the raw power and strength to be effective as a 2-gap NT as well. He just needs to continue to refine his fundamentals.

13. Dontavius Russell DT Auburn 6'3 319 lbs

Strengths: Russell is a well-built interior defender for the Tigers who has been a 4-year starter for the defense. Highly regarded by the coaches for his leadership and hard-working personality. Good snap anticipation abilities in combination with a really good 1st step. Shows some active and aggressive hands utilizing a really good swim move at the line of scrimmage. Plays with good pad level, utilizing his length and explosive characteristics to get some movement and push at the line of scrimmage. A high-motor player who brings it on every snap of the ball. A versatile defender, he shows the power and anchor ability to play as a gap-control NT, explosive 1-gap or as a 3-tech DT. Shows potential and flashes as a pass rusher to get better and better given more time. Does a nice job of utilizing his length in the run game, to maintain a healthy distance between himself and a blocker to free up his non-club hand.

Weaknesses: Russell has had very limited production as a pass rusher with only 6 career sacks and 1 forced fumble. Not a finisher, gets really close to making a lot of plays but finishes very few of them. Has some sloppy weight in the midsection. A 'flash' player who will frustrate. Quicker than fast, lacks the closing speed to cut off running lanes or chase a QB down on the move. Can get stuck on blocks far too often, failing to have any kind of counter ability.

Best Fit: 4-3 DT (1-tech or 3-tech)

Player Ranking (1-100): 76.3 – Russell is a really good player where stats don't show the whole picture. I like that despite his experience he remains an 'upside' player and has the athletic traits to work with. He has pass-rush potential despite his limited production. He's a strong and physical guy who is highly regarded and athletic. To me, that is worth something. A 3rd round player.

14. Jerry Tillery DT Notre Dame 6'7 305 lbs

Strengths: Tillery is a rare physical specimen displaying outstanding size and length, rare for the position. An experienced lineman for the Fighting Irish who has played significant snaps all 4 seasons in college. Versatile player, he has experience playing in 3 and 4 man fronts, both inside and outside. Has shown improvement in each of his seasons for the Irish, and had an outstanding senior season with 7 sacks. A relentless style who plays with a nonstop motor, fighting to the end of the whistle. Powerful upper body delivering devastating blows when he's able to engage first. Tremendous leg drive in his lower half showcasing the ability to drive piles backward or push lineman into the QB with his bull rush. Frequently takes on double teams, freeing up his teammates. Violent upper arms, showing the ability to use an impressive rip move to disengage quickly when rushing the passer. Good snap awareness coupled with good initial quickness allows him to get a good jump at the snap of the ball.

Weaknesses: Upright rusher who can easily be controlled by a lineman that can play with a low pad level and get under him. Lacks the agility and side to side movement skills to play with any kind of counter or 2nd effort. Sits on blocks for far too long. Has had some maturity concerns in regards to some dirty plays early on in his career, and a suspension by the team his freshman season. Some concern whether he truly loves football. Wins more with motor and 'never give up' mentality than he does pure talent. A very raw guy who doesn't quite know how to fully utilize his length. Not a great athlete who can close quickly or effectively win off the snap of the ball in pass rush situations.

Best Fit: 4-3 DT. Has experience playing as a 0-tech NT but is best used as a 1-gap DT who doesn't have to worry about gap control. Will likely be attractive to some 3-4 defensive teams due to his length and possibly playing a 5-tech. I personally just don't see that translating well with his style of play or experience.

Player Ranking (1-100): 74.2 – Tillery is a talented guy who will likely go higher than the 4th round, but that's where I have him. He's raw and never quite lived up to his potential. His tape is inconsistent, every game I felt different about the player. Some games he's dominant, other's he can't get off a block all game. The major concerns are going to be off the field.

15. Isaiah Buggs DT Alabama 6'3 295 lbs

Strengths: Buggs is a JUCO transfer from Mississippi Gulf Coast, and played his final 2 seasons for the Tide. Buggs has really come on and has improved tremendously, rebuilding his body. Possessed with outstanding and prototypical defensive line size with long limbs and a power-packed physique. As a senior, he produced tremendously with 9.5 sacks and 2 forced fumbles during the season. Buggs is a heavy-handed athlete who commits himself to win the leverage battle, quickly winning inside hands and controlling blockers in the run game. While pass rushing, he shows the grip strength to violently shed blocks. A versatile lineman who plays all over the Alabama front, showing the power and anchor to hold up for all 3 downs. Possesses the upper body strength to finish plays and bring down ball carriers with ease. While playing on the outside, he understands gap control and setting the edges in the run game.

Weaknesses: His 9.5 sacks his senior year is a bit misleading and really doesn't tell the story of his pass rush ability. He's frequently stuck on blocks, failing to have the lateral quickness to get off blocks. There have been some questions in regards to his motor and giving it 100% on every snap, and it shows when plays aren't going in his direction. Tight-hipped in space, failing to redirect or counter in any capacity. Slow reflexes, failing to react quickly or get a good jump at the snap of the ball. Not a great athlete, fails to have any kind of closing quickness.

Best Fit: 3-4 DE (5-technique)

Player Ranking (1-100): 73.2 – 4th round player. Buggs had a really good season but his athletic ability is extremely limited and will never be a 9 sack guy at the next level. He's the best playing in a 2-gap defensive end role in a 3-4 defense where he can utilize his anchor and strength to effectively stuff the run with limited responsibility in getting after the QB.

16. Renell Wren DT Arizona State 6'4 315 lbs

Strengths: Wren is a 3-year starter for the Sun Devils who is built with tremendous size and wingspan. A freakish athlete, he utilizes an impressive blend of initial quickness off the snap of the ball and snap anticipatory skills to get a good burst at the line of scrimmage. It's rare to see guys who display the combination of physical tools that Wren possesses, including his size, length, and athleticism. Very good upper-body strength showcasing the ability to possess some POP in his hands at the line of scrimmage. Utilizes his large tackle radius to cut off running lanes on zone and counter-style runs. Good make-up speed with the ability to work back towards the ball and regain any lost steps. Shows the lower body explosiveness to generate serious push on his bull rushes, overpowering single blockers routinely. Has anchoring ability in the run game to set the edge against double teams.

Weaknesses: A talented guy who never quite lived up to his talent with only 3 career sacks and 14.5 tackles for loss. An upright rusher, he allows his pad levels to rise far too quickly post-snap, allowing smaller blocks to easily control and sustain him. Very marginal lateral movement skills to counter or get off blocks. His stiffness prevents his frame from redirecting or changing direction. Lacks any kind of plan when rushing, and far too often appears to run out of gas at the end of games. Needs to do a better job of utilizing his hands mid-rush to disengage and shed, sits on blocks too routinely. Questionable awareness, failing to see things pre-snap or locate the ball mid-play. Very marginal pass-rusher who gives very little despite the athleticism, might be limited to a 2-down player.

Best Fit: 3-4 DE (5-tech)

Player Ranking (1-100): 72.9 – I think Wren will get over-drafted due to his physical makeup, leading some teams to overvalue his 'potential.' He's an upside player who needs to be coached up properly to fully maximize his combination of size, length, and speed. I think he will be especially attractive to 3-4 defensive teams that want a guy who maintains the strength to play 2-gap as a 5-tech DE.

17. Daylon Mack DT Texas A&M 6'1 317 lbs

Strengths: Mack is a 4-year contributor for the Aggies who really impressed his senior season showing good production with 5.5 sacks and 10 tackles for loss. Mack's best quality is his rare explosiveness for a 320 pounder, getting incredible jump on the snap. He utilizes his twitchiness in conjunction with snap anticipation to consistently beat blockers off the snap of the ball. A gap-penetrator, he shoots gaps incredibly quickly. Despite not having great length, Mack certainly maximizes his production, consistently slowing down backs out of his reach. Immovable at the point of attack, displaying tremendous power in his legs and a low center of gravity. Prevents blockers from winning inside hands, keeping his frame clean in the run game. An absolute bull in the run game who will frequently take on double teams.

Weaknesses: Very inconsistent pad level. Flashes when he fires low out of his stance, but far too often allows his pads to rise to prevent him from disengaging. An upright rusher who fails to consistently engage his lower half to generate any kind of movement in his bull rush. Lacks the lateral movement to offer anything on a counter move. Completely reliant on getting penetration with his 1st step, and fails to do anything if he's initially blocked. Lacks much of a pass rush arsenal. Might be limited to a 2-down role despite his explosive traits.

Best Fit: Nose tackle in either scheme

Player Ranking (1-100): 72.6 – I really like Mack's explosive characteristics for a guy of his size. It's rare. But I'm not sure he consistently offers enough as a pass rusher to be a 3-down player for most teams at the next level. He's developed more pass rush moves during his time, but still lacks much of an arsenal. A 4th round player who can be a Day 1 nose tackle for a team in either scheme.

18. Greg Gaines DT Washington 6'1 307 lbs

Strengths: Gaines is a powerfully-built man who shows incredibly thick and compact limbs. Gets a good jump off the snap of the ball with good ball anticipation and timing. Shows good ball awareness, quickly finding and locating the football and working towards it. Quick to notice things, Gaines shows good anticipatory and play recognition ability to sniff out misdirection and screens. An absolute load to have to handle in the run game, showing tremendous power in his upper-body to quickly offset and move powerful blockers. Eats up double teams, showing the power and the anchor to sustain combination blocks. Utilizes his club arm to engage and his other arm to slow down runners. Possesses the finishing ability in his upper-body to consistently bring down and tackle. Plays with good leverage, keeping his pad level low to stay balanced upon contact.

Weaknesses: Tore his pec muscle during the offseason after his sophomore season. Very minimal pass rushing upside and lacks the quickness and the closing ability to win with anything other than hustle. A marginal athlete who lacks the change of direction skills necessary to redirect his large frame. Strictly a 2-down player. Gets turned around far too often, playing with his back towards the ball as the play goes directly past him. Despite his power, he doesn't seem to be able to convert speed-to-power and get any push or movement with his bull rush. Appears to have minimal length with a stubby build.

Best Fit: 0-tech NT in either scheme

Player Ranking (1-100): 71.9 – A powerful guy who had a really good season replacing Vita Vea for the Huskies. Not a guy who is going to offer any upside as a pass rusher, but possesses tremendous power and strength to assist in the run game, or at the very least open it for his teammates. A 4th round player.

19. Chris Slayton DT Syracuse 6'4 309 lbs

Strengths: Slayton is a 3-year starter for the Orange who possesses an outstanding overall frame for the next level with long limbs and the room for additional growth. Slayton has experience playing all over the Syracuse defensive front and offers systematic versatility for 3-4 and 4-3 teams. He displays the 1st step quickness and leverage ability to play as a 1-gap penetrator, but he also displays the power and lower body strength and double team ability to play as a 2-gap nose tackle. A strong guy at the point of attack who commits himself to keep his pads low, making him an immovable force in the run game. A good overall athlete who shows some looseness in his lower body. Utilizes his length to keep his frame clean in the run game, quickly winning inside hand leverage.

Weaknesses: Minimal production during his career with the Orange, with only 7.5 career sacks. Isn't IN on enough of the action, failing to have any kind of situational and play awareness, quickly losing track of the ball. Can have some concentration lapses, leading to him being a tick late off the snap. Lacks the counter ability to disengage on the 2nd move and doesn't appear to have a secondary move. Despite having the length to cut off run lanes, he doesn't finish enough plays when he gets his hands on a ball carrier or the QB. Needs to take better advantage of 1 v 1 opportunities in pass rush situations.

Best Fit: NT in either scheme

Player Ranking (1-100): 71.6 – Slayton is a really interesting player who had an excellent East-West Shrine week and I can see why. He's a really good player on tape who will offer a defense tremendous versatility. He doesn't have a true weakness, and I believe he can offer some 3-down ability at the next level. 4th round player.

20. Edwin Alexander DT LSU 6'3 331 lbs

Strengths: Alexander is a massive man with tremendous girth and size. He eats up a lot of space in the middle of a defense occupying multiple blocks on almost every snap. Despite his size, Alexander is impressive in his ability to get off the ball. Displays a tremendous 1st step, showing the skill to get into the backfield and even make stops behind the line of scrimmage. Plays with natural leverage ability, keeping his pads down and generating serious movement with his leg drive. A reliable tackler in the open-field showing forcefulness and strength in his upper-body. Alexander is a schematically-versatile NT in either a 3-4 or a 4-3 defensive system. Tremendous anchoring ability, very rare to see him moved off his spot even by 2 or 3 guys. Converts speed to power using his natural momentum to barrel through bodies and open up opportunities for his teammates in the passing game.

Weaknesses: Has had a number of injury issues throughout his career, most notably a lingering knee injury throughout his 2018 season. Has had surgery on both knees. There will be questions as to whether he is a 3-down player at the next level with only 2 career sacks. Has had some academic and disciplinary issues. Motor runs hot and cold, a very inconsistent player on film. Average length, fails to have the ability to consistently make plays outside of his frame. Really struggles when asked to redirect or move in space. A tight-hipped player in space who can easily be avoided by athletic quarterbacks.

Best Fit: NT in either defensive scheme

Player Ranking (1-100): 71.0 – There are just too many questions for the player. There's no doubt he's a talented guy, but his off-the-field concerns are troubling. Some have questioned his love of football, his desire and his work ethic which are all very troubling signs. If he lives up to his true potential, he can be the best nose tackle in this entire draft class. His strength and size coupled with his 1st step abilities make him a nightmare matchup for offensive lines. I wouldn't' take him until the 4th.

21. Byron Cowart DT Maryland 6'3 297 lbs

Strengths: Cowart is an Auburn transfer who played his final year of eligibility with the Terrapins, and had a real good final campaign, finally living up to some of his 5-star hype coming out of high school. Built with a chiseled and power-packed frame, Cowart shows the size and versatility to play all over the defensive front at the next level, just like he has for both Auburn and Maryland. Played mostly as a defensive end for the Terrapins this past season, showing his ability to hold the point of attack and beat power with power. A physical presence who possesses a nasty punch at the line of scrimmage, displacing and generating serious movement. A schematically-versatile defender with 81-inch arms showing the wingspan and length to play in both 3 and 4 man fronts. At his best when playing with an angled front, utilizing his outstanding burst at the line of scrimmage. Shows the lower-body strength and anchor ability to 2-gap in the run game, a bull who rarely gets moved off his spot. Utilizes his length to keep his frame clean, controlling the point of attack. When playing with good pad level, demonstrates excellent speed to power to walk offensive lineman back to the QB.

Weaknesses: Battled nagging injuries during his time at Auburn, causing him to miss several games and never truly living up to his potential. Was arrested for marijuana possession while at Auburn. Has shown maturity and off-field concerns on multiple occasions, and will need to prove he's moved past that stuff. Was a rotational guy at both Auburn and Maryland, never having been relied upon to play 60 or 70 plays a game. Has never had great production in any of his years, his career best is 3 sacks. Inconsistent pad level, can play too upright, allowing his chest to be too exposed. Doesn't always play with great ball awareness, and can be slow to diagnose. Needs to learn how to utilize his athleticism more, attempting to win with speed/power, and lacks hand finesse.

Best Fit: 5-technique DE in a 3-man system

Player Ranking (1-100): 70.1 – Cowart is an exciting player who certainly shows upside. His lack of great production and finishing ability worries me, in addition to his off the field concerns. He certainly flashes and can be a better NFL player than he was in college. I think he possesses power at the point of attack and his length would best be used in a 3-man defensive front at the next level. He can play as a 5 or 7 technique DE. A 4th round pick who has the potential to far exceed his draft valuation.

22. Ricky Walker DT Virginia Tech 6'2 304 lbs

Strengths: A 2-year starter for the Hokies who is one of the defensive and team leaders. Had his best season as a junior with 12.5 tackles for loss and 4.5 sacks. An intangibles guy who is beloved by the coaching staff for his hardworking nature. Walker is a perfect 3-tech candidate with a good 1st step, firing low out of his stance and quickly generating penetration. Plays with active and relentless hands, showing the upper-body strength to disengage and counter, and utilizing his core flexibility and lateral mobility to keep his frame slippery. Good overall functional strength, noticeably in his upper body with his ability to finish and make tackles away from his frame. Plays with an urgency and energy which is contagious for the defense. Reads the game really well with good overall awareness, quickly locating the football. When he can't make the play, he does a nice job of extending his arms and affecting the throw.

Weaknesses: Walker had a disappointing and down senior campaign. Suffered an injury missing his final game of the season. Lacks the length and lower-body power to be able to be a schematically-versatile player and only really fits in a 4-3 defense. Can take overaggressive pathways to the football, leading to some missed fits in the run game.

Best Fit: 4-3 DT (Three Technique)

Player Ranking (1-100): 69.9 – I really like Walker overall as a player. I think he should be a borderline 4th/5th round player. He's a slippery rusher who keeps his frame clean. He's a better player than his production would seem to indicate. I was disappointed by his senior season, but I genuinely think he's a better player than he showed. I wouldn't be surprised if he gained some snaps as a rookie.

23. Kevin Givens DT Penn State 6'1 283 lbs

Strengths: Givens is a compactly-built defensive presence who has had starts in all 3 seasons, showing good overall production with 13.5 sacks and 22 tackles for loss. Givens plays with a natural pad level, keeping a low center of gravity, almost always winning the leverage battle on the snap of the ball. Due to his leverage, he generates outstanding movement on his bull rushes, quickly putting blockers on skates in pass sets. At his best when he's playing with an angled front, where he can utilize his good 1st step to quickly generate penetration into the backfield. Quick, explosive hands showing the ability to displace quickly. Good core flexibility and strength to get skinny and fight through tight spaces. A better athlete than would be expected for his size, showing good closing ability and burst. A wide diversity of pass rush moves who can win in a variety of different ways.

Weaknesses: Struggles locating the ball in the run game, getting blown off the ball and failing to disrupt. A rotational player who was never relied upon to play down after down for a full game, allowing him to remain fresh. Lacks ideal length to be able to control the line of scrimmage, giving away inside hand placement against longer blockers. Length concerns affect his ability to disengage on the counter, getting caught and stuck on blocks for the duration of a play. Lacks ideal height to disrupt passing lanes. Lacks a plan of attack on down after down, consistently crashing down into a wall of blockers.

Best Fit: 4-3 DT (3-technique)

Player Ranking (1-100): 67.6 – Givens is an experienced and above average pass rusher who shows the ability to get really good initial penetration. He lacks the length and the anchoring ability to be an effective player against the run at this point. He shows the ability to be a nice rotational player for a team, who can be used early on in obvious passing situations. 5th round player.

24. Trysten Hill DT Central Florida 6'2 315 lbs

Strengths: Hill is a massive, big-bodied man in the heart of UCF's defense. Hill is a 3-year starter for the Knights who has shown improved production in each season despite changing defensive schemes and coaches. Had an impressive final campaign, totaling 10.5 tackles for loss and 3 sacks. Hill makes a living on slipping gaps, generating an excellent 1st step. Does a great job of timing the snap count to beat blockers off the snap of the ball. Hill has a HOT motor, works his butt off on every snap, always in pursuit. Plays with a natural leverage advantage, doing a good job of keeping his pads down to get underneath blockers. A hard guy to move, showing good anchoring ability. Strong lower-half, fully engaging his legs and his hips when attacking the pocket, showing good speed to power ability.

Weaknesses: A little bit of a stubby built guy who lacks great length and height. Missed a lot of tackles, having some trouble extending and consistently making tackles outside of his frame. Stiffness in his core, preventing him from moving or redirecting his frame. Lacks any kind of counter ability if he gets blocked initially. Doesn't know how to fully utilize his hands to disengage. Lacks the height to be able to consistently affect passing lanes. Limited in his recovery ability, a marginal athlete who lacks makeup speed.

Best Fit: 4-3 DT or 3-4 NT

Player Ranking (1-100): 66.1 – Hill would be an effective 1-technique in a 4-3 who can also play as a NT in a 3-4 scheme as well. He's a powerful, squatty built guy who is difficult to move. UCF coaches rotate their defensive lineman constantly, so he was never relied upon to play every snap. He's a better athlete than you would expect.

25. Demarcus Christmas DT Florida State 6'4 302 lbs

Strengths: Christmas is a 5th year senior for the Seminoles who displays impressive size and length. Christmas wasn't exactly utilized to the best of his traits/characteristics throughout college, limiting his level of production. A big bodied guy who displays the ability to hunker down and anchor well in the run game. Won't easily get pushed off his spot showing the lower body strength and point of attack power. Aggressive hands showing the ability to make the initial contact. Plays like a bully showing an impressive ability to convert speed-to-power to walk back offensive lineman into the QB in pass rushing situations. Really good against the run, showing the ability to consistently take on double teams and free up his linebackers.

Weaknesses: Terrible production throughout college with only 3.5 career sacks and 11.5 tackles for loss. Plays with power, but lacks the consistency and explosion to attack plays or reach the backfield whether it's in the running or the passing game. Typical space eater who doesn't know how to stack/shed to disengage. Will get hung up on 1 block for the duration of a play time in/time out. Lacks any kind of lateral movement skills to shed on a counter move. Fails to have any kind of burst or closing ability to consistently make plays. Lacks much of a pass rush array, focusing solely on utilizing a bull rush.

Best Fit: 2-Gap DT (1-technique or 0-technique NT)

Player Ranking (1-100): 63.2 – Christmas is a guy who plays with power but not much else. He's a 2-down player in today's NFL and asking him to do too much in clear passing situations is expecting failure. But utilizing him in the run game and taking up blocks is where he can succeed. A 6th round player.

26. Youhanna Ghaifan DT Wyoming 6'4 282 lbs

Strengths: A 3-year contributor for Mountain West program Wyoming who has declared after his redshirt junior season. Had his best year as a sophomore with 7 sacks, 15.5 tackles for loss, 69 tackles, and 2 forced fumbles. When playing with good technique and pad level, Ghaifan shows tremendous quick-twitch ability. He quickly shoots gaps and closes down, showing real finishing ability with good closing speed. Violent with his hands, quickly displacing and shedding. Flashes a wide array of pass rush moves, showing an ability to attack with precision and diversity. Accelerates fluidly to chase ball carriers down backside. Really good bend, showing flexibility throughout his frame.

Weaknesses: Was suspended indefinitely for a false imprisonment charge and a harassment charge at the end of the season, causing him to miss the last few games of his college career. Didn't compete against elite competition in college. A smaller frame who lacks the adequate lower body strength and anchoring ability to be effective in the run game. An undisciplined player who plays overaggressive and needs to maintain proper positioning to contain better. Has balance concerns, always on the ground, as a result of his lack of lower body strength. Very inconsistent at the snap of the ball, and can be several ticks too slow. Not a guy who is going to threaten with power, failing to play with adequate power at the point of attack. Serious tightness in his core, preventing him from redirecting his frame if initially blocked.

Best Fit: 4-3 DT (3-technique)

Player Ranking (1-100): 57.2 – Flashes some brilliance, but everything has to be 'JUST RIGHT.' His off the field concerns need to be looked into. I think there are traits to work with, but he needs to gain functional strength to play on the inside at the next level. It wasn't exposed much in college, but it will be at the next level. A 7th round player who has some athletic traits to develop.

27. Terry Beckner Jr DT Missouri 6'3 295 lbs

Strengths: Beckner Jr is an experienced guy who has played against top-tier competition for 4 seasons in the SEC. He had his best season as a junior with 7 sacks. A physical guy, he embraces the physical side of the game. Plays with a relentless motor, going all-out on every snap, always in pursuit. Power-packed frame, displaying strength and thick limbs throughout his upper and lower body. Very quick and active hands, utilizing a wide array of hand tactics. Commits himself to win inside hand placement upon snap of the ball. Shows good ball awareness, quickly working toward the football. Nice 1st step quickness with the long speed to close on the ball as well.

Weaknesses: Has had injury concerns, tearing ligaments in both of his knees during his career. Was suspended as a freshman with possession of marijuana. Had a disappointing senior campaign with only 2 sacks. Really struggles to bring ball carriers down, bouncing off them instead of utilizing good mechanics to break down. Fails to utilize all his length and extend his arms to cut off lanes. Keeps his frame far too exposed in the run game, allowing himself to quickly get hooked and sustained. Locked on blocks far too often, failing to see an escape route or utilize his hands to shed.

Best Fit: 4-3 DT (1 or 3-technique)

Player Ranking (1-100): 54.3 – Beckner Jr has some good tape, some not so much. I'm afraid his injury concerns might cause him to get undrafted. He's going to have to prove in training camp he can make an NFL roster.

28. Amani Bledsoe DT/DE Oklahoma 6'5 287 lbs

Strengths: Bledsoe is a 2-year starter for the Sooners who possesses tremendous length and size. He played mostly as a 5-tech 3-4 DE in Oklahoma's base defensive system and will likely best be suited in that role at the next level. Does a nice job of taking on blockers and stacking them at the line of scrimmage with his length, controlling through the duration of the snap. Understands how to utilize his length in the passing game, almost always getting his long arms up to disrupt passing lanes and had 7 pass knockdowns his last season. Plays with a relentless motor. Has the strength to anchor and sustain the outside edges in the run game.

Weaknesses: Bledsoe was suspended for 1-year following a suspension for a banned NCAA drug. He took the NCAA to court after arguing one of his protein powders was contaminated. Teams will likely look into this situation. A 2-down player at the next level who fails to have any kind of pass rush arsenal, only having 4 career sacks and 8.5 tackles for loss. Lacks a plan when attacking the pocket, settling to just bull rush on every snap. Fails to utilize his hands in any kind of way to disengage. A very upright rusher who allows smaller blockers to easily win the leverage battle and control him through the snap. Balance concerns as he is on the ground a lot.

Best Fit: 3-4 DE (5-technique)

Player Ranking (1-100): 53.9 – Not a fan of the player at all. Besides his length and motor, he offers very little else as a player. I would be very surprised if he makes an NFL roster at this point in time. Undrafted free agent.

29. Olive Sagapolu DT Wisconsin 6'2 342 lbs

Strengths: Sagapolu is a 4-year starter for the Badgers who has mostly played at nose tackle. The definition of a big-bodied guy, he possesses a strong upper body and a good natural leverage advantage. Despite his size, Sagapolu shows a surprising amount of agility and lateral movement skills, with quick feet and loose hips. Very active hands, and puts them on overdrive due to his lack of length. When playing with a good pad level, Sagapolu explodes out of his stance and generates really good initial movement with his bull rush. Frequently occupies double teams and demands attention from the interior.

Weaknesses: Missed most of his final season after needing surgery on his right arm. Very limited production during his career with only 6 sacks and 10 tackles for loss. A minimal threat to do anything in the passing game, frequently getting stuck on double teams. Doesn't fight through double teams and generally is completely washed out of plays when taking on combination blocks. Despite his huge frame, most of it is in his upper body and he fails to possess any kind of anchor ability to sustain at the point of attack. A stubby-built guy who lacks the necessary skills to disengage and shed blocks. Very inconsistent pad level.

Best Fit: 2-gap NT

Player Ranking (1-100): 53.2 – Sagapolu is an 'OK' player in every sense of the word. He's not going to blow anyone away, but he isn't bad. He's a 2-down guy who will need to show he can effectively 2-gap at the next level. Undrafted free agent.

Defensive Tackles (Interior Players) Top-10 Rankings

1. Ed Oliver
2. Quinnen Williams
3. Jeffrey Simmons
4. Rashan Gary
5. Christian Wilkins
6. Dexter Lawrence
7. Daniel Wise
8. Marquise Copeland
9. Dre'Mont Jones
10. Khalen Saunders

Chapter 11

Middle Linebackers

1. Devin Bush ILB Michigan 5'11 233 lbs

Strengths: Bush is a highly productive interior linebacker for the Wolverines who had a great sophomore and junior seasons. An athletically-built linebacker who possesses leanness with practically 0 body fat. Has a real knack for getting after the QB as a blitzer, with 5.5 sacks his sophomore season and 4.5 sacks his junior year. Bush perfectly fits in with today's hybrid linebacker/safety role that many defenses are deploying. Will only be 20 years old for the draft. A downhill, heat-seeking missile Bush possesses explosive POP on contact, utilizing his short-area bursts coupled with hip torque to deliver powerful blows. A highly intelligent and disciplined football player who was tasked with many responsibilities by the Michigan defense, including a number of different looks. A relentless motor guy who brings it on every snap of the football, never lacking from effort. A tremendous athlete who displays functional movement skills all over the field, showing the ease of movement and flexibility through his core. Outstanding agility with the start/stop and change of direction ability that is rare to see in linebackers. Possesses the range and body control in space to cover large portions of green. Is at his best when he's able to utilize his explosive 1st step quickness to shoot gaps and make stops behind the line of scrimmage. Showcases the long-speed to chase down plays backside or run down plays down the field. Is used routinely in man-coverage situations against slot receivers, not looking out of place or lost.

Weaknesses: A bit of an undersized linebacker who lacks ideal bulk and length. Due to his lack of size, he can get completely engulfed by larger offensive lineman who can reach his chest and latch on. His lack of length prevents him from stacking and shedding effectively at the 2nd level. Tends to take indirect pathways to the football in order to avoid blockers. Lacks the ability to make a lot of tackles outside of his frame, due to his lack of length. Goes for the big hit all the time, keeping his pad level too high causing him to miss some tackles and not securely wrap up.

Best Fit: Hybrid LB/Safety for a team. The best fit is in a non-traditional linebacker role where he can have a number of assignments and responsibilities including some pass rushing and coverage.

Player Ranking (1-100): 85.9 – Bush is a hot commodity in today's NFL. His change of direction and sideline to sideline ability is ridiculous. It's rare to completely trust a linebacker in coverage against NFL slot receivers, but with Bush, I wouldn't be afraid one bit. I hope he goes to a creative defensive coordinator who can maximize his ability in space. You don't want Bush having a lot of 'take on' responsibilities against offensive lineman. I wouldn't think twice about taking him at the end of the 1st round if I wanted to speed up my defense. He's going to improve a team a lot.

2. Mack Wilson ILB Alabama 6'2 239 lbs

Strengths: Wilson is a productive 2-year contributor for the Tide defense who had 65 tackles, 5 passes defended and 4.5 tackles for loss this season. Wilson has a good overall frame, showing the room to continue adding additional weight and muscle. Really impressive ball production with 6 interceptions the last 2 seasons. Wilson is really good with his hands, showing the ability to keep his frame untouched, maximizing his length. Possesses a good awareness of passing lanes, constantly getting his hands up and disrupting QB's line of vision. Quick to diagnose with good reactionary skills, possessing quick reflexes. Completely comfortable in a wide variety of coverage assignments, showing the fluidity and movement skills to mirror in man. While in zone, shows the awareness and short-area bursts to close windows quickly. A good overall athlete, he has the range to cut off running lanes, shortening the field.

Weaknesses: Inconsistent pad level when taking on bigger backs in the hole, leading to drag down tackles or completely bouncing off. Needs to utilize better fundamentals when tackling to wrap up securely. When Wilson gets hooked or reached in space, he will really struggle to shed, lacking ideal length or power in his hands. Has a slighter frame and will get washed out on a lot of plays. Plays as physical as his frame suggests he should, but needs to add additional strength to his lower body to better sustain and anchor when teams run towards him. Flashes quick diagnostic ability, but it's inconsistent and he can suffer from mental lapses.

Best Fit: Scheme-versatile ILB

Player Ranking (1-100): 84.1 – Wilson is a good overall prospect who shows the fluidity of movement and the athleticism to be a rangy middle linebacker who can play as a true 4-3 MIKE linebacker. He's a really good cover linebacker that will likely cause him to get drafted high, but he's still a work in progress and needs to continue learning the position. 2nd round player.

3. Devin White ILB LSU 6'1 240 lbs

Strengths: White is a 2-year starter for the Tigers who has displayed tremendous production in the last 2 years with 255 tackles, 7.5 sacks, 3 forced fumbles, 25.5 tackles for loss and 9 passes defended. A compactly-built linebacker who is a rock solid 6'1, 240 pounds with power throughout his frame. White is young and will have just turned 21 right before the draft. White is a downhill, physical player who looks to deliver a shot every time he touches the ball carrier. Shows the fluidity throughout his frame to click/close in the blink of an eye in coverage. A really good overall athlete who flashes the mirror ability to stick with assignments in man-coverage, granting very little separation. An excellent blitzer, he shows violence with his hands and the core flexibility to shoot through tiny gaps. Impressive range in lateral situations, showing the ability in his hips to cross-field without losing any built up speed. A twitchy athlete with good reaction time. Good strength throughout his frame, displaying excellent upper-body power and lower-body anchor ability.

Weaknesses: White's motor runs hot and cold, playing 100 mph one snap and the next he looks disinterested and passive. Needs major play-recognition work. Not always disciplined in his assignment, looking like a chicken without his head on occasion, taking overaggressive angles and getting fooled by every pump-fake and misdirection style play. Goes for the big hit constantly, leading to missed wrap-up opportunities. Plays with a poor pad level at the 2nd level, leading to upper-body tackle attempts. Lacks the length to consistently tackle out of his frame. Takes far too many steps in his pursuit of the ball. Gets caught on blocks, lacking the length to shed.

Best Fit: ILB in any defensive scheme

Player Ranking (1-100): 82.2 – White is the tale of two players who looks explosive and exciting on some snaps, and disinterested and stuck on blocks on others. He needs major work in recognizing things pre and post snap to put himself in good positions, instead of constantly running back toward the ball. He has the range and athleticism to cover loads of space, showing the potential to be a solid MIKE linebacker in a 4-3 system. Has the agility and looseness in his frame to be solid in all coverage alignments with more experience. 2nd round player.

4. Te'Von Coney ILB Notre Dame 6'1 244 lbs

Strengths: Coney is a well-built and compactly built inside linebacker for the Fighting Irish. He's a tough kid who shows toughness and positional instincts for the linebacker position. Coney is a 4-year contributor, he has played almost every snap on defense the last 3 years and is a guy that never gets hurt. Each of the last 2 seasons, he has shown an ability to get 3+ sacks a year showing good awareness in blitzing situations. Smart guy who understands disguising coverages and not showing his hand too early in the snap count. Quickly diagnoses plays and shows good read/reactionary skills to locate the ball. Does a nice job of staying off blocks, rarely getting stuck on a block for more than a second. A long-levered frame who plays with good length and an understanding of utilizing his upper body power. Has a really nice feel for drops and zone-based coverages rarely allowing too much spacing on underneath routes. Rarely too far out of position, taking good angles to the football. Not the most fundamentally sound tackler, but will bring a ball carrier down on almost every occasion. Shows an ability to play different linebacker positions.

Weaknesses: Coney is a good athlete when things are in front of him, but his stiff hips can get him in trouble on horizontal routes. Was arrested with possession of marijuana and a firearm in his sophomore year causing him to have probation for a period of time. Not the most fundamentally sound guy, allowing his pad level to rise mid-play causing him to drag guys down rather than bringing them down cleanly. Can struggle with too much space, and was often times put in positions to succeed rarely having to cover much in man-to-man situations. Lacks ideal size and bulk to play as a stand-alone MIKE linebacker in a 4-3 system. Kind of a tweener who lacks elite physicality, toughness or athleticism.

Best Fit: 3-4 ILB or 4-3 WILL

Player Ranking (1-100): 80.7 – Coney is a good and reliable prospect who has a high floor. He isn't going to WOW you at any 1 aspect of the game, but he's a smart kid who understands the game and plays disciplined. I like him best running at the ball backside and keeping things in front of him without getting caught on an island. His size traits make him ideal in either a 4-3 WILL role or a 3-4 ILB spot. 2nd round player.

5. TJ Edwards ILB Wisconsin 6'1 245 lbs

Strengths: Edwards is a 4-year starter for the Badgers who has had tremendous production with over 360 tackles during his career. A well-built, big and physical LB who is always looking to play downhill. Edwards shows natural coverage ability, always being at the right place at both zone and man coverage. Showing instincts, play recognition and awareness, Edwards puts himself in good position to make a lot of plays in coverage, with 7 interceptions and 22.5 tackles for loss the last 2 seasons. When playing in space, Edwards shows a nice ability to slip off blocks and disengage by shedding and stacking. He also has the powerful upper body to deliver a jolt upon impact, causing blockers to be set back. Plays with outstanding contact balance, always staying on his feet ready to make a play. He's a reliable tackler who will bring ball carriers down consistently with good fundamentals. Edwards is a production machine, almost always putting himself in good position to make plays.

Weaknesses: What Edwards has in play-recognition and instincts; he lacks in physical ability. His body is a bit too compact, and you can argue, he could stand to play at a lower weight at the next level to impact his movement skills. Lacks great height and length for the position. Reliant more on his awareness and a pre-snap idea of what is going on than great movement skills in coverage. Plays with a bit of stiffness in his core and hips that limit his change of direction. Has a bad tendency of getting caught in traffic, not possessing the ability to get skinny and play through tight windows. Very limited range in the amount of field he can cover.

Best Fit: ILB in a 3-4 but can play as a sub-package LB as well

Player Ranking (1-100): 79.0 – I like Edwards quite a bit. He's a really good coverage LB for a MLB. He lacks the ideal range/length to play as a 4-3 MLB in the run game but shows the ability to play in coverage on all 3 downs.

6. Cameron Smith ILB USC 6'2 230 lbs

Strengths: Smith is the definition of a well-built guy with a compact and muscular frame from head to toe with little body fat. Smith plays with nice length, showing the ability to outstretch his arms and corral opponents before bringing them down. Smith played on every snap for USC and in all their sub-packages as well. Plays with a relentless motor and tremendous strength. Smart kid who diagnoses and reads plays pre-snap and knows exactly where he needs to be on the football field. When he can't make the play, he constantly gets his hands up in the air to disrupt the pass and he knocks down a lot of balls. Excellent react ability with natural instincts to always be at the right place at the right time. Understands pursuit angles, taking the most disciplined routes to the play. A twitchy athlete who moves exceptionally for a guy of his size, showing short-area quickness as well as the pursuit and speed to chase plays down. Shows a really good awareness of passing lanes. Even used at times to play as a man cover guy against slot receivers or tight ends. Very reliable tackler who uses good technique in bringing guys down.

Weaknesses: Smith had a really down senior season with his production greatly dropping. Smith has had numerous injury concerns throughout his time in college, including tearing his ACL his freshman season. Gets a bit handsy in coverage grabbing down the field when receivers attempt to break on a route. Has a tendency to play too upright, and with too high a pad level mid-play causing him to have some balance issues in coverage.

Best Fit: ILB in 4-3

Player Ranking (1-100): 77.3 – Smith is an outstanding prospect and really impressed me on tape. He shows the athletic ability, the body, instincts, and the football IQ to really excel at the next level. He displays the range and athletic ability to cover a ton of ground and play as a true 4-3 MLB. 3rd round player. The biggest question mark with Smith is going to be his medical report.

7. Tyrel Dodson ILB Texas A&M 6'2 242 lbs

Strengths: Dodson is a 2-year starter for the Aggies who had his best season as a sophomore with 104 tackles, 5.5 tackles for loss and 3 interceptions. Dodson is an athletically-built interior linebacker who possesses good overall weight distribution. Dodson is an explosive, playmaking linebacker who is always around the football and has had touchdowns in each of the last 2 seasons. Instinctual, quickly reading and diagnosing things, and then utilizes his twitchiness to spring himself in any direction. Possesses the range and body control to play in loads of space, very comfortable in a variety of coverage situations. A team leader who is known to have a high football IQ. Does a nice job of working back towards the football, sorting through the trash and getting to the ball carrier. Takes sharp angles to the ball, beating ball carriers to the action. Loose-hipped, showing fluidity in movements, looking comfortable in man-coverage situations.

Weaknesses: Dodson's final season, as a junior, was greatly disappointing after a stellar sophomore season. His production was down greatly. A bit overaggressive, lacking necessary discipline in gap-assignments, taking poor pathways to the football. Lacks ideal length to consistently make tackles away from his frame or close down gaps with length. Upright in space, keeping his frame far too exposed. Poor pad level when tackling, attempting to drag down from the upper-body, leading to additional yardage after contact.

Best Fit: ILB in either scheme

Player Ranking (1-100): 77.0 – Dodson is an impressive guy to watch on film, especially during his sophomore campaign. He possesses the fluidity in his movement to cover loads of space. He's one of the few guys in this draft class that displays the range and athleticism to play as a MIKE linebacker in a 4-3 defense. 3rd round player.

8. Khalil Hodge ILB Buffalo 6'1 235 lbs

Strengths: Hodge is a 3-year starter for MAC conference Buffalo having over 120 tackles in each season. A quick and instinctive linebacker, he displays good instincts and awareness to cover crossing and drag routes across the field. Nice fluidity and flexibility in his hips to cross the field and change direction. Impressive quickness, showing the ability to run stride for stride with slot receivers or joker TEs. Excellent football IQ who shows the ability to read things pre-snap and has excellent play recognition. Impressive in coverage, showing a good feel for zone coverage or straight man to man. Quickly stacks and sheds, showing the upper body strength to disengage and not sit on blocks. Plays all 3 downs on every snap and has shown reliability starting in every game the last 3 years for the Bulls.

Weaknesses: Lacks adequate anchor and lower body power to stop runners dead in their tracks, tends to allow runners additional yardage. Quick but not real fast. Played in the MAC conference and didn't compete against the best of competition on a week in week out basis. Needs to continue to add strength/muscle/weight to his frame.

Best Fit: 4-3 MIKE

Player Ranking (1-100): 76.7 – While Hodge certainly shows the strength and movement skills to play as a MIKE in a 4-3, I genuinely believe he can play the WILL spot or as an interior LB in a 3-4 system as well. His consistency, awareness, quickness, and instincts make him a really good prospect. I would select him early in the 3rd round.

9. Joe Giles-Harris ILB Kentucky 6'2 240 lbs

Strengths: Giles-Harris is a well-built linebacker with long limbs and an athletic frame. An outstanding and fundamental tackler, utilizing both arms to wrap up securely. Had his best year as a sophomore notching 125 tackles, 16 tackles for loss, 3.5 sacks, 4 passes defended and 1 forced fumble. A smart linebacker and very quick decision maker, rapidly reading keys pre and post snap. Very good athlete who displays good long speed, as well as the secondary burst to close down plays. An effective blitzer, showing good instincts and timing to affect the pocket. Understands how to effectively disguise coverages pre-snap. Has a good understanding of passing lanes, maintaining disciplined eyes and putting himself in good position in zone-coverage. Displays the loose hips and light feet when used in man-coverage, generally staying stride for stride with receivers. Utilizes his length effectively to close down outside lanes or disrupt passes at the catch point. A rangy athlete, he has the ability to break quickly and play sideline to sideline. Takes sharp angles to the football, utilizing his acute diagnostic skills and often times funneling ball carriers to his teammates.

Weaknesses: Giles-Harris had a knee injury at the end of his final season, causing him to miss the last few games of the year. Doesn't always trust his eyes in pursuit, causing some hesitations and getting stuck in traffic while working back towards the football. Needs to utilize quicker, more active hands when shedding blockers. Gets stuck far too long, struggling to disengage. Plays with too high a pad level in space, causing him to sometimes drag down as opposed to forcefully utilizing lower-body explosion. Has a tendency to get too grabby when playing in coverage down the field.

Best Fit: ILB in either defensive system

Player Ranking (1-100): 76.6 - Giles-Harris is not a flashy player, nor will he blow you away on film. He's just a consistent performer who showed outstanding production in each season. He quietly does his job and will be a solid contributor at the next level. He will absolutely be an effective special teams' player immediately and can possibly gain some additional snaps early on in passing situations due to his athleticism. Should be a 3rd round player.

10. Jeffrey Allison ILB Fresno State 5'11 242 lbs

Strengths: Allison is a compactly-built production machine for Fresno State the last two seasons, totaling over 120 tackles in each season. Allison is a highly intelligent MLB who reads the game pre-snap. A disciplined linebacker who understands where he needs to be, maintaining good depth on zone drops in coverage. In the running game, he fully trusts his eyes and maintains disciplined gap control. Does a good job of sorting through the trash and finding the ball carrier. Good overall speed, showing an impressive secondary burst to quickly close on the ball. A heat-seeking missile who plays downhill and delivers bone-rattling hits due to his acceleration and compact frame. Despite lacking great length, Allison displays the ability to extend and make tackles outside of his frame. A relentless athlete who plays 100 mph on every snap showing light feet and loose hips when moving laterally. Allison possesses good range and body control in space. Shows 0 hesitancy when taking on backs head-on in the hole.

Weaknesses: Allison lacks ideal size and length to play as a standalone MIKE in a 4-3 setup. An overly-aggressive linebacker at times, and needs to do a better job of training his eyes to read keys. Allison frequently bites hard, showing undisciplined eyes causing him to quickly fall for misdirection-type plays and play-action. Goes for the big hits in space, and fails to always wrap up securely.

Best Fit: 3-4 ILB or 4-3 WILL

Player Ranking (1-100): 72.4 – Allison is an undersized linebacker who is a really good football player. He's going to fall lower in the draft than he should, and I honestly believe he's an NFL starter. His athleticism, movement skills, and physicality, despite being a bit undersized are impressive. Going to be a great special teams player as well. He's worth a 4th round pick.

11. Tre Lamar ILB Clemson 6'4 255 lbs

Strengths: Lamar is a 3-year contributor and 2-year starter for the Tigers defense who had really impressive junior season production with 79 tackles, 3 sacks, and 1 interception. The first trait you'll notice with Lamar is his size, possessing an outstanding wingspan and a next-level physique. Lamar is an impressive blitzer who understands how to attack the pocket, as evidenced by his 7 sacks the last 2 seasons. A good straight-line athlete, he shows great closing bursts in vertical spaces. Fully extends his length to close down running paths, and makes tackles consistently away from his frame. Knows how to utilize his length when taking on blockers, keeping his frame clean. A strong upper-body showing finishing ability to routinely bring tacklers down with good form. Awareness of passing lanes, understanding where he needs to be disruptive. Rarely hung up on blocks, quickly sorting through the trash in the run game, and working back towards the ball with a good, relentless motor. Reads things quickly in the backfield, quickly diagnosing and plugging holes.

Weaknesses: Lamar is a limited athlete who shows stiffness throughout his lower body, minimizing his explosiveness and change of direction. Has had some balance concerns when taking on blocks, due to his uprightness post-snap. Minimal range in space, preventing him from playing laterally, immediately gearing down and losing speed. Lacks the short-area bursts to deliver impactful hits or close down in the passing game. Most likely a 2-down player at the next level. Inexperienced in man-coverage. Looks vulnerable and uncomfortable in space in zone coverage.

Best Fit: 3-4 ILB

Player Ranking (1-100): 71.7 – Lamar is a guy who will likely get overdrafted because of his rare size and wingspan. He's a stiff athlete who will get exposed at the next level in coverage. There are certainly some traits as a run player, with his diagnostic ability and plugging run holes. An immediate special teams' player who is physical and can offer some snaps on defense as a sub-package guy. 4th round player.

12. Jahlani Tavai ILB Hawaii 6'3 245 lbs

Strengths: Tavai is a 3-year starter for Hawaii who had tremendous junior and sophomore seasons with over 120 tackles and 5.5 sacks in each season. Built with good length for an inside linebacker, showing the necessary frame to continue adding additional muscle and size. Smart guy who obviously watches a lot of film, quickly reading plays pre-snap understanding what the offense is about to do. Shows the ability to get himself skinny and shoot closing gaps. A relentless motor who gives it 100% on every snap, always around the football. A really good blitzing linebacker, he understands how to get home by utilizing pre-snap recognition and awareness. Tavai is impressive in coverage, showing the ability to cover in man situations down the field. Has a good understanding and feel for zone concepts as well.

Weaknesses: Missed the final 4 games of his senior season with a shoulder issue. Was arrested and suspended for a nightclub incident. Shows some hesitancy when taking on a back in the hole, leading to low-impact collisions, allowing rushers to gain additional yardage after contact. Lacks elite change of direction and sideline to sideline range to play as a MIKE at the next level. Has some athletic limitations, forcing him to chase down plays rather than being in front of plays.

Best Fit: 3-4 ILB

Player Ranking (1-100): 70.5 – Tavai is a late riser for teams that possesses incredible leadership and toughness. His experience in a variety of coverage situations is going to draw him to defenses of both schemes. He's tough as nails and shows an incredibly high football IQ. He has some limitations physically, but he's a dang good football player.

13. Deshaun Davis ILB Auburn 5'11 233 lbs

Strengths: A 3-year starter for the Tigers who had a tremendous senior campaign with 112 tackles, 15 tackles for loss and 3.5 sacks. A compactly-built defender who possesses a power-packed frame. Davis is a team leader who plays with outstanding fundamentals and leadership intangibles. A tough, downhill linebacker, he always looks like a hammer in search of a nail. Plays with a contagious motor and energy that is infectious to the defense. The signal-caller for the defense who reads the game well pre-snap, frequently shouting out orders to his teammates. A really good and forceful tackler, he delivers impactful blows to runners, utilizing his short-area bursts and powerful hip torque. Slippery in space, showing the ability to keep his frame clean in space. Has a good understanding and is comfortable in zone-sets, allowing little space.

Weaknesses: Davis lacks ideal size and length to play as a stand-alone middle linebacker. Shows some hip and lower-body stiffness when asked to change direction or play in loads of space. Gets exposed when having to cover in man-coverage, lacking the overall speed and movement skills to be an effective coverage linebacker in sub-packages. A 2-down linebacker who won't be playing in clear passing situations. Good pre-snap, but lacks the mental recognition and decisiveness post-snap.

Best Fit: 3-4 ILB

Player Ranking (1-100): 68.2 – I really like Davis and the energy he brings to a defense is outstanding. He's not a great overall athlete and has serious size/coverage limitations. But I'm convinced he will be a dynamic special teams' player and a really good 2-down linebacker in a 3-4 defense. A 5th round player.

14. Joe Dineen Jr ILB Kansas 6'2 235 lbs

Strengths: Dineen Jr is a 5-year senior for the Jayhawks who has been really impressive his last 2 seasons as a starter, combining for over 275 tackles, 5.5 sacks and 32 tackles for loss. Dineen is built with a muscular and lean physique, showing the necessary girth to play LB at the next level. A natural-born leader who calls the defensive signals and play calls. A physical player showing toughness and an understanding of the physical aspects of the game. Good awareness and reading of the game, picking up free runners down the field when uncovered. Inches towards the line of scrimmage keeping his frame and pad level down, exploding on the snap of the ball. An aggressive player, he isn't afraid of taking on bigger lineman in the hole. Solid tackler who uses nice fundamentals to get the guy on the ground.

Weaknesses: Stiff athlete who lacks any kind of misdirection or cross-field movement skills. Not a guy you want playing in too much space in the open field. Lacks great size or power. Despite his smaller frame, lacks great speed and athleticism to make enough plays consistently. Had a hamstring injury early in his junior season causing him to get redshirted that year.

Best Fit: Special Teams' and developmental linebacker

Player Ranking (1-100): 61.2 – Good player but will need to show he can play on special teams to be given a fair shake to make an NFL roster. 6th round player.

15. Dakota Allen ILB Texas Tech 6'1 235 lbs

Strengths: Allen is a 3-year starter and team captain for the Red Raiders who possesses compactness and muscular girth to play inside at the next level. Community college transfer. An instinctive guy, he quickly finds and locates the football. A reliable tackler who finds a way to bring ball carriers down. Fast mental processing time to be able to quickly read/react. Forceful tackler who brings guys to the ground quickly. A natural born leader who plays with ranginess and sneaky athleticism. Excellent blitzer, he times it perfectly and utilizes his closing burst to get in the backfield quickly. Trusts his eyes and immediately follows.

Weaknesses: Serious behavioral issues which caused him to get kicked off the team, he was eventually let back on. Gets washed out of too many plays, failing to shed blocks and disengage. Easily manipulated by play fakes and misdirection style of plays. Overaggressive nature can lead to some missed tackles and gap assignments. A drag tackler who allows additional yards upon contact. Lacks great length to play in too much space.

Best Fit: Special teams' player and backup MIKE linebacker

Player Ranking (1-100): 57.3 – Good player who shows impressive movement skills and toughness. Plays aggressive and would be an immediate special teams player. Could develop more at linebacker and be a solid player in the future. 7th round guy.

16. Ryan Connelly ILB Wisconsin 6'2 237 lbs

Strengths: A 3-year starter who has had 2 tremendously productive years, with almost identical levels of production in each year. Connelly is a rangy-built linebacker who shows good overall length to cut off running lanes and keep his frame clean in the run game. Plays with a HOT motor, showing good contact balance to stay on his feet. Takes good pathways to the football, and uses his length to direct runners to the sidelines. Plays downhill and delivers some big hits. Limited experience in coverage situations, but flashes the movement ability and overall speed to limited spacing.

Weaknesses: Connelly possesses a leggy-build who needs to continue to strengthen his anchoring ability to better hold up in run support when taking on blocks, frequently getting washed out of plays. Lacks the short-area bursts and explosiveness to consistently win behind the line of scrimmage. Lacks the power and strength in his upper-body to deliver blows to blockers or disengage in sufficient time. Shows some lower-body stiffness when asked to change direction or play laterally. Misses a lot of tackles due to poor pursuit lanes, failing to accurately wrap up.

Best Fit: MLB in either scheme

Player Ranking (1-100): 55.9 – Connelly is an average player in every sense of the word. Nothing about him excites me other than his size, length, and some flashes of coverage ability. He's going to need to prove he can win a spot on a team by playing awesome on special teams. 7th round player.

Middle Linebackers Top-10 Rankings

1. Devin Bush
2. Mack Wilson
3. Devin White
4. Te'Von Coney
5. TJ Edwards
6. Cameron Smith
7. Tyrel Dodson
8. Khalil Hodge
9. Joe Giles-Harris
10. Jeffrey Allison

Chapter 12

Outside Linebackers (Strong Side or Weak Side)

1. Vosean Joseph OLB Florida 6'1 226 lbs

Strengths: Joseph is an athletically-built and explosive linebacker for the Gators, who has started each of the last 2 seasons. As a junior, Joseph was tremendous totaling 93 tackles, 9 tackles for loss, 4 sacks, and 5 passes defended. Joseph plays with a nonstop, relentless motor always flying to the football. Joseph is at his best in space, showing outstanding quickness surprising ball carriers with his speed. He converts that speed to power to deliver some bone-crushing blows to runners in space. Follows his eyes, constantly keeping his head up throughout the duration of a play, rarely getting stuck through traffic. Slippery, understands how to use his hands to disengage quickly. Tremendous secondary burst to close quickly on plays. Shows light feet and loose hips in traffic, showing the ability to fluidly change directions laterally. Disciplined eyes, rarely getting fooled on misdirection or play-action type plays. Knows how to key in pre-snap, recognizing things before they happen. Takes disciplined and acute angles to the football. Outstanding blitzer, showing the ability to stay skinny through contact and get home.

Weaknesses: Joseph played inside with the Gators and will likely have to learn a new role as an outside guy at the next level. He lacks necessary body armor and size to consistently play inside. Played in more of a free-roaming linebacker role that the Gators used, and rarely was used in coverage situations. Has some issues tackling when he doesn't have built-up speed and his feet are stopped. Allows his pads to occasionally rise mid-snap to keep his frame far too exposed in space.

Best Fit: 4-3 WILL linebacker

Player Ranking (1-100): 85.3 – Absolutely love the player. Despite his lack of experience in coverage, he showed on quite a few snaps that he can turn and run and move laterally. That was enough for me to be convinced he can do it at the next level consistently with more technique and practice. As a rookie, he can be used in blitz situations and as a base WILL linebacker. He's going to be a perfect player in today's modern NFL. Late 1st round player.

2. Josiah Tauaefa OLB UTSA 6'2 245 lbs

Strengths: Tauaefa is a 4th year junior for UTSA who has started in all 3 straight seasons. Has played both DE and linebacker during his career, but will most likely play as an outside linebacker at the next level. A tackling machine where in both full seasons as a starter he had over 110 tackles. A proficient blitzer, showing tremendous timing and quick-twitch explosion off the snap. A tireless worker with a ridiculous motor, Tauaefa is always working towards the ball and is truly a magnet to the football. A chippy defender who battles to the echoes of the whistle, bringing a level of physicality that toughens up an entire defense. Possesses above-average length, does a nice job of contorting in space to get his arms up to disrupt the pass. Good ball awareness, he breaks real fast once the pass is released. Takes sharp angles to the full, quickly diagnosing post-snap. Good athlete who shows a tremendous closing burst delivering some big collisions with backs.

Weaknesses: Missed half of his sophomore year with a bad knee injury. Will have a big step-up in competition levels playing at the next level. Struggles when asked to change direction, getting stuck in quicksand with his feet. A bit of a tweener who lacks a true position at the next level. Has a tendency to arrive at the ball carrier with poor pad-level causing him to have issues bringing down consistently, sometimes bouncing off. Very little experience in man-coverage situations.

Best Fit: 4-3 SAM or 3-4 OLB

Player Ranking (1-100): 84.9 - After former teammate, Marcus Davenport had a successful rookie season for the Saints, Tauaefa's stock has certainly risen. I liked this kid's tape a lot more than I was expecting to. While his level of competition wasn't the greatest, Tauaefa was all over the field! He shows up in almost every snap, affecting the play in one way or another. I want him on my team! A beast who plays with physicality, always coming downhill. I wouldn't hesitate to take Tauaefa in the 2nd round.

3. Kendall Joseph OLB Clemson 6'0 225 lbs

Strengths: Joseph is a smaller but rangy MLB for Clemson. He possesses outstanding instincts, showing his short-area quickness and closing burst on every snap. He's a smart kid who understands pursuit angles and maintaining good angles at all times. Shows the range to play sideline to sideline. Generates explosiveness from his hips to generate bone-crunching hits. Longer arms than average, and shows an ability to control blockers in the run game by winning the leverage battle. Does a nice job of finding the ball carrier quickly and is always in pursuit. Joseph is a leader of the Clemson football team possessing all the attributes defensive coaches are looking for. Shows fluidity in his movements with great change of direction, light feet, and loose hips. Always tends to be at the right place at the right time.

Weaknesses: Lacks great size for the ILB position at the next level and will likely have to transition to a weak-side backer. Not the most physical LB and will get overwhelmed at the point of attack by bigger, longer tackles and guards at the next level. Needs to do a better job of shedding quickly. Has a tendency to get stuck in traffic quite a bit. Shows some indecision with wasted movement, causing a second or two delays. Gave up some big plays in pass coverage when attempting to cover backs and TEs. Jumps at guys' ankles far too many times when trying to tackle, creating additional yards for the backs.

> **Best Fit:** 4-3 OLB (Will backer)

Player Ranking (1-100): 82.2 – Joseph is a talented linebacker with top-notch explosion and athleticism. He deserves to be a high selection in the draft and has all the intangibles teams want. Will likely need to transition to a new position at the next level though. 2nd round pick.

4. Ulysees Gilbert III OLB Akron 6'1 230 lbs

Strengths: Gilbert is a 3-year starter who has had tremendous production throughout his career with over 350 tackles and 8.5 sacks. An impressive and natural athlete who shows the ability to take sharp angles to the football, acutely diagnosing plays pre-snap. Extremely impressive in his ability to work through the garbage and quickly find a way to the football. Impressive hand strength to quickly disengage and get off blocks, rarely getting hung up. Plays with good pad level, maintaining his balance and staying skinny through tight lanes. Does a nice job of making linemen miss in the open-field working his way to the ball. Has shown experience and fluidity in man coverage at times. Loose-hipped athlete who shows the ability to flip his hips and cross-field while losing little speed. Really good sideline to sideline range, showing the ability to break quickly.

Weaknesses: A bit of an undersized linebacker who can struggle when taking on bigger backs in the hole. Not a forceful tackler, rather a 'DRAG' or an ankle-biter tackler. Can be overaggressive at times, falling for play-action or misdirection type of runs. Needs to maintain his low pad level through the direction of plays, leading to poor tackling technique.

> **Best Fit:** 4-3 WILL

Player Ranking (1-100): 79.1 – Gilbert III is a really good player who shocked me how effective he was playing in space. He's one of my favorite small-school guys in this draft, and one of the best outside linebackers in this class. He's always looking for a way to quickly get to the football without taking on blockers head-on, and he has an effective way of doing it. 3rd round player.

5. Terrill Hanks OLB New Mexico State 6'2 234 lbs

Strengths: Hanks is a 4-year starter who has had over 100 tackles in each of his last 3 seasons in college, playing for New Mexico State. A production machine, even having 8 interceptions and 11 sacks from the linebacker spot. A modern-day linebacker possessing outstanding coverage ability, showing smoothness in his hips and the flexibility to turn and run without gearing down. A former defensive back who shows it in his coverage ability. A twitchy athlete, he shows outstanding quickness out of his stance. He couples that with his long-strides showing the recovery ability and the speed to track down ball carriers from behind. Plays with some power and pop in his hands, frequently knocking blockers to the ground. A forceful tackler who displays impressive hip torque when driving to the ground. Comfortable in blitz situations, showing good timing and instincts to shoot gaps and affect the QB. Excellent play recognition coupled with read/react to quickly put himself in a good position. Used quite a bit in both man and zone coverage, comfortable and reliable in both.

Weaknesses: Takes some very poor pursuit lanes in space, leading to misses in the open field. Leverage concerns, plays far too upright in space, minimizing his strike zone. Relies on big, forceful hits rather than good form tackling. If he doesn't have built-up speed, he fails to bring ball carriers down. A bit of a lanky guy who lacks adequate lower body power when taking on blocks. An 'avoid' linebacker rather than a 'take on blocks' kind of guy.

Best Fit: 4-3 WILL linebacker

Player Ranking (1-100): 78.9 – Hanks is a really good player who perfectly fits in with today's NFL. Could he be this year's version of Darius Leonard? He certainly demonstrates the physical traits to be. A real sideline to sideline football player who will immediately help out on special teams. He a perfect fit as a WILL (weak-side) linebacker in a 4-3 defense who can run to the ball. He's a lot more physical and tough than his size would indicate. I just wish he would be a bit more consistent with his tackling. 3rd round player.

6. Germaine Pratt OLB North Carolina State 6'3 240 lbs

Strengths: Pratt is a converted linebacker who played safety his first 2 years with the Wolfpack. His senior season was his first year as a full-time starter at linebacker. He led the ACC in tackles and led his team for tackles for loss and sacks as well. Pratt is an athletic linebacker who displays the movement skills and athleticism to play all 3 downs at the next level and is included in all sub-packages. Impressive short-area quickness and burst to be able to make plays behind the line of scrimmage and close in a flash. Impressive in his ability to stay skinny through contact and make plays. Shows the desired height/length with the ability to add more muscle and strength onto his frame. Really good range, showing the sideline to sideline speed to play horizontally. Comfortable even in man coverage situations, showing the movement skills and the loose hips to line up against slot receivers at times. Reliable tackler who is able to use his long arms to contort in space. Can be used in pass rushing situations, showing his ability to attack from the inside or the outside.

Weaknesses: Inconsistent physicality who struggles to consistently get off blocks. More of an 'AVOID' linebacker that a 'take-on' linebacker. Needs to learn how to use his hands better when taking on blockers. Would like to see him add some more strength in a NFL strength & conditioning program. Has some struggles in zone situations, failing to always cover the right route, granting far too much spacing to receivers.

Best Fit: 4-3 WILL

Player Ranking (1-100): 77.2 – I really like Pratt and I think he can be an awesome 4-3 WILL linebacker at the next level. That position would suit him best because of his athleticism and would allow him to run toward the ball. Pratt can be used in all coverage packages for a defense as well. You don't want him consistently taking on blockers, that's not his strong suit. I don't believe he's an ideal MLB. 3rd round player.

7. Otaro Alaka OLB Texas A&M 6'3 240 lbs

Strengths: Alaka is a 5th year senior who has started the last 3 seasons for the Aggies defense. He's been tremendous the last 2 seasons especially, with 157 tackles, 9.5 sacks, and 26.5 tackles for loss. Alaka is an impressive physical specimen with good girth and muscle throughout his frame, showing the length teams are looking for. A physical bull who plays with power throughout his frame, especially notable in his ability to generate speed to power on pass rush attempts. When picked up by a tight end or a running back, Alaka routinely bulls them back into the quarterback. A reliable form tackler who utilizes outstanding fundamentals to bring ball carriers down. Plays with a hot motor, always running 100 mph on every snap, tending to put himself in good position. Has a really good feel for the game, reading the quarterback's eyes and throwing arm. Possesses 3-down ability due to his skill in attacking the pocket and consistently generating a pass-rush. Tremendous at sorting through the trash and either making the tackle in heavy traffic or funneling ball carriers back inside. One of the better linebackers in this draft class at taking on blockers, rarely getting hung up and hooked. Possesses some range ability, saw him make quite a few stops on the opposite side of the field and turn/run on a dime

Weaknesses: His eyes can deceive him at times, leading to incorrect guesses and wrong pathways to the football. A slightly above average athlete who plays with some tightness in his core and hips leading to struggles when playing in too much space. Lacks the short area quickness in space to deliver powerful blows to tacklers. While he has some experience in coverage, his stiffness throughout his core and lack of agility is going to prevent him from being used in that role at the next level.

Best Fit: 4-3 Strong-Side

Player Ranking (1-100): 74.7 – I really love the player a lot more than most. I've heard some concerns in regards to his athleticism, and I think it's completely overblown. While he's not an elite athlete, he's above average and displays some range and closing speed to play in space. The physicality and toughness he brings to a defense are contagious. He can routinely take on blocks so is best suited for the strong-side position due to his pass-rush versatility and physicality. 4th round player.

8. David Long Jr OLB West Virginia 5'11 230 lbs

Strengths: Long Jr is a smaller, athletically-built linebacker who had a tremendously productive final season with West Virginia totaling 108 tackles, 19.5 tackles for loss, and 2 forced fumbles. Long is an impressive blitzer who frequently gets home on his blitzes, utilizing snap anticipation and low pad level to get through the line of scrimmage unblocked. Excellent pre-snap, showing outstanding play-recognition to put himself in really good position, he obviously does a lot of film work. A downhill guy that is always flying around the ball, beating ball carriers to the spot of the ball. Keeps his pad level low through impact, allowing him to slip around guys or get under them in space. Always keeps his feet moving, rarely getting stuck in the mud. Does an excellent job of keeping his frame skinny through contact, sorting through the trash and finding the football. An aggressive guy who shows fearlessness and no hesitancy in his style of play. The defensive team leader, he is known for having a tremendous work ethic and high football IQ. Does a nice job pre-snap of disguising coverages and blitzes.

Weaknesses: Tore his meniscus in the spring before his sophomore season causing him to miss the first 4 games of the season. Long is an undersized linebacker who will likely be limited to strictly a WILL linebacker role at the next level. Due to his smaller physique and lack of length, once he gets locked up by a bigger moving target in space, he's stuck. Tends to be a 'drag down' tackler lacking the necessary hip-torque and upper-body power to bring down upon impact. Lacks much experience in coverage situations. And when he does cover, he tends to look out of his element and gets caught looking in man. An overly aggressive downhill linebacker who will bite hard on misdirection style of plays and guess wrong quite a bit. On tape, it appears that Long isn't the most athletic linebacker despite being smaller. Relies on his instincts and anticipation abilities rather than pure speed.

Best Fit: 4-3 WILL linebacker

Player Ranking (1-100): 73.2 – In today's day and age it's always good to have mobile linebackers who can fly to the football. While Long isn't a great athlete, his instincts and anticipatory abilities frequently put him in great position. He's a tough kid who plays much bigger than his size would seem to indicate. I think he's an NFL starter at the next level and really impressed me this year. He likely will be limited to 2-down duties and special teams early on, as he lacks experience in coverage.

9. Bobby Okereke OLB Kentucky 6'1 231 lbs

Strengths: Okereke is a 2-year starter for the Tigers who has had really impressive production with 90 tackles in each season and 9.5 sacks playing as a middle linebacker. Okereke is a long and rangy built linebacker who is an ideal WILL (weak-side) linebacker in a 4-3 system. A really good athlete who displays the secondary burst to close cushions or recover after false steps. Despite being a smaller linebacker, he shows better than average toughness and physicality. Shows the sideline to sideline range with the speed to shoot gaps and make plays in the hole. Really impressive in his ability to stay skinny and find narrow holes to attack the pocket and create sacks when rushing the passer.

Weaknesses: Despite his athleticism and straight-line speed, he struggles with the change of direction stuff. Far too reliant on his upper-body strength to tackle rather than driving them down with his hips, causing ball carriers to pick up additional yardage. Takes far too aggressive angles to the football, leading to far too many steps and missed opportunities. Lacks great instincts and is slow to react quickly. Leaves his frame much too exposed when working back towards the ball. Far too passive when taking on blocks, getting caught in traffic never finding a way to get to the football. Shows some hesitancy when tackling, preventing him from forcefully taking down ball carriers.

Best Fit: WILL backer (weak-side linebacker) in a 4-3 system

Player Ranking (1-100): 72.2 – Good athlete that a team will likely take a chance on due to his speed and athleticism. Won't see much of the field as a rookie unless he really impresses early on special teams. 4th round player.

10. Ben Burr-Kirven OLB Washington 6'0 221 lbs

Strengths: Burr-Kirven is an athletically-built linebacker with a tapered midsection. Really came onto the scene this year after his ridiculous 165 tackle, 2 interceptions, 4 forced fumble senior season. Is at his best when he's playing off-ball, showing his ability to put himself in good position to make plays. He's a pursuit player who is always working towards the football with a relentless motor. Shows 0 hesitation when it comes to playing the run, or stacking lineman that are 80 pounds heavier than him. A tough, physical linebacker who plays with a chip. Does a nice job of slipping blocks in space, utilizing active hands with good-positioning. Always looks to track the QB's eyes in coverage. Almost on every tackle, he goes to knock the ball out from the runner, as evidenced by his 4 forced fumbles his senior season. Takes good angles to the football in the run game. Comfortable in zone-coverage with good ball awareness, showing the ability to read situations and maintain good cloud/zone positioning.

Weaknesses: Burr-Kirven will likely have to learn a different position at the next level due to his lack of size. Was hoping to see a better athlete on tape, lacks the speed to close down on plays. Will get exposed on in-cutting routes where he lacks the looseness in his hips and deep-speed to cover effectively in man. Lack of length limits his tackle radius to tackle outside of his frame. Not a forceful tackler who has the closing burst to deliver powerful blows in space, tends to be a drag down tackler.

Best Fit: WILL LB or a Box-Safety

Player Ranking (1-100): 71.9 – His level of production this year absolutely warrants some credit and recognition, but unfortunately his overall size/athletic limitations are going to cause him to most likely be a special teams' player as a rookie. His physicality and toughness could make him an outstanding special teams guy while he learns a new position at the next level. 4th round player.

11. Drew Lewis OLB Colorado 6'2 225 lbs

Strengths: Lewis is a productive 2-year starter for the Buffaloes who has played at both middle linebacker and outside linebacker for their defense. He had his best year as a junior with 94 tackles when he was playing in the middle. Lewis is an athletic freak, showing tremendous twitchiness and explosive characteristics in his lower body. He's a great fit for today's NFL showing 3-down ability with his ranginess in coverage, showing adeptness moving in space. Despite his smaller physique, Lewis plays fearless, taking on bigger lineman at the 2nd level. He's a hard guy to reach at the 2nd level due to his elusiveness and lateral movement ability. An effective blitzer who shows some ability to attack the pocket, utilizing impressive strength in his hands to jolt backs or tight ends. Maximizes his frame, showing the ability to extend and make plays outside of his frame.

Weaknesses: Lewis is aggressive to a fault, almost always playing downhill and reckless, taking some poor pathways to the ball. Questionable instincts and slow to process things, having to always play catch up and make up lost steps and ground. Allows his pads to rise mid-play causing him to leave his frame exposed against lineman, leading to poor leverage when taking on blocks. Situational and play awareness is very suspect, losing the ball carrier in traffic.

Best Fit: 4-3 WILL

Player Ranking (1-100): 70.5 – Lewis had a stellar pre-draft workout process showing his smoothness and athleticism in coverage. There's always more room for that at the next level, and teams are desperate for undersized athletic linebackers who can cover. That's exactly why I think Lewis can be a really good special teams' player early on and develop into a nice sub-package player. 4th round player.

12. Dre Greenlaw OLB Arkansas 6'0 227 lbs

Strengths: Greenlaw is a 4-year contributor who has started almost every game during his college career, possessing outstanding overall production with 320+ tackles. Greenlaw is a twitchy athlete who displays rare athleticism and sideline to sideline range to beat backs to the spot. Has rare instincts and reactionary ability, showing little processing time. Breaks incredibly quick once the pass is released. Shows 0 hesitancy in the hole, playing fearless, and is almost always in the frame of the play. Doesn't have a ton of coverage experience, but due to his flexible and looseness, he will succeed in all situations. Takes sharp angles to the football, initiating contact just as the ball arrives.

Weaknesses: Greenlaw is aggressive to a fault, committing himself to poor pursuit angles and incorrect running lanes, leading to consistently running into walls of traffic. A very slight frame who will get blown off the ball by tight ends. Doesn't have an understanding of how to utilize his hands to stack/shed at the 2nd level, causing him to get stuck on blocks. Lacks power throughout his frame, preventing him from finishing plays consistently. His lack of upper-body power prevents him from consistently wrapping up and bringing down bigger ball carriers. His lack of lower body strength limits his ability to anchor down and handle strength at the point of attack. Greenlaw needs to be utilized in space and can't handle having to take on blocks at the next level. Broke his foot during his sophomore season, leading him to miss the final month and half. Had some ankle concerns this season, leading to a couple of missed games in the beginning of the season.

Best Fit: 4-3 WILL

Player Ranking (1-100): 69.4 – Greenlaw is a really good athlete who shows impressive instincts and fluidity in his movements. He's a liability in the run game, lacking the strength and power to win at the point of attack at any level. He movement skills and athleticism is going to cause him to get overdrafted. He will likely need to prove himself on special teams early on. 5th round player.

13. Drue Tranquill OLB Notre Dame 6'2 228 lbs

Strengths: Tranquill is a 5th-year hybrid safety/linebacker hybridwho has had a really good career at Notre Dame. Coaches love the player, a 2-year captain who shows outstanding character. Possessing an athletically-built muscled up physique with good overall size. An athletic linebacker, he displays good twitchiness and short-area bursts to shoot gaps and make a lot of plays in the backfield. He combines his play recognition and cover awareness to be in good position. Sinks his hips pre-snap, maintaining good leverage, and keeping his frame wide and square in the hole. Physical point of attack tackler, especially when taking guys head on. A sideline to sideline athlete who utilizes his high motor anticipatory abilities to put himself in a good position. Takes really good angles to the football, often times beating blockers to the spot. A good coverage linebacker, bringing his former safety experience into play, with good mirror abilities in man-coverage situations. A physical guy who shows the ability to set the edge and maintain a solid anchor at the point of attack.

Weaknesses: A bit slow to recognize things post-snap, showing some hesitancy in reaction time. Struggles tackling in too much space, failing to utilize his full wingspan to make tackles outside of his frame. Lacks ideal length and it can get exposed in run support, as he fails to disengage and shed blockers. Can be a bit upright in space, lacking ideal change of direction when crossing field. Tore his ACL in back to back seasons in college and it shows with his long-speed and overall athleticism having taken a toll.

Best Fit: SAM or WILL linebacker in a 4-3

Player Ranking (1-100): 63.9 – I really like Tranquill as a prospect if his medical checks out OK. He's a better than average athlete and he possesses some good traits, including his blitzing ability and his physicality, despite being a bit undersized. His experience as a defensive back certainly will help his value, showing impressive man-coverage experience. 6th round player.

14. Jordan Jones OLB Kentucky 6'1 221 lbs

Strengths: Jones is a 4-year contributor for the Wildcats who has been a valuable piece for their defense playing in the heart of the defense as a middle linebacker. He's a super aggressive guy who plays with nonstop aggression and motor, always running full speed. An effective blitzer who times his rushes to perfection, frequently getting home. Shows good awareness pre-snap, quickly diagnosing and reading/reacting. Plays with a natural pad level, showing good bend to be able to get through narrow gaps when rushing the QB.

Weaknesses: Jones is an injury-prone guy who has had nagging and different concerns in every season at Kentucky. Has had some disciplinary concerns with some terrible personal foul issues. Misses a lot of tackles, and is frequently an ankle biter when trying to tackle. Reliant on upper-body power to drag guys down, rather than forcefully drive them down with his lower body. Has some tightness in his core and lower-body, causing him to struggle when playing sideline to sideline and changing direction. Despite his lack of size, he isn't a great athlete. Takes overly aggressive paths to the ball, leading to poor pursuit angles and missed tackles. Gets caught in traffic and stuck on blocks, rarely finding a way off or through.

Best Fit: WILL linebacker in a 4-3

Player Ranking (1-100): 53.4 – Jones is a relentless athlete who plays with a mean streak and aggression level that teammates love. He has major concerns as a player but is worth a flyer as an undrafted free agent.

15. Chase Hansen OLB Utah 6'3 230 lbs

Strengths: Hansen is a senior linebacker for Utah who has had an interesting college career, to say the least. He has bounced around from QB to defensive back to linebacker. Possessing a long and lean frame with good length, Hansen is an ideal sub-package linebacker at the next level. His only year playing linebacker, he had 114 tackles, 5 sacks, and 2 interceptions. At outstanding blitzer, Hansen shows a real knack for timing the snap count and finding open gaps. In coverage, Hansen shows his defensive back background, playing with outstanding situational and ball awareness. A smart guy who plays with a very high football IQ. Hansen is a downhill, heat-seeking missile always looking to make an explosive collision. A high-motor guy who brings it on every snap. Good initial quickness out of his stance, showing the ability to play sideline to sideline. Shows some play-recognition pre-snap quickly reading and diagnosing screens. Shows some ability in man-coverage responsibility, despite his limited experience.

Weaknesses: Limited experience as a linebacker, only 1 year of starting experience. An older prospect who will be a 26-year-old rookie. His overaggressive style of play leads to too many false steps and poor pursuit angles. An upright tackler, far too often bouncing off runners. Gets enveloped by blockers, failing to shed in the run game. A thinner-framed guy who might be limited to a WILL role only, making him systematically dependent. An average athlete, lacking great change of direction or long-speed to run plays down. Late to respond to things, showing some hesitancy and a slow mental processor.

Best Fit: Special Teams' and WILL linebacker in a 4-3

Player Ranking (1-100): 52.8 – Hansen is a developmental type of player who unfortunately has changed positions far too often. Couple that with the fact that he's already 25 and will be 26 in a couple of months, selling the player is very hard. He isn't a great athlete, nor is he a proven commodity in any aspect of the game.

Outside Linebackers Top-10 Rankings

1. Vosean Joseph
2. Josiah Tauaefa
3. Kendall Joseph
4. Ulysees Gilbert III
5. Terrill Hanks
6. Germaine Pratt
7. Otaro Alaka
8. David Long Jr
9. Bobby Okereke
10. Ben Burr-Kirven

Chapter 13

Cornerbacks

1. Amani Oruwariye CB Penn State 6'2 204 lbs

Strengths: Oruwariye possesses outstanding size and strength for the position. Really physical player who dominates and out muscles receivers when the balls in-flight showing the ability to high point and box out. Utilizes his long arms and strong hands to knock the ball out upon arrival. Disciplined in his assignment and completely in control, never falling for double moves or making an incorrect step. Good athlete who runs and accelerates fluidly sticking to the hip pocket of his assignment. Excellent secondary burst showing the ability to close quickly on the ball. A physical kid who fights through blocks in the run game. A schematically-versatile kid who has experience playing in off-man, zone coverage, or press-man. Reliable wrap-up tackler who shows little hesitancy in the hole or on the perimeter. Rare to see a bigger corner like Oruwariye that displays the looseness and agility in his hips to play as a slot corner, but he can. Impressive ball production with 3 interceptions and 11 passes deflected as a senior. 4 interceptions his junior year as well despite not starting. Impressive balance and coordination at the top of routes. Excels at play-recognition and awareness frequently jumping routes. Shows the ability to use his hands at the line of scrimmage to alter, misdirect and disrupt receivers' routes. Shows the capability to be used in blitz situations and reach home.

Weaknesses: Despite being a 5-year senior, Oruwariye only has started 1 season (senior) since being there. The interview process with his coaches will be interesting to find out 'why.' A little bit of an older prospect who is already 23. Can sometimes take bad angles to the football when in pursuit.

Best Fit: Outside corner in any scheme

Player Ranking (1-100): 90.2 – An outstanding prospect who has little in the way of negatives. Possesses the size, athleticism, movement skills, toughness and physicality teams are looking for. I would just be interested to know why Nittany Lions coaches didn't use him earlier in his career, what were there concerns? He's going to be a top notch # 1 CB at the next level. 1st round player.

2. Byron Murphy CB Washington 5'11 182 lbs

Strengths: Murphy is a 1-year starter for the Huskies who has declared as a redshirt sophomore and will only be 21 years old his rookie season in the NFL. Murphy has had tremendous ball production with 4 interceptions, 1 forced fumble and 13 passes defended in his final season. Murphy is physical and aggressive in run-support showing the ability to fight through blocks and quickly shed blockers to make the tackle. Equally comfortable in the slot, off-man, zone, and press-man. Murphy displays tremendous awareness of route recognition and awareness pre-snap, reading keys and utilizing his excellent diagnostic abilities to disrupt plays immediately. Outstanding on a vertical plain, knowing how to utilize boundaries, angling his body to cut off lateral routes. Aggressive at the catch point, fully utilizing his length, toughness, physicality and strong hands to make almost everything contested. Mentally-alert, always playing on the balls of his feet showing the flexible joints to change direction and accelerate and close quickly. Top notch short-area bursts coupled with very good long speed to quickly recover if he takes any false steps. Completely comfortable transferring weight to smoothly open up his hips and turning and running without gearing down. Plays the game with excellent football IQ and awareness, understanding route concepts down the field, smoothly and effectively coming off his guy to make plays in the run game or against an uncovered receiver. An instinctual blitzer who understands how to time it properly to disrupt the QB. A physical presence who is not afraid to lay the wood, utilizing his short-area bursts to deliver knock out blows.

Weaknesses: 1 full year of starting experience, although he did start some freshman games. I've noticed he can have some balance issues against savvy route-runners who run effective lateral routes, conceding some separation at the top of routes. A slighter-built guy with an average NFL corner frame, lacking ideal bulk and height.

Best Fit: Can play in any defensive scheme due to his coverage ability and tackling

Player Ranking (1-100): 88.3 – Murphy is a 1st round player, there's no doubt about that. His coverage skills are exceptional, showing elite movement and mirror ability at all levels of a route, in addition to excellent ball skills. He makes receivers compete for everything. He still needs more time and experience considering he's only started in 1 full season, but his potential is through the roof. I would imagine he might have some growing pains due to his lack of experience, but he could end up being a top # 1 corner for a team in a year or two.

3. Deandre Baker CB Georgia 5'11 183 lbs

Strengths: Baker is an extremely productive 3-year starter at corner for the Bulldogs. Baker is an intelligent kid who has a good understanding of the game, quickly reading and diagnosing plays pre-snap. He plays with excellent instincts and awareness, getting good reads on the ball and quickly recovering any lost steps. He really does an impressive job of releasing and closing quickly on the ball mid-flight to get his hands on the ball. Does a nice job of utilizing his feet and angles to cut off inside access on slants and underneath routes. Plays far bigger than his size, showing toughness and physicality to assist and help out in the run game. Is never satisfied and is a tireless worker in all facets of the game, always running and putting himself in position to be near the ball carrier. Has experience playing in all kinds of different defensive systems, including press man, zone, and bump-and-run coverages. Plays with really strong hands capable of pulling and ripping the ball out. Understands how to play the position, showing a nice ability to utilize the sidelines to shorten the field and cut off routes on receivers. Patient cover guy, rarely playing too aggressive on routes. Shows good closing burst after sometimes getting beaten initially.

Weaknesses: Will not impress in the athletic aspects of the game. Lacks ideal height, length or straight-line speed. A slightly above-average athlete who can sometimes get beaten initially off the line of scrimmage granting some spacing for receivers. Can get far too physical with his hands and arms down the field getting too grabby. At the next level will be prone to pass interference and holding calls downfield. Despite his smaller stature he doesn't have outstanding elasticity or bend in his hips, allowing shorter and shiftier receivers some separation. This will prevent him from being an ideal inside slot player. Can get turned around a bit by good route runners. Not a great man-to-man corner as he really struggles when he fails to engage at the line of scrimmage.

Best Fit: Zone-based corner who can use his instincts to play on the outside.

Player Ranking (1-100): 84.6 – Not as huge a fan as some are of the player. He's a solid corner but isn't truly an elite shutdown type of player. He's a cross between Morris Claiborne and Tre'Davious White. Shows a good feel for the game and plays with excellent positional awareness. That coupled with the fact that he's a physical guy who isn't afraid to tackle makes him an ideal zone-based outside corner. Worth a 2nd round pick.

4. Rock Ya-Sin CB Temple 6'0 189 lbs

Strengths: Ya-Sin moved and transferred to Temple prior to his senior season after his former school Presbyterian dropped their football program. Ya-Sin possesses a good overall frame with a good wingspan, showing the ability to utilize his full extension while playing and competing at the catch point. Highly competitive at the catch point, literally competing and fighting for everything thrown in his vicinity! Ya-Sin wins a good majority of the 50/50 balls showing outstanding timing and high-point ability. A quick-footed athlete who shows fluidness in his backpedal, remaining mentally alert perfectly mirroring on vertical or horizontal routes. His fluidity is evident in his ability to smoothly transfer weight and open/drop his hips without gearing down. An explosive athlete who possesses outstanding long-speed and the secondary burst to quickly recover any lost steps. A mentally-alert guy, he plays with outstanding play-recognition to beat receivers to the spot of the ball.

Weaknesses: Played against weaker competition and very little NFL caliber receivers. Ya-Sin frequently fails to get his head turned around when the ball is in mid-flight, which will lead to some pass interference calls at the next level. His overly aggressive style can make him prone to play-action and misdirection style of play. His aggressive pursuit can also lead to some poor pursuit angles in the run game. A bit of a lankier frame guy who should continue to put on additional muscle mass without losing his explosive traits.

Best Fit: Press-man corner

Player Ranking (1-100): 84.2 – Absolutely love this kid. His movement skills and fluidity are outstanding. He's going to need time to adjust to NFL level of athletes, but he really impressed when going up against Anthony Johnson this year. He's perfect for a man-cover scheme where he can match up and cover against all routes. He shows the movement skills and athleticism to eventually play on an island at the next level. 2nd round player.

5. Greedy Williams CB LSU 6'2 185 lbs

Strengths: Williams is a supremely talented and twitchy redshirt sophomore for the Tigers who will only be 21 years old his rookie season. Williams is built with impressive height and length, exactly what teams are coveting for their corners. Despite his height, Williams isn't strictly an outside corner. His fluidity, agility and horizontal movement skills rival that of a 5'9 slot corner. Impressive ball production skills his freshman season with 6 interceptions, his numbers dropped as sophomore mostly because teams weren't throwing in his direction. Williams is the ultimate competitor, showcasing the fearlessness you want in a corner. A mentally alert guy who plays with self-assured confidence. Isn't afraid to get right up on guys at the line of scrimmage and play bump-and-run. Versatile, showcasing abilities in the slot, press-man, or in off-man coverage schemes. A quick-footed guy who mirrors with ease, showing impressive cover awareness and range in coverage. An instinctive player who plays with outstanding route anticipation and closing quickness. Overall a really good athlete who is even an effective blitzer.

Weaknesses: Williams is slight, and I mean really slight. He came to LSU as a 155 lb kid, and despite gaining muscle he still plays a bit passive in run support. He's a classic ankle biter in run support, frequently jumping at the feet of runners, missing a lot of tackles. Plays a bit flat-footed pre-snap. Other discernible balance issues with his footwork, both at the line of scrimmage and at the top of routes, allowing some separation. Has a bad habit of grabbing when panicked. His over-aggressive style can lead to incorrect guesses and poor pursuit angles when tracking the football. Fails to always get his head turned around when the ball is in flight.

Best Fit: Man-to-man defensive system who can utilize his ability to mirror

Player Ranking (1-100): 83.7 – Williams to me is a bit of an overrated player. Yes, he's talented and has upside but his downsides are very troubling. His slight frame, hesitancy and lack of ability in run support, and balance concerns in coverage make me worried. He's young and will absolutely get better but he's not a 1st rounder in my opinion. A 2nd round player who needs to be given time.

6. Chauncey Gardner-Johnson CB Florida 6'0 207 lbs

Strengths: Gardner-Johnson is an impressive prospect out of Florida who has transitioned from safety to nickel his junior season. Built with compactness and toughness throughout his frame, Gardner-Johnson displays the body type and physicality to play as a safety or corner. A fiery and competitive kid, he is the definition of a 'talker,' but also backs it up with his play on most occasions. The kid just loves playing football and it is obvious and infectious in his style of play. Smart kid who has a knack for being around the football at all times, getting good jumps on blitzes and often getting home, with 3 sacks his junior year. Smooth back peddler coming out of his stance, quickly flipping his hips and changing direction. Outstanding athlete who possesses the ability to out jump bigger receivers and knock the ball away at the high point. Good anticipatory skills getting a good read and jump on the ball pre-throw. Has the closing speed to deliver big blows to ball carriers, or quickly jump the route. Outstanding open-field ability with the ball in his hands and it's clear on his interception returns.

Weaknesses: As a safety, he really struggled consistently bringing ball carriers down in the open field, missing a lot of tackles. Takes some bad angles to the football when playing against the run. Can get grabby down the field when covering in 1 on 1 situations, which would result in holding calls at the next level. Strictly a nickel back or a slot player at this point, with no experience playing on the outside. Has bounced around from safety to corner a few times during his career, and lacks consistency playing in 1 position. Overaggressive style of play which can lead to bad 'misses' in open space.

Best Fit: Nickel corner or a hybrid type of FS who can cover

Player Ranking (1-100): 83.0 – Chauncey Gardner is a really impressive football player who displays the physicality, toughness, awareness, and athleticism to exceed at the next level. Plus, he loves football. The key is deciding what position he plays best. I personally feel it's the nickel spot he played for Florida this past season as a junior. But limiting him to just a slot player is a mistake, this kid can do everything. 2nd round player.

7. Julian Love CB Notre Dame 5'11 193 lbs

Strengths: A 2-year full-time starter for the Irish who possesses an athletic and leanly-built frame, possessing little body fat. Despite Love's smaller size, he plays far bigger than his listed size. One example of this is in his willingness in run-support. An impressive tackler who has posted 60+ tackles in each of his 2 years of starting. Love is a terrific short-area athlete, displaying elite click/close ability. A quick-footed guy who sinks in his stance and remains controlled and disciplined. Utilizes his agility and movement skills to perfectly mirror down the field, remaining on the hip pocket of receivers. Remains on the balls of his feet, showing the innate ability to time the ball perfectly down the field, trusting his eyes all the way. An explosive athlete who shows physicality at the catch point, making every throw his way a contested one. Is at his best when he can showcase his instincts in off-man coverage.

Weaknesses: Love lacks the ideal height and length for a lot of defensive schemes at the next level. Despite his toughness, he will get absolutely blown backwards in run support by wide receivers, lacking the strength at the point of attack. A quick but not especially fast athlete, he lacks elite top-end speed to recover lost steps in a linear path. His lack of size is evident in red-zone situations, getting boxed out by bigger receivers. When in press-man coverage, he fails to always utilize his hands effectively at the line of scrimmage to redirect. Despite his short-area movement ability, Love has very little experience playing in the slot. Inconsistent footwork at all levels, taking far too many steps, leading to space being given at the top of routes.

Best Fit: Outside corner

Player Ranking (1-100): 82.5 – A good overall player, but not an elite corner. Lacks that "ONE TRAIT" that makes you think he has a huge ceiling to continue to grow. He's a good overall cover guy, but isn't a great athlete. I think he can be a solid starting corner, but never an elite type of guy. 2nd round player.

8. Saivion Smith CB Alabama 6'1 200 lbs

Strengths: Smith is a 1-year starter for the Tide who has had a really interesting career thus far. A former 5-

star recruit for LSU before transferring to community college, and then playing his final season at Alabama. Smith only played 1 season for the Tide, having an impressive season with 60 tackles, 5 pass breakups, 3 interceptions, and a forced fumble. Built with an outstanding frame, showing the length and size defenses are looking for. Smith is a physical 'rough you up' corner who is aggressive at the line of scrimmage, using good jam technique and strong hands to redirect. A good boundary corner who understands how to utilize the sidelines to cut off and close one side of the field. Smith is a flexible mover, showing fluidity and loose hips in his movements to change direction without gearing down. A gifted athlete who possesses rare burst, body control and reflexes. A finisher in the run game, showing the ability to drop his pads and take out ball carriers. Plays with mental confidence and swagger, frequently playing on an island in loads of space.

Weaknesses: Smith is indecisive at the line of scrimmage, failing to always displace at the line of scrimmage, or overreaching leading to him getting beaten over the top. Minimal starting experience and is a bit of a raw player. Needs to clean up his footwork at all levels of routes.

Best Fit: Press-man corner

Player Ranking (1-100): 81.9 – Smith is one of the gems in this draft class. Rare to find a guy who has the size, strength and overall movement skills of Smith. While he is RAW in every sense of the word and needs additional experience, few players in this draft class have the raw talent as Smith does. He's a 2nd round player with a HUGE ceiling.

9. Joejuan Williams CB Vanderbilt 6'2 208 lbs

Strengths: Williams is a 2-year starter for the Commodores who had a really impressive final season, and was 2nd in the SEC in interceptions with 4, and had 61 tackles. Williams is built with prototypical NFL size and length. Williams is comfortable in zone, off-man and in press-man, but is best used at the next level in press-man. When playing press-man, Williams shows good jam technique to disrupt and redirect at the line of scrimmage. Contests almost every ball, and is extremely physical at the catch point with strong hands to disrupt. Despite his large frame, Williams shows the agility and lateral quickness of a 5'9 slot corner. A mentally-alert guy who plays with swagger and self-assured confidence. Possesses good mirroring ability to stay on the hip pocket of receivers. A disciplined guy in coverage who has a good understanding of route concepts. Rarely falls for double-moves or misdirection type of plays. As a tackler, Williams is adept, showing good reliability. He always swipes at the ball, attempting to rip the ball out.

Weaknesses: Williams needs to do a better job of playing the ball when his back is turned and fails to get his head turned around before the ball arrives. Can sometimes get very handsy down the field, which would get called as holding at the next level. Would like to see him utilize his length and size more in run-support, getting stuck on too many blocks in space. Can struggle a bit against smaller, shiftier route-runners who can get him caught off-balance on in-breaking routes. Not always engaged against weaker competition, was at his best against the top-tier competition. Not a great straight-line athlete.

Best Fit: Press-man corner in a man-to-man defensive system

Player Ranking (1-100): 80.1 – Joejuan Williams is a highly intelligent and gifted corner who possesses rare size for a corner. His battles against the Ole Miss receivers this past season were outstanding! They took turns winning their share of snaps, but Williams still impressed thoroughly. He's a competitive and highly physical guy who plays with swagger. He's not a top-tier athlete, but he isn't a slouch either. He's worth a 2nd round pick.

10. Sean Bunting CB Central Michigan 6'1 181 lbs

Strengths: Bunting is a 4th year junior who has had a really impressive career for the Chippewas. An absolute production machine and ball magnet throughout his years in college, forcing 2 fumbles and creating 9 interceptions. Bunting possesses outstanding length and ball skills. Rare key and diagnostic skills with outstanding reactionary ability. Good athlete who shows both the short-area and closing bursts to make plays on the football and also the long-speed to play on an island by himself in man coverage. Really aggressive jam technique, outmuscling smaller receivers at the line of scrimmage. Flexible joints to change direction and accelerate fluidly. Impressive lower-body explosive traits, showing good leaping ability. Possesses good timing and anticipation to jump routes. Can play on an island and is outstanding in mirror coverage, staying on the hip pocket of his assignment at all areas. Comfortable in zone as well, utilizing his instincts and eyes to read the field and anticipate.

Weaknesses: Can be overaggressive at the line of scrimmage with his hands, leading to getting outmuscled by bigger, stronger receivers. It also results in some grabbing and holding calls. Not aggressive enough in run support, showing some hesitancy and not fighting through blocks. Lacked elite competition in college, rarely playing against NFL quality receivers.

Best Fit: Either defensive system, I prefer in man-coverage due to his mirror ability and loose hips. His tackling concerns would be too noticeable in zone.

Player Ranking (1-100): 79.1 – Outstanding athlete who has barely cracked the ceiling of his potential. His size, length, and movement skills will make him extremely attractive to teams. This kid is going to be a good 3rd round player.

11. Jamel Dean CB Auburn 6'2 208 lbs

Strengths: Dean is a 2-year starter for the Tigers who possesses outstanding size and length. Built with a power-packed frame, showing physicality and toughness throughout. Had good ball production his final season at Auburn as a junior with 9 passes defended and 2 interceptions. Sinks in his stance, staying on the ball of his feet remaining under control. A physical corner who shows good hand usage at the line of scrimmage to disrupt and redirect routes. At his best when he's in off-man, showing outstanding mirror ability with easy movement skills. Aggressive at the catch point, showing strong hands and good body control to compete mid-flight. An experienced blitzer, he shows good instincts and timing. Utilizes his length effectively to disrupt at all levels. Disciplined in his assignment, showing good route-recognition rarely allowing a completed pass farther than 10 yards. Smooth in transition, showing smoothness and flexibility in his hips/core to easily change direction.

Weaknesses: Has had multiple knee surgeries and issues in high school and in his freshman year of college, causing him to miss his entire freshman year. Was declared medically ineligible by Ohio State team doctors after originally declaring for the Buckeyes. Not a speed maven, can struggle a bit on a vertical plain against top-tier athletes. Has a tendency to get overly handsy down the field, leading to some pass interference calls. Very little experience in zone coverage. Would like to see him be more aggressive in run situations, far too often he's passive and away from the ball.

Best Fit: Man-coverage corner

Player Ranking (1-100): 77.9 – The biggest question mark with Dean is going to be his injury history. He's had multiple knee surgeries now, and it might scare some teams away. If it checks out OK, he's a really good cover guy. A bit reminiscent of his former teammate Carlton Davis. He isn't quite as physical as Davis, but he's got better ball skills than Davis. 3rd round player.

12. Iman Marshall CB USC 6'1 203 lbs

Strengths: Marshall possesses the long, stout and muscled up physique defensive coaches are looking for at the next level. He has a ton of experience in all kinds of defense, from press man to off-coverage to zone coverage. He does a really nice job of playing physical with receivers and not giving them free access out of their routes. He shows the fluidity to play zone, quickly reacting and diagnosing. Keeps his body low to the ground with knees bent always looking to play on the balls of his feet. Shows flexible joints to be able to change direction and accelerate smoothly and quickly. Aggressive in run support, willing to come into the box to make the tackle. Does a nice job of utilizing the sidelines and cutting off routes against receivers. A 4-year starter who started immediately as a freshman, and has a lot of experience and played in a lot of big-time games against big-time receivers. Aggressive and physical, not afraid of laying the wood and delivering a big hit.

Weaknesses: Needs to utilize his size better at the catch point, allows himself to get boxed out against bigger receivers. Inconsistent ball skills, sometimes he's great, but a lot of times he fails to get his head turned around to even make a play on the ball. Had 0 interceptions his final two years at USC, some will attribute that to teams not throwing in his direction. His aggressive and physical style causes him to get some pass interference calls, as he has the tendency to get handsy. Inconsistent tackler who misses quite a few tackles due to poor technique. Struggles when he fails to get his hands on receivers at the beginning of their route. Good athlete as a whole, but doesn't have great closing speed if initially beaten.

Best Fit: Can play anywhere but I like him best in zone coverage.

Player Ranking (1-100): 75.2 – Marshall possesses most of the traits teams are looking for. Tough, physical, willing, aggressive and above average athlete. He's versatile and can play in a lot of different spots for teams. He's worth an early 3rd round pick.

13. Isaiah Johnson CB/FS Houston 6'2 207 lbs

Strengths: Johnson is a long and rangy-built corner who was a former wide receiver, and has only played corner the last 2 seasons. An aggressive athlete, he shows physicality and fearlessness in his style of play. A magnet to the ball, possessing good cover awareness with the ability to play as a deep-playing zone corner or a ball-hawking free safety. Possesses really good deep-speed showing the range to cover up the field vertical routes and quickly make-up ground on any lost steps in coverage. Johnson possesses rare fluidity and movement skills for a 6'4 corner, showing the ability to match up against bigger receivers or the flexibility to cover shiftier, quicker receivers. Hyper-aggressive in run support, showing very little hesitation when it comes to assisting in run support and fighting through blockers. Plays with self-assured confidence in both press-man and in off-coverage. A tireless work ethic who plays with a relentless motor.

Weaknesses: Johnson has a wiry and lanky frame lacking ideal body armor to assist in the run game. A raw athlete who is still learning and developing the nuances of playing in coverage, most notably his footwork. Shows some erratic footwork, failing to remain on the balls of his feet and losing his balance at multiple points of a route. Has some slot experience but his experience is mostly limited to playing on a vertical plain, rarely having to cover inside routes. Can be a bit slow to react to things, showing lapses in concentration, causing slow reaction times. Over-aggressive when playing in press-man looking to strike a devastating blow at the line of scrimmage instead of just redirecting.

Best Fit: Cover-2 or Cover-3 corner

Player Ranking (1-100): 74.3 – An awesome athlete with excellent size, Johnson's potential is through the roof. The question is, how long is it going to take him to be NFL ready. 1 year, 2 years, 3 years? It's not going to be immediate for him. A good team should draft him and develop him. Has the potential to be a top-5 corner in this class. 4th round player.

14. Michael Jackson CB Miami 6'0 200 lbs

Strengths: Jackson is a well-built corner who displays prototypical NFL corner size with long limbs and good length. Shows the physicality at the line of scrimmage to bully and outmuscle smaller receivers. Really good react ability with outstanding route recognition to quickly close and make a play on the ball. Does a nice job of competing against receivers every step of the way, especially at the catch point. Shows the ability to track the ball really well down the field with outstanding ball skills. Plays the ball like a receiver with his ability to high point the ball and knock it away. Really good athlete showing the fluidity in his movements and the long speed to keep up with speedy receivers. A mentally alert guy who plays with self-assured confidence. Good length to be able to contort his body in space to knock down the ball.

Weaknesses: Lacks experience and is a 1-year starter. Has an overaggressive gambler-style of play which leads to him biting on fakes and misdirection style of plays. Struggles if initially beaten and doesn't get a good jam at the line of scrimmage.

Best Fit: Press-man corner

Player Ranking (1-100): 73.1 – Jackson is a talented kid who has the length and the athleticism to thrive at the next level. Needs time to continue to gain more experience, but certainly displays the confidence and swagger. 4th round player.

15. Trayvon Mullen CB Clemson 6'2 190 lbs

Strengths: Mullen is a tall, rangy outside corner for the Tigers who has started in each of the past 2 seasons. Mullen's career is especially memorable for his tremendous final game in the championship against Alabama with an interception and a critical sack. Mullen thrives and is at his best when he has the opportunity to play press-man on the outside. He utilizes his length to disrupt and redirect at the line of scrimmage, altering routes. His length also comes in handy when he gets beaten initially, showing the ability to extend and use his arms to help make up for lost ground in coverage. Mullen keeps his eyes in the backfield, quickly reading and diagnosing pre-snap. This allows him to be an effective blitzer, timing it perfectly. Plays bigger than his size, showing toughness and physicality against receivers, both in the run game as well as outmuscling on contested throws. A deep-speed guy who rarely grants any separation on a vertical plain. Times and anticipates the ball well, displaying an ability to get a good jump and break up the play.

Weaknesses: Would like to see him put on a bit more muscle. He has a bit of a lankier frame, lacking ideal width to compete against next-level outside targets consistently. Mullen struggles when having to play on a horizontal plain, failing to have the looseness in his hips or the agility to change directions fluidly. Has a tendency to get far too handsy down the field, grabbing when panicked. Flashes some ball skills at times, but his overall ball production is minimal, totaling only 1 interception and 3 passes defended in his final season. Tends to be a drag down tackler as opposed to a forceful tackler, failing to engage his lower body. Struggles when playing off-man, failing to have the short-area burst to close quick enough on the ball before the catch arrives.

Best Fit: Outside press-man corner

Player Ranking (1-100): 72.9 – Mullen is a 4th round player with loads of experience in big-time games. He's at his best when he is covering big, possession type receivers who attempt to beat him on vertical routes. When asked to cover too much ground on an island or have to run laterally, he really struggles, granting far too much separation. I think he can continue to develop but his stiffness, flexibility, and lack of short-area quickness will cause him to struggle a bit at the next level. #3 or #4 corner for a team.

16. Jordan Brown CB South Dakota State 6'1 199 lbs

Strengths: Brown is a 3-year starter and team captain for FCS South Dakota State, he has had really impressive ball production during his career with 21 passes defended, 6 interceptions and 4 forced fumbles. Brown possesses an NFL physique, with long arms and good overall weight distribution. Brown offers upside and experience as a return specialist. Brown is a twitchy athlete who is at his best in off-man coverage, utilizing his ability to click and close. A former track star, Brown is an outstanding athlete who shows tremendous closing ability to regain any lost steps. His quick reflexes and mental processing ability is rare, closing down and rapidly taking away passing windows. Fluid in all aspects, Brown shows looseness in his hips and the ability to mirror and remain in the hip pocket of receivers in man. Impressive ball skills, he is a magnet to the football with innate timing ability. When playing in press-man, shows good hand placement and physicality at the line of scrimmage.

Weaknesses: Brown is a bit of a liability in run-support, taking some poor routes to the football. He allows his pads to rise in the run game, playing far too upright, seemingly disinterested in the physical parts of the game. If he does make contact in run-support, he hangs on for dear life or bounces off. Has played against FCS competition, failing to compete against NFL quality opposition. Limited experience with zone concepts or playing inside. Tends to play on a vertical plain, rarely having to cover lateral routes.

Best Fit: Outside man-cover corner

Player Ranking (1-100): 72.2 – Brown impressed me quite a bit. Quarterbacks tended to avoid his side of the field in his final season because he was clearly the best athlete on the football field. He's a bit of a developmental guy who will need time adjusting to NFL speed, but he's got the fluidity and the pure athleticism to be an NFL starter at some point. 4th round player.

17. Kris Boyd CB Texas 5'11 195 lbs

Strengths: Boyd is a well-built corner with above average size who has shown improvement in each of his seasons. He's an ultra-competitive guy who plays with fire and feistiness. Outstanding in coverage, rarely leaving the receivers hip pocket. Does an awesome job of tracking the ball in the air to go up and play the ball like a receiver. Tough run defender, showing the aggression, willingness, and sound tackling fundamentals. Offers experience on special teams as well and has been the Longhorns primary kickoff return specialist. Versatile cover guy, showing the ability to play in the slot and on the outside. Plays with awareness and instincts, having a good read of what's going on around him. Has a real feel to time his blitzes and get to the QB in an instant. Good athlete, he shows above-average long speed to cover vertical routes, while also displaying tremendous agility and short area quickness to cover horizontal routes. Understands how to leverage routes and play the sidelines, cutting off routes and pinning receivers.

Weaknesses: Boyd lacks prototypical size and length to play as an outside corner at the next level for some teams. Has little ball production with 0 interceptions as a senior and only 3 in his career, despite playing all 4 seasons and in over 40 games. Has some balance concerns, getting caught off balance at the top of routes. Overaggressive nature leading to some incorrect guesses and making him vulnerable to play-action and play fakes. Needs to do a better job of getting his head turned around, affecting his ability to make plays on the ball. Will get called for PI penalties quite a bit at the next level if he doesn't correct this.

Best Fit: Played in a Cover-2 in college and would best be suited in a zone-coverage defense

Player Ranking (1-100): 71.7 – Boyd is a really solid all-around cover corner who displays the coverage ability and the toughness to be a good next-level player. Will compete for snaps early on at the next level. 4th round player.

18. Lonnie Johnson Jr CB Kentucky 6'2 210 lbs

Strengths: Johnson is a 2-year starter for the Wildcats who came onto the scene a few games into his junior year. Built with NFL size, length, and toughness, Johnson shows impressive physical traits and makeup. Johnson is one of the best special teams' players on the Wildcats, offering value in that area at the next level. Johnson is a great and explosive athlete, having been one of the best track & field athletes in high school in the state. His size allows him to run downfield with elite receivers on vertical routes, limiting separation. Johnson has experience in off-man and press-man in college. Johnson stays bent at the knees, maintaining good leverage while inching closer to the line of scrimmage despite his large frame. Johnson shows the ability to compete at the catch point, showing physicality at all levels. Utilizes his length down the field, limiting separation for receivers and forcing QB's into tight window throws.

Weaknesses: When playing in man-coverage, Johnson really struggles with jam consistent technique at the line of scrimmage missing far more often than hitting. Very little ball production in college with 0 career interceptions and only 8 career passes defended. Johnson is incredibly raw as a defender lacking lateral quickness/balance in his feet, quickly losing his balance to nuanced route-runners. Lacks the flexibility in his joints to change direction and accelerate fluidly. Lacks great cover and situational awareness, rarely putting himself in position to make a play on the ball.

Best Fit: Developmental press-man

Player Ranking (1-100): 71.0 – Johnson is a developmental type of player who displays good size and overall explosiveness. He needs to learn how to better translate his athleticism into consistency and coverage ability. His tape is just 'OK' and fails to impress in any 1 area. 4th round pick with huge developmental upside.

19. Xavier Crawford CB Central Michigan 6'1 180 lbs

Strengths: Crawford is a 4th-year junior who transferred from Oregon State following his sophomore season. Crawford plays with an aggressive and confident style, frequently getting in the faces of receivers disrupting their routes at the line of scrimmage. Shows good short-area burst and agility to break on underneath routes before receivers. Shows impressive diagnosis ability and cover awareness down the field. Transfers weight to smoothly open up his hips, turning and running without gearing down. Most comfortable in man coverage situations, showing the ability to win inside position and box out receivers to make plays on the ball. A fluid mover in space, showing the ability to mirror and stay in the hip pocket of receivers on horizontal or vertical routes. An instinctual player who understands how/when to time blitzes. A good athlete, he can run with all types of receivers down the field.

Weaknesses: Limited ball production throughout his career with only 2 career college interceptions. Came off a really bad back injury his sophomore season causing him to miss a large percentage of his season. A very slight frame who takes 'business decisions' when it comes to tackling. Would like to see him gain additional functional strength to be able to assist in run support and better fight through blockers. Loses track of the football in the air and lacks the necessary body control to play the ball when his back is toward the QB.

Best Fit: Press-man outside corner

Player Ranking (1-100): 70.8 – A really good cover corner, he displays the footwork and quickness to mirror shifty, quick receivers or up-the-field speed receivers on seam routes. I don't like his hesitancy and disregard for the running game, therefore I wouldn't feel comfortable taking him until the 4th round.

20. Derrick Baity CB Kentucky 6'3 188 lbs

Strengths: A 3-year full-time starter for the Wildcats who has had really solid production in each season. Possessing rare height and length for a corner, Baity holds the size and frame to continue to add additional girth and muscle without sacrificing his athletic ability. Baity is experienced playing in off-man, zone or in press-man coverage. Patient at the line of scrimmage while in press, waiting for precisely the perfect time to engage and redirect. A disciplined corner who rarely falls for misdirection type plays or double moves. Shows impressive overall mirror ability in man-to-man, giving very little cushion on in-breaking routes. Stays balanced at all levels of his routes, sinking in his stance and remaining on the hip pocket of his assignment. His long speed is evident in vertical routes, rarely allowing any separation down the field. Utilizes his length at the catch point to disrupt, making everything contested.

Weaknesses: Despite his ability to mirror, Baity fails to get his head turned around and only possesses marginal ball skills and body control. A lanky framed defender who lacks the girth in his lower body to consistently take on blocks. Rarely in good positions in the run game, looking passive and consistently getting stuck on blocks.

Best Fit: Press-man coverage corner

Player Ranking (1-100): 70.1 – I like Baity and think he has a future at the NFL level. Between his size, his deep speed, and his good man-to-man cover ability, Baity has the ceiling to continue to develop. A 4th round player who should have a role early on.

21. Blace Brown CB Troy 6'0 184 lbs

Strengths: A 3-year starter who was a former wide receiver for Sun Belt conference Troy, he has had tremendous ball production with 12 interceptions and 16 passes defended. A good-sized athlete with long arms, showing the frame to continue adding additional weight/size. Brown is a terrific athlete who shows the ability to go from 0-60 in the blink of an eye. Is at his best in off-man coverage, utilizing his acceleration, instincts, and quickness to quickly close any gaps and time the ball to perfection. Remains disciplined and controlled, reading the QB's throwing motion, rarely biting on double moves. A twitchy mover, who shows fluidity and ease of motion in his hips to quickly change direction. Fearless in run support, showing toughness and the willingness to drop his pads to make impactful hits to bigger backs. A bend but not break CB who will give up underneath throws, but rarely will get beat down the field.

Weaknesses: Brown possesses a lanky-built frame, needing to put on some additional bulk and muscle in his lower body. A bit of a gambler who likes to bait quarterbacks into throwing in his direction, leading to some big plays down the field. Had a bit of a down year, production-wise, mostly due to teams not throwing his way. Strictly has experience in off-man coverage on the outside. Has very little experience in the slot, in

DTP's 2019 NFL DRAFT GUIDE

zone or in press-man coverage. Tore his ACL at the end of his junior season.

Best Fit: Cover-3 corner

Player Ranking (1-100): 69.8 – Brown is a really intriguing prospect with outstanding upside. His athleticism and play-making skills will make him a target for Cover 3 defenses. He's at his best in off-coverage where he can utilize his instincts and downhill style of play to keep balls in front of him. 5th round player.

22. Jordan Wyatt CB SMU 6'0 195 lbs

Strengths: Wyatt is a 4-year starter for the Mustangs who is one of the team leaders for their defense. A true magnet to the ball due to his cover awareness, field vision, and range in coverage. Outstanding at using his hands to rip at the ball, forcing 8 fumbles in his career. Much tougher and more physical than you would expect looking at his frame. A better tackler than you would expect for his size, showing the ability to consistently wrap up runners. Impressive in his ability to play the ball mid-flight, quickly locating and attacking, and then knocking it out at the perfect time. Quick-footed athlete, he has the lower body explosiveness to close quickly, displaying outstanding short-area bursts. An agile guy who shows the ability to easily transfer his weight to smoothly open up his hips and turn and run without gearing down to cover horizontal routes up the field.

Weaknesses: Wyatt has a long and wiry frame, and could stand to gain some additional weight and strength. Tore his ACL after the end of his junior season. A bit of an inconsistent player. Rarely was challenged much in the AAC conference, teams tended to throw away from him. Quicker than fast, I worry about Wyatt's long speed to play on the outside.

Best Fit: Slot/nickel player

Player Ranking (1-100): 69.2 – Wyatt is an explosive athlete who shows good short-area speed and quickness. He wasn't tested by top-level receivers much in college and will have to be dynamic in pre-draft workouts. But he's a natural playmaker and ball magnet. I would take him in the 5th round.

23. Clifton Duck CB Appalachian State 5'10 175 lbs

Strengths: Duck a 3-year starter for Sun Belt Conference Appalachian State, greatly impressed in all 3 seasons. His ball production dropped his final year as a junior, but that was due to teams avoiding throwing to his side of the ball. As a whole, Duck shows tremendous ball skills and body control, frequently getting his head turned around at the perfect time to make a play on the ball. An instinctual guy who remains on the balls of his feet, anticipating and quickly responding to the QB's arm motion. Has experience in off-man, press-man and also in zone. Is at his best when he's playing off-coverage, allowing him to bait the QB into throwing in his direction. Duck is a feisty little corner, he brings it on every snap and plays far bigger than his size would seem to indicate. Especially notable in his aggressiveness and downhill nature when playing the run. Excellent fluidity in his lateral movements, showing the turn/run ability to stay on receivers' hip pockets at all times. Shows outstanding route-recognition, frequently jumping routes. Brings it as a blitzer, showing the ability to utilize his closing bursts to get home.

Weaknesses: Duck is extremely small and lacks ideal length to play as an outside corner at the next level. Gets completely overmatched in the run game when a body gets on him at the 2nd level. His aggressive style of play can lead to some poor tackling attempts, not always taking the best, most acute angles to the football. Quicker than fast, lacks the long-speed to track plays down from behind, or make up lost ground on vertical routes.

Best Fit: Slot corner

Player Ranking (1-100): 68.8 – Duck is a really good athlete who shows quick-twitch and mirroring ability in coverage, especially on lateral-breaking routes. His hip fluidity and change of direction ability could give him a chance to be an effective slot receiver. His lack of size/length will turn him off to many teams, despite his ability, causing him to drop more then he should. He should absolutely get picked in the 5th round, and no later. Duck is a good player.

24. Justin Layne CB Michigan State 6'3 185 lbs

Strengths: Layne is a long and rangy built corner for the Spartans who is a converted WR. Outstanding ball skills showing anticipatory skills and ball tracking ability to find the ball mid-flight and knock it away. Had 15 passes defended this season. His receiver traits are extremely evident in the way he extends, high points and attacks the football in flight always getting his head turned around at the right time. Very young still and will only be a 21-year-old rookie. Rare to see guys that have the height, length, and speed of Layne that play corner. Plays tougher than his size indicates, a willing tackler who shows no hesitancy when attacking the run. Does a nice job of utilizing his long arms and strong hands to time the balls' arrival. Remains disciplined in his assignment, rarely falling for the double move. Shows nice recovery ability to regain any lost steps. Possesses the closing burst to make impact tackles as well as allowing receiver little chance to do anything with the ball in his hands.

Weaknesses: Layne is still a major work in progress, having only played the position for 2 seasons. Despite his ball skills, his lack of production has been very subpar with only 1 interception in each of the last 2 seasons. A very lanky frame, he needs to continue getting stronger to improve his functional strength. Gets stuck playing on his feet far too often at the line of scrimmage, getting caught off-balance on horizontal routes granting far too much separation. Inconsistent physicality in the run game, playing with too high a pad level. Poor pursuit angles to the football affect his ability as a tackler. Has some stiffness in his core and lower body, lacking the elite agility levels to be a mirroring corner. Tends to grab when panicked down the field.

Best Fit: Outside press-man corner

Player Ranking (1-100): 68.0 – Not as huge a fan as others are. His lack of mirroring ability is evident, and he's still a major work in progress. Will need some time, but I don't believe he possesses the traits to be a starting CB in this league. 5th round player.

25. Hamp Cheevers CB Boston College 5'10 180 lbs

Strengths: Cheevers is a 1-year starter for the Eagles who had a tremendous year with 7 interceptions, 7 more passes defended, and 1 forced fumble. Cheevers has experience playing in zone, off-man, and press-man but seems at his best when playing off-man. An instinctual guy who remains on the balls of his feet throughout the play. Reads the quarterback's arm motion and quickly reacts. When in off-man he utilizes his awareness, route recognition, and short-area quickness to close on the ball in the blink of an eye. He loves to bait quarterbacks to throw in his direction by seemingly leaving spacing but then breaks on the ball. A springy mover, Cheevers shows the lower body explosiveness to burst in any direction without losing any built-up speed. Plays with confidence and self-assuredness, remaining mentally alert at all times. Shows the looseness and agility in his hips to cover lateral routes, remaining in the hip pocket of receivers at all times on both vertical/horizontal plains. Elite ball skills with good body control, always attempting to compete at the catch point.

Weaknesses: Cheevers is poor in the running game, showing hesitancy and disinterest when it comes to getting off blocks. Very upright and poor tackler who refuses to keep his pads down, attempting to bring ball carriers down from up top, allowing them additional yards after contact. A slight-built guy, he seems to have skills that translate to the slot corner, but has mostly played as an outside corner in college. Can be overly aggressive against disciplined quarterbacks, always attempting to jump routes. Experienced quarterbacks will use his aggressiveness against him on double moves, etc. Struggles against bigger receivers who can utilize their frames against him and box him out at the catch point. Likes to keep things in front of him at all times, and can struggle in coverage with his back towards the ball.

Best Fit: Off-man coverage corner

Player Ranking (1-100): 67.5 – Cheevers is a really good player with elite ball skills. The problem is, he's a gambler and will absolutely give up some big plays at the next level due to his mindset and mentality to attack the football. The main problem with Cheevers is he's slight and probably won't figure to play in an outside role at the next level, but he has limited inside experience. The other problem is he's a major liability when it comes to tackling, one of the worst tackling defensive backs I've studied this season. Cheevers is a frustrating prospect who has so many positives skills, but so many negative traits as well. I wouldn't take him until the 5th round.

26. David Long CB Michigan 5'11 198 lbs

Strengths: Long is a well-built corner for the Wolverines who has started in each of the past 2 seasons. Long is a physical corner, he is at his best when playing as a press-man corner, getting in the face of receivers and utilizing good hand-technique to disrupt. Plays with good natural leverage ability and initial quickness out of his stance, showing the good overall change of direction with fluid hips. A physical guy in run-support, showing toughness and finish to fight through blocks. Packs lower-body anchoring ability and the upper-body strength to bring down ball carriers with solid fundamentals. Long is a confident corner who trusts his eyes and his physicality to allow him to shadow in space and misdirect receivers at the line of scrimmage.

Weaknesses: Long hasn't had great ball production during his career, with only 1 interception his final season, and 3 during his career. Lacks ideal height/length to play as an outside boundary corner. Has a tendency to get grabby down the field, especially when panicked. Has some balance concerns, granting some separation at the top of routes, getting caught off-balance. Lacks the necessary reflexes and awareness ability to get his hands up and play the ball in the air, reacting far too slowly to the ball. Had some miscommunication/coverage lapses against bunch formations down the field.

Best Fit: Outside press-man corner

Player Ranking (1-100): 66.1 – A physical corner with good overall girth and strength to play at the next level. My concern is he gives up far too much separation against effective and savvy route runners. I don't see him as an elite cover corner and therefore I don't think he will be a starter at the next level. He's going to have to prove he can be a #4 or #5 corner for a team and play special teams effectively. 5th round player.

27. Montre Hartage CB Northwestern 5'11 187 lbs

Strengths: A 3-year starter who started in 37 straight games for Northwestern. Hartage is a playmaker who has had terrific ball production, totaling 9 interceptions and 26 passes defended during his career. Really impressive read/recognition ability in run support, quickly closing and breaking on the ball. A tough player, he shows impressive physicality and toughness when tackling. A mentally alert defender who plays with confidence and swag. Is at his best close to the line of scrimmage where he can utilize his physicality and anticipatory abilities.

Weaknesses: An average athlete with some some deep speed concerns, getting beat on a number of vertical routes during his career. Fails to locate the ball down the field, far too often playing with his back to the ball, minimizing his ability to make a play. Limited movement ability, failing to mirror in space against quicker, shiftier targets.

Best Fit: Zone corner or box safety

Player Ranking (1-100): 62.3 – Hartage has some really nice traits, physicality, ball skills and toughness being 3 of them. He's a limited man-cover corner, and is at his best in zone or when used as a blitzer or an 'in the box' defender. He reads and reacts quickly, showing good football intelligence and short-area quickness. 6th round player.

28. Alijah Holder CB Stanford 6'2 188 lbs

Strengths: Holder is a long and rangy senior CB for the Cardinals who displays impressive physicality and 'WIN' ability at the line of scrimmage. Holder is an outstanding open-field tackler, rarely missing a tackle. Holder is a tough kid who will fight through blocks in the run game and rough up receivers fighting until the whistle. Plays with sound footwork and fluid at the line of scrimmage, rarely losing much ground in coverage at the snap of the ball. Has experience both playing in press-man or off-coverage.

Weaknesses: Has had an injury-plagued career at Stanford missing almost all of 2016 with a shoulder injury and several games in 2017 with a knee injury. Lacks great recovery ability, closing quickness or the long speed down the field to keep up with speedier receivers when playing in too much space. A stiff-hipped player, he struggles when asked to change directions or when covering a tidy route-runner. Is a peaker that likes to play facing the QB at all times, and can quickly lose the receiver behind him. Doesn't trust his athleticism, generally giving up 8-10 yards of cushion pre-snap to avoid getting beat down the field. Rarely does he play the ball in the air or affect the catch point mid-flight.

Best Fit: Outside press corner or might be converted to safety by teams because of his physicality/tackling ability

Player Ranking (1-100): 54.3 – Holder is a tough, physical kid who is likely to be a UDFA due to a lack of movement skills and injury-plagued history.

29. Donnie Lewis Jr CB Tulane 6'0 190 lbs

Strengths: Lewis is a 4-year starter for AAC conference Tulane. Lewis is a competitive corner who does a really nice job of playing routes and fighting every reception. Shows the secondary burst to close cushions and recover after false steps. Sinks his hips and plays on the balls of his feet at all times, Lewis reacts quickly and decisively. Shows the flexibility and coordination to change direction and quickly accelerate. Shows willingness and toughness in the run game, always pursuing and working towards the ball. Excellent route recognition and anticipation.

Weaknesses: Fails to always disrupt at the line of scrimmage, causing him some missteps at times. Lewis is a thinly-built corner, he could use to gain some additional muscle and functional strength. Struggles against bigger bodied receivers who can easily box him out and out muscle him at the catch point. Takes too many short, choppy steps in his backpedal leading to some separation being granted on breaks. Gets manhandled in the run game, easily sustained by most receivers. Balance concerns, conceding far too much separation at the top of routes getting caught off-balance. Might be best suited to play in the slot at the next level, but has little experience doing it.

Best Fit: Slot corner

Player Ranking (1-100): 53.2 – Donnie Lewis Jr is a good athlete with impressive quickness and a closing burst. But he got dominated in some games in the AAC against bigger receivers when playing on the outside. I think he needs to play in the slot and utilize his quickness and agility better. Has a chance to make it as an undrafted free agent.

Cornerbacks Top-10 Rankings

1. Amani Oruwariye
2. Byron Murphy
3. Deandre Baker
4. Rock Ya-Sin
5. Greedy Williams
6. Chauncey Gardner-Johnson
7. Julian Love

8. Saivion Smith
9. Joejuan Williams
10. Sean Bunting

Chapter 14

Safeties

1. Taylor Rapp S Washington 6'0 200 lbs

Strengths: Rapp is a well-built safety with a developed and pro-ready NFL physique. A 3-year starter who has had a tremendous college career, showing excellent ball production numbers with 7 career interceptions, 2 forced fumbles, 6 sacks, 1 defensive touchdown and 6 passes defended. The definition of reliable, having played in all 36 games of his college career. Rapp has played in a variety of roles but mostly played as a single-high safety, completely comfortable in acres of space. An excellent and comfortable blitzer, he shows tremendous timing and closing ability to get home. An extremely physical guy who is always coming downhill, like he's shot out of a cannon, delivering big hits. Not just a 'big hitter', he is also a reliable open-field tackler and is a great last line of defense, securely utilizing the good form to bring down opponents. An instinctual guy who shows very good play-recognition, often times beating receivers/backs to the spot. Takes acute diagnostic angles to the football, almost always in good position. Disciplined eyes, rarely falls for double-moves or misdirection type plays. Doesn't play in a lot of man-coverage situations, but at times he does cover in the slot and shows excellent movement skills with the short-area quickness to stay on the hip pocket of receivers. Stays disciplined in his zone-drops, keeping his eyes up and reading the QB's eyes. A tough, hard-nosed guy who refuses to come off the field, fighting through minor injuries.

Weaknesses: Not a "play-maker" per se, seemingly preferring to play the physical sides of the game then make plays on the ball. A quicker than fast athlete who lacks elite deep-speed to run vertically with the more explosive receivers at the next level. Very little experience in tracking the ball with his back towards the ball almost always is set up to keep things in front of him. Lacks a tremendous amount of experience in coverage situations, rarely being asked to play in man.

Best Fit: I would keep him in the box, despite his single-high experience.

Player Ranking (1-100): 88.2 – I absolutely love Taylor Rapp as a player. While he's not the ball hawk like some of the previous 1st round safeties, he's the physical and reliable presence a defense needs. He possesses good range, anticipatory abilities and play recognition to put himself in good positions on every snap of the ball. While he doesn't make a ton of "game-changing" plays, he's ALWAYS around the football due to his awareness and field vision. He brings so much toughness and discipline to a defense, making so many game-saving tackles in the open-field. He possesses the short-area quickness and movement skills to be good in coverage with more experience. 1st round player.

2. Deionte Thompson S Alabama 6'2 196 lbs

Strengths: Thompson had a tremendous season this year, really coming onto the radar for 1st round discussions, after having 78 tackles, 3 forced fumbles, 2 interceptions, and 6 passes defended. Thompson took over the role as the center-field safety, responsible for covering huge percentages of the field. A downhill safety who plays like he's been shot out of the cannon. A physical presence, he plays bigger than his size, always looking to deliver a big hit. An instinctual athlete who quickly diagnoses and reads/reacts. Excellent flexibility and change of direction to flip his hips and cross the field without gearing down. Outstanding athlete who shows the short-area burst to quickly close, as well as the long-speed, to chase plays down from behind or to shorten the field. Has shown the ability to line up in man coverage in certain games this season, showing an ability to do it comfortably with good fluidity and overall movement skills. Makes every ball in his direction a contested ball, competing at the catch point, utilizing his length and strong hands to knock the ball away. Reads the quarterbacks eyes and throwing motion to time the ball to perfection, breaking on the ball at the precisely perfect moment. Really good hands to finish interceptions, showing the ability to high-point and make contested grabs.

Weaknesses: Thompson is only a 1-year starter, which was this past season. Overly reliant on delivering the wood, and fails to keep his pads down in run support, leading to missed tackles or additional yards after contact. An ankle biter who frequently jumps at ankles or feet in space, showing some hesitancies to take on bigger runners. A bit of a lanky frame with room to put on additional weight, he needs to increase his functional strength. His overaggressive pathways to the ball led him to poor pursuit angles, failing to utilize his length and the sidelines to cut off runs. Started the season in outstanding fashion, but tapered off near the end of the campaign.

Best Fit: Single-high FS

Player Ranking (1-100): 86.5 – Thompson is a 1-year starter who needs to gain some additional functional strength and experience. He plays with a gambler's mindset and is overaggressive at times. But he's no doubt, a gifted athlete who plays with an unbelievable combination of burst, body control, and overall athleticism. He's going to be perfect for a team that will utilize him in loads of space, and he's the best in this draft class at playing single-high with his unique instincts and click/close ability. 1st round player.

3. Mike Edwards S Kentucky 5'11 204 lbs

Strengths: Edwards is a 4-year starter for the Wildcats who has played in almost every game of his career. Edwards possesses impressive size and length, ideal for a next level FS. Really impressive ball production in his career with 10 career interceptions, 23 passes defended and 2 forced fumbles. Not going to WOW anyone with off-the-chart measurables, but he's just a solid, smart football player who plays with discipline. Good blitzer, he finds a way to get home and make a play in the backfield. Aggressive in run support showing the awareness to sniff out misdirection plays. Comfortable in man coverage situations when he has to cover the nickel receiver. Shows some ability to stack/shed against receivers or TE's to fight through blocks and make the tackle. Shows the ability to transfer weight smoothly to open up his hips and turn and run without gearing down. A team leader, coaches rave about his work ethic and intangibles.

Weaknesses: Edwards limits his effectiveness as a tackler by taking wild pursuit angles to the football. Needs to clean up some of his mechanics when breaking down to be a better finisher. A bit inconsistent with his physicality and leverage. Limited experience playing as a deep safety, generally playing in a Cover-2 or as a nickel player. Good athlete, but isn't a great one.

Best Fit: FS or a Dime/Nickel CB

Player Ranking (1-100): 83.9 – Edwards to me is a really, good player who is everything you want in a defender. Smart, disciplined and savvy. Not going to WOW you in the physical areas of the game, but he makes plays in every game I watched and is a true "playmaker." An ideal safety or nickel player who can fulfill alot of roles on defense. Absolutely worth a 2nd round pick. Reminiscent a bit of former 49ers draft pick Jimmy Ward.

4. Darnell Savage Jr S Maryland 5'11 199 lbs

Strengths: Savage is an athletically-built and lean safety who took over halfway through his freshman year as one of the starters at safety. Improved each season at Maryland, displaying an outstanding senior year, showing tremendous ball production. An aggressive guy, he plays with a real feistiness and swagger. Really good athlete who shows impressive movement and flexibility through his midsection and hips. Quick feet and reflexes which allows him to accurately and quickly close on the football. Magnet to the football who always is in a good position, displaying outstanding cover awareness and range. Completely comfortable in off-man or in man coverage situations, showing fluidity, balance, and short-area quickness to disrupt at the catch point. Really acute diagnostic ability, quickly reading and processing the action in front of him.

Weaknesses: Undersized safety who might end up having to move back to a nickel/slot role at the next level which he played his first couple of seasons at Maryland. Lacks the necessary physicality and 'want' when it comes to the running game, looking disinterested at times to play in the box and make stops in the running game. A bit of a reckless, kamikaze style of play which leads to missed assignments and failed assignments. Also takes some very risky paths to the football.

Best Fit: Hybrid safety who can be used in sub- packages as a nickel player

Player Ranking (1-100): 81.1 – Savage is a really good player who can affect the defense in a lot of different facets. His movement/athleticism and range make him a versatile guy who can play either a deep-lying safety or a nickel back. Really love this kids' passion and swag. 2nd round player. His size and lack of length might cause him to drop lower than he should.

5. Nasir Adderley S Delaware 5'11 195 lbs

Strengths: Adderley is an impressive small-school Colonial Athletic Association prospect who possesses prototypical free-safety size. Adderley is the definition of a ball hawk, always finding and locating the football. It shows in his production with 10 career interceptions and 31 career passes defended. A 4-year starter for Delaware, he has experience as a return guy as well, with some big-time returns. Good closing speed, showing good recognition skills and the ability to break quickly on the ball. Reliable open-field tackler who shows fearlessness. Outstanding athlete who possesses quick feet and loose, flexible hips to change direction and play horizontally. A twitchy athlete, he plays downhill utilizing his closing speed to deliver big blows. A chippy guy who plays with a swagger and plays to the whistle every snap. Relentless motor plays all-out on every play. Does a nice job of disguising coverages pre-snap. Has experience playing in a variety of different schemes. Plays mostly Cover-2 but plays some single high and Cover-3 as well. Forceful tackler who plays stronger than his size would indicate.

Weaknesses: Overaggressive style of play which can lead to bad angles to the football in the run game, or getting beat on double moves down the field. Obviously hasn't played against elite competition. Limited experience being used in blitz situations. Has a bit of a reckless, kamikaze style of play.

Best Fit: FS in any defense

Player Ranking (1-100): 80.8 – Adderley is a guy who really impressed me. There are concerns about him competing against elite levels of competition, but he shows the toughness, athleticism, and physicality to do so. I think this kid really has a chance to be a stud at the next level. He should be a 2nd round player but I believe he might actually play above that. A natural football player who plays with rare ball skills and instincts.

6. Marquise Blair S Utah 6'1 180 lbs

Strengths: Blair is a leanly-built safety with good overall size and length. A twitchy athlete who possesses lower body explosiveness to spring in any direction. Stings in run support and reacts without hesitation, maintaining good leverage, showing the ability to take on bigger backs in the hole head-on. Delivers the wood in the run game, displaying outstanding short-area bursts which allow him to utilize his hip torque to make violent collisions in space. A versatile guy, he has played all over the defense, even playing some in the slot. Very aggressive and physical guy who brings toughness to a defense. A sideline to sideline athlete who possesses the ball awareness, reflexes and range to quickly find the ball. An outstanding athlete with the secondary burst and closing speed to recover after false steps. A slippery guy in space who utilizes his high motor and physical makeup to disengage quickly.

Weaknesses: Has had some disciplinary issues during games this season, getting ejected for targeting hits in 2 separate games. Suspect ball skills, he has shown very minimal production in the passing game with only 1 career interception and 4 passes deflected. Has very limited experience in coverage situations, has played mostly in the box as a free-roaming player. Takes some very risky angles to the football, putting him in bad spots to make tackles in space. Has some questionable body control when playing the ball in mid-flight, failing to accurately locate and find the ball with his back to the ball. Has had some knee concerns, including tearing his ligaments in 2017.

Best Fit: Box safety close to the line of scrimmage

Player Ranking (1-100): 79.2 – I really like Marquise Blair, he was a pleasant surprise for me. He's ALWAYS around the football and his ability to be a magnet to the ball is his best attribute. His athleticism and size are also top-notch! While he is raw as a cover safety, his instincts and physicality will garner him valuable snaps as a rookie either on special teams or as a box safety. 3rd round player.

7. Darius West S Kentucky 5'11 207 lbs

Strengths: West is a compactly-built safety who had a really impressive senior season for the Wildcats. Possessing a muscled-up physique, West certainly brings the toughness and swagger to a defense. West is a versatile safety, possessing the size and frame to play as a strong safety, but has the experience in coverage to play a FS role as well. West is physical in every sense of the word, almost always coming downhill. Hyper-aggressive in run support, West shows 0 hesitancy when it comes to filling a hole or squaring up to take on a back head on. West maintains good leverage pre-snap, inching his body toward the line of scrimmage and exploding on the snap. A gifted athlete who shows a good blend of burst, body control and reflexes to play in loads of space as a single high. Shows good situational awareness in zone coverage, remaining disciplined and locking his eyes on the QB at all times.

Weaknesses: Has had an injury-plagued college career, missing 2 full seasons due to bad leg injuries to the same leg. Got ejected for a game this past season for a targeting penalty. A bit of a squattier built guy who lacks ideal length or height, failing to have the ability to tackle outside of his frame.

Best Fit: Single-high FS

Player Ranking (1-100): 78.2 – If West's medical comes out clean, I really like the player. While he isn't an elite athlete nor does he possess great size, he reads things quickly and puts himself in a great position to make plays. Plus, he isn't afraid to really lay the wood in the run game or when a receiver is crossing the middle of the field. Love his downhill, physical nature. 3rd round player.

8. Johnathan Abram S Mississippi State 5'11 205 lbs

Strengths: Abram is a physical, downhill and thumping strong safety, he was a Georgia transfer after his freshman season. Abram really came onto the NFL scene this year after an outstanding senior year, totaling 99 tackles, 9 tackles for loss and 3 sacks. Abram possesses a big, strong and powerful frame showing the ability to withstand the NFL rigors. An effective blitzer with 4.5 career sacks, he understands how to time it properly to get a good jump on the football. Abram is a typical box safety who plays with toughness and swagger. Despite being a box safety, Abram has shown the ability to line up over tight ends and running backs. Outstanding against the run, showing hyper-aggressiveness in run support. Smart kid who plays with discipline and precision in all areas of the game, showing reliability to be in the right place at the right time. Shows the ability to stack/shed in the run game and make the play.

Weaknesses: Has lacked great ball production in college with only 2 career interceptions. Despite being a bigger safety, he attempts to deliver the knock out blow leading to bad form and too many missed tackles. Good athlete but not a great one and lacks the great speed to be used in too many coverage situations at the next level. Takes terrible angles to the ball carrier on far too many occasions, attempting to jump at the legs. Doesn't play with the physicality you would expect for a guy of his size/stature.

Best Fit: Strong-safety and special teams'

Player Ranking (1-100): 77.9 – A good player but I'm not as big a fan as others are. Not an elite athlete, not a reliable open-field tackler and can really struggle in space. A 3rd round player who needs to play in the box. Will absolutely be a stud on special teams' as a rookie.

9. Khari Willis S Michigan State 5'11 213 lbs

Strengths: Willis is a big, physical and nasty safety for the Spartans who plays hard on every snap. Willis utilizes his length to cut off running lanes and wrap up securely away from his frame. An outstanding athlete, he flies all over the field, displaying tremendous range in run support. A fluid athlete who displays suddenness, change of direction and the secondary burst to quickly close. Disciplined eyes that read the game really well, showing outstanding instincts and anticipation to beat blockers to the ball carrier. A relentless motor who brings it on every snap of the ball. Effective as a blitzer, had 3 sacks his junior season. Sets the tone of the defense with the physicality and toughness he brings. When used in man-coverage, Willis shows some reliability and comfort, overwhelming smaller receivers at the line of scrimmage. An excellent special teams' player who has made a ton of big-time plays. Willis is a quick processor who makes snap decisions, needing very little processing time.

Weaknesses: Had a tremendous junior season, but dropped off a bit as a senior. Takes very risky and aggressive pathways to the ball, leaving him exposed in space, whiffing on some open-field opportunities. Quicker than fast, Willis has some deep-speed questions. He was exposed a few times in man coverage, getting burned down the field by 3-5 yards. Lacks elite ball skills, failing to play the ball in the air, very limited ball production numbers in college.

Best Fit: Box safety

Player Ranking (1-100): 77.5 – Willis is a really good box safety who reads the field exceptionally. His short area quickness and sideline to sideline range make him an NFL starter quality safety. He's been very reliable throughout his career and will immediately play a vital role on special teams for a team. He wasn't asked to cover much down the field in college and was mostly used as a free roaming safety who can rely on his instincts and downhill nature to quickly find and locate the football close to the line of scrimmage. He would be best used in that role at the next level as well. 3rd round player.

10. Sheldrick Redwine S Miami 6'0 202 lbs

Strengths: Redwine is a well-built thick safety displaying the next-level size to be an effective safety at any role he plays. Redwine is a 2-year starter who has fulfilled a variety of different roles in the Hurricanes defense, including as a slot corner and a single-high safety. Redwine has proved to have good ball production numbers in each season, with 4 turnovers in each of his 2 years starting. Redwine is a physical presence who shows toughness and soundness in all areas of the game. A reliable tackler, he takes good sharp angles to the football, utilizing good fundamentals and wrap-up skills to be a reliable last line of defense. Shows the size and strength to cover bigger tight ends in man coverage scenarios. Physical when used in man-coverage, getting his hands on receivers and altering their route course. Stings in run support, reacting without hesitation, showing the ability to take on blocks. Effective when used in blitzing situations, had 3 sacks this past season. Sees things quickly, showing the intelligence and physicality to put himself in good position to sniff out plays.

Weaknesses: Redwine is an average athlete, and doesn't possess any elite athletic traits. He has the tendency to grab on lateral routes when a receiver attempts to cross his face. Needs to learn to engage his lower half when tackling, allowing runners to gain additional yards after contact. Lacks the short-area bursts to quickly close on the ball after seeing a play develop, preventing him from making additional plays. Lacks elite instincts and agility to play in too much space as a single-high at the next level.

Best Fit: FS that can be used in a variety of different roles

Player Ranking (1-100): 76.1 – Redwine is a really good player who hasn't gotten as much hype as he deserves. While he isn't a great athlete capable of playing in loads of space at the next level, he still is an effective overall safety. His best attribute is his toughness and physicality, bringing it on every snap. He should and will be a starter at the next level. His coverage ability is an added benefit, being able to assist in dime/nickel packages for an NFL team. 3rd round player.

11. Mike Bell S Fresno State 6'3 203 lbs

Strengths: Bell is a 3-year starter for Fresno State who took over during his redshirt freshman year. Possessing outstanding height and length, Bell has the wingspan to be a real pest in coverage. Bell is also a stalwart for their special teams' unit. The last 2 years, he's really shown outstanding production with over 75 tackles in each season. His final season as a junior, Bell showed excellent and improved ball production with 3 interceptions and 8 passes defended. Bell is a highly-intelligent safety who remains disciplined in a wide variety of coverage assignments. Plays mostly in a Cover-2 showing outstanding anticipatory skills, route concepts and instincts. Possesses excellent range in large amounts of green to quickly close. Reliable hands to finish interceptions. Shows a good secondary burst to quickly close cushions, or when used to blitz.

Weaknesses: A drag down tackler who lacks the strength and hip torque to consistently bring down tacklers. Often times, Bell is an ankle biter, tending to jump at ankles to trip bigger runners over. Can have some slight hesitations in coverage, not always reading things as fast as he should. Very inconsistent physicality and leverage when taking on blocks in the running game. Would like to see him gain additional functional strength on his frame. An average athlete whose deficiencies are hidden due to his instincts and anticipatory skills.

Best Fit: Deep-lying FS

Player Ranking (1-100): 74.8 – Bell is a very refined cover safety who shows outstanding ability to be in the right place at the right time, putting himself in great positions. He's not a great athlete per se, but he makes up for it with his instincts and ball awareness. I want him playing in space, not close to the football. His tackling/physicality are a concern; therefore he shouldn't be used as a box safety. 4th round player.

12. D'Cota Dixon S Wisconsin 5'10 198 lbs

Strengths: Dixon is a 5th year senior for the Badgers who transitioned from corner to safety before his junior season. Team leader and signal caller for the defense, having a good understanding of the necessary communication/coverage assignments. Dixon possesses a filled-out and maximized frame, showing good muscularity and compactness. His corner movement and ability show up in his play, showing fluidity and flexibility in his lower half, maintaining outstanding positioning throughout plays. A downhill player who shows fearlessness and 0 hesitancy when coming into the hole. Shows commitment and sacrifice often times taking out the lead blocker to set up his teammates for the stop. A twitchy athlete, he shows impressive short-area bursts to sting in run support. Versatile athlete very comfortable in playing both in the box or in slot coverage. Times the ball really well in the air, showing the body control to disrupt at the perfect time to make a play or break up the ball. Natural blitzer who shows the ability to time effectively and take direct routes to the QB. Sinks low in his stance, inching toward the line of scrimmage playing controlled, and on the balls of his feet pre-snap at all times. Impressive man coverage ability sticking to the hip pocket of even quicker receivers.

Weaknesses: Undisciplined in his vision, easily manipulated on misdirection and trick plays. Lacks great strength and consistency in run support, failing to bring down in the open field when playing in too much space. Doesn't have center field anticipatory ability, nor can he play with his back towards the ball.

Best Fit: Box safety/slot corner

Player Ranking (1-100): 74.4 – I really like Dixon as a prospect. His man coverage abilities are outstanding, showing the ability to truly be a versatile next-level prospect. His box ability is really impressive considering his lack of great size. Utilizing his instincts and short-area bursts, he should be kept closer to the line of scrimmage. He struggles in too much space, with limited experience playing as a centerfielder and it shows. A 4th round player who can absolutely have a role at the next level. There's something nice about "knowing" what a prospect is and having a vision for the player. He has size limitations but he's a really good football player.

13. Jaquan Johnson S Miami (FL) 5'10 186 lbs

Strengths: Johnson is a 4-year starter for the Hurricanes with loads of experience in big-time games. Impressive turnover numbers, producing 13 on his own during his career. Johnson is a tackling machine, producing almost 100 his junior season. Johnson is a downhill player who is always looking to lay the wood. He is a perfect box safety that quickly reads, diagnoses and closes on the ball carrier. Johnson is a powerful and explosive hitter but he's not just a 'BIG' hitter, but a reliable form tackler who will take his ball carrier down on almost every occasion. Johnson possesses a never-ending motor who is always running full-speed on every snap. Johnson plays much bigger than his size playing with physicality and toughness throughout his frame. Stings in run support and reacts without hesitation possessing a large strike zone and is always around the football on every snap. A team leader who possesses impressive intangibles off the field.

Weaknesses: Lacks the great movement skills to be able to play in man coverage or in deep zone situations. A bit of an undersized guy who lacks the typical size of a box safety. Straight ahead athlete, he really struggles when his back is toward the ball. Lacks the lower body agility and flexibility to spring in any direction and play horizontally. Inconsistent timing on his ability to attack the football at the high point. Risky decision maker who plays an aggressive style which can lead to some incorrect guesses and bites on play fakes and misdirections. His size makes him more of an ideal FS, but he fails to possess typical FS qualities and is more suited to play as a SS.

Best Fit: Box Safety

Player Ranking (1-100): 73.2 – Really like the player but I absolutely have concerns. He's going to have to make his way on special teams early on and continue to get bigger and stronger for the next level. Teams will probably want him closer to 200 lbs. to play as a true 'box safety.' But the kid is aggressive and is always around the football. This kid has traits and I really think he has a chance. 4th round player.

14. Juan Thornhill S Virginia 6'1 202 lbs

Strengths: Thornhill is a 3-year starter for Virginia who displays NFL size with a prototypical safety physique. Thornhill has improved in each of his seasons, with a tremendous senior year totaling over 90 tackles and 5 interceptions. A versatile guy who has switched between playing as an outside corner and strong safety the last couple of seasons. Also played some wide receiver as a freshman. A modern NFL safety who shows experience and is comfortable when playing in coverage, showcased in his ability to cover slot receivers or even bigger TEs. Thornhill utilizes his length rarely allowing an uncontested catch, fighting and competing at the catch point on almost every instance. Impressive instincts and awareness in space, showing the ability to understand where he needs to be in zone coverage and attacking the football. Really good ball skills to play the ball in flight, keeping his eyes in the backfield. Understands how to deal with bigger targets, rarely allowing them to get inside leverage, beating them to the spot. Displays the short-area bursts to make plays in the backfield or in pursuit by utilizing sharp angles. Has a knack for getting home on blitzes, quickly reaching the backfield or disrupting the throw.

Weaknesses: Thornhill doesn't consistently play with the physicality you would expect for someone with his size. A bit passive when going in for tackles, preferring to trip runners up at the ankles, leading to many broken tackles. Struggles when his back is toward the ball, lacking the necessary foot quickness and recovery speed. Quicker than fast, Thornhill will get beat in 1 v 1 situations on vertical routes. What is his best position? Tackles badly like most cornerbacks, but has the size and skill set of a safety.

Best Fit: Strong Safety

Player Ranking (1-100): 72.4 – Thornhill is a solid prospect who displays some physicality and has the length to succeed. He shows familiarity and is comfortable in coverage and is a magnet to the football. 4th round player.

15. Amani Hooker S Iowa 6'0 210 lbs

Strengths: Hooker is a compactly-built safety hybrid who has played in the STAR position for the Iowa defense this past season, where he really excelled. (It simply means he fulfilled a variety of different roles for the defense depending on the situation, including covering in the slot or being used as a linebacker) Hooker had an outstanding final season, with 65 tackles, 4 interceptions, 7 passes defended and 3.5 tackles for loss. Hooker's versatility is his best trait, having shown success from all his different roles. Hooker is an explosive athlete who shows the fluidity and lower body explosiveness to spring in any direction. Engages his lower body and short area explosiveness when tackling, delivering some powerful pop-on contact. Stings in run support showing little hesitancy. Excellent when attacking the pocket, showing good timing and acceleration to make stops in the backfield. A playmaker who is excellent when the ball is in mid-flight showing vertical ability and very good hands to catch the ball outstretched. Mentally alert in coverage, showing good instincts and little processing time, especially when things are kept in front of him.

Weaknesses: Hooker tends to be too upright in space, minimizing his ability to have an accurate strike zone when tackling. A better straight-line athlete than a lateral athlete. Has some stiffness in his core preventing him from redirecting his frame and stopping/starting. Little deep-coverage experience, and is limited to a box role at the next level.

Best Fit: Strong Safety who should play in the box

Player Ranking (1-100): 71.0 – Hooker is an explosive athlete who has really good size. There's some stiffness to his movement skills preventing him from playing in too much space or utilizing him in deep-coverage situations. But he plays with physicality, explosiveness, and fearlessness. He also has the skillset to be used in special teams and in the return game.

16. Ugo Amandi S Oregon 5'10 203 lbs

Strengths: Amandi is a 4-year contributor for the Ducks who has had tremendous back to back seasons his last 2 years. Amandi is a low center of gravity safety who possesses compactness and stoutness throughout his frame. An excellent athlete, he shows terrific long speed as well as short-area bursts to come downhill and deliver big shots. Generally plays in the box, but shows some success when lined up in man-coverage displaying smoothness and fluid hips. Plays with urgency and determination on every snap. Demonstrates impressive makeup speed to recover any lost steps when initially beaten. An effective blitzer who understands how to properly time it to get home and affect the interior of the pocket.

Weaknesses: Marginal processing time, seems to see things late and take too long to respond. Grabs when beaten downfield, leading to some interference calls. Undisciplined eyes lead him to fall for every double move and misdirection type play, taking him completely out of plays. Doesn't always drive through his tackles, attempting to always deliver the big shot. Lacks the ideal height and length teams are looking for in a centerfield type of safety.

Best Fit: Box safety who is best closest to the line of scrimmage

Player Ranking (1-100): 70.3 – I like Amadi and I think he's an outstanding and gifted athlete who continuously plays 100 mph. He's not always the most instinctual guy and certainly lacks the necessary height and length for some teams. His explosive characteristics will get him drafted somewhere in the middle rounds. I would take him in the 4th.

17. Marvell Tell III S USC 6'2 195 lbs

Strengths: Tell III is a senior safety for the Trojans who is built with the prototypical size and frame for an

NFL safety, showing broad shoulders and heavily muscled limbs. 4-year contributor who has started in over 30 games. Tell is an outstanding special teams' player making some big-time plays for USC on special teams. Has experience playing as a single high or as a box safety and can do both. Impressive vision and instincts for a safety, quickly scanning and following his eyes. Plays on the balls of his feet inching up pre-snap and driving quickly on the ball. Good short-area quickness to quickly close openings and make up for any lost steps in coverage. Sees the mental sides of the game with a good understanding of route concepts. Disciplined in his assignments in coverage, rarely playing overaggressive.

Weaknesses: Tell was suspended by the team this past season in one of the biggest games of the season against Notre Dame for an undisclosed reason. Missed some other games for a neck stinger. Has lacked great ball production with only 5 career interceptions during his career. Mediocre tackler who will miss some important tackles at key spots in games. Not the most physical of safeties and will need to improve his consistency in his physicality. His wild pursuit angles dent his batting average as a tackler, putting him in awful positions. Not an impact tackler, rather relying on dragging ball carriers down while they pick up additional yardage. Gives up on plays failing to consistently fight and work through blocks. Quicker than fast, failing to have the long speed to chase ball carriers from behind.

Best Fit: Single-high FS

Player Ranking (1-100): 70.1 – Tell III is a good player but has serious flaws when it comes to the physical parts of the game. Not overly physical and not a great athlete, which is very concerning. He can be an immediate special teams player but I'm not quite sure he has what it takes to be a starter at safety in this league. 4th round player.

18. Andrew Wingard S Wyoming 5'11 209 lbs

Strengths: Wingard is a compact safety who plays both as a box safety and a Cover-2 safety for Wyoming. Wingard is a smart kid who understands the mental part of the game, shouting defensive commands for the defense pre-snap. He's a mentally alert guy who plays with confidence and assurance, rarely panicking or seemingly out of position. Hyper-aggressive in run support, Wingard is always inching his way forward to impact or make the stop in the backfield. He plays with good short-area quickness showing the ability to make stops quickly, and sniff out screens and tosses to the edges. Shows good man coverage abilities, doing a nice job of flipping his hips and staying across the middle or down the field with backs and tight ends. A thumper, Wingard isn't afraid of delivering the big hit. Trusts his eyes and follows the ball decisively, showing no hesitancy. Physical through the whistle, and shows a real toughness in doing the dirty work.

Weaknesses: Takes some wild pursuit angles which leads to a poor average as a tackler. Has some range limitations, and it is especially noticeable when he plays as a center field single high safety. Lacks the ideal size and length. Shows some stiffness and lack of coordination in his lower body. Not the greatest of athletes and it shows when playing in too much space.

Best Fit: Special teams and backup safety

Player Ranking (1-100): 68.9 – Definitely has some limitations as a starter at the next level. I wasn't overly impressed or convinced he can do it after watching his tape. But he can still be developed and get better, and absolutely have a role on special teams for a team. 5th round pick.

19. Rob Rolle S Villanova 5'11 190 lbs

Strengths: Rolle is a 5th year senior and team leader who had his best season in 2016 with 63 tackles, 7 interceptions and 12 passes defended. Rolle possesses natural read/react ability and instincts, quickly reading and processing, and then putting himself in good position. Disciplined in the run game, stinging and reacting without any hesitation. Takes acute angles to the football, cutting off run lanes and quickly finding and locating the ball carrier. The definition of versatile, frequently lining up over slot receivers, playing as a deep Cover-2 safety, playing as a boundary corner or even playing as a dime linebacker. A playmaker with the ball, having a few long interception/fumble returns for touchdowns.

Weaknesses: Got a medical redshirt in 2017 after tearing his ACL in 2017. A slighter-built guy who lacks the necessary power and muscle in his frame. A quicker than fast guy, lacking the long speed to cover deep routes. Needs to tune up his tackling fundamentals, attempting to cut off the legs, rather than wrap-up securely.

Best Fit: Box safety

Player Ranking (1-100): 67.3 – I really like Rolle and I think he's the perfect versatile defender for the modern day NFL. While he's not a great athlete and he's a 'hit or miss' tackler, he's got the range and instincts few do. A 5th round player who will make his mark on special teams as a rookie.

20. Jah'Shawn Johnson S/CB Texas Tech 5'10 185 lbs

Strengths: Johnson is a 5th year senior for Texas Tech. Johnson is an impressive read/react athlete who shows impressive instincts, reflexes and reactionary ability. Versatile safety, he plays both in a single-high role, Cover-2, and has experience at lining up in the slot and covering. Johnson is the defensive team leader who calls signals for the defense. A downhill, fearless guy who shows 0 hesitancy when it comes to being aggressive. Johnson is a magnet to the football due to his movement skills and cover awareness. A twitchy athlete, he has the lower body explosiveness to spring in any direction. A competitive guy who plays with a fieriness and will compete at all levels of the field. Good ball skills and shows the ability to attack the ball at the high point.

Weaknesses: Johnson possesses a very slight frame and might be required to move to a nickel player at the next level. Has a tendency to take some "business decisions" when it comes to tackling, preferring to slow down as opposed to forcefully bring down. Needs to do a better job of staying square and keeping his pad level down in run support as opposed to keeping himself too upright bouncing off runners. Will get outmuscled and boxed out when lined up in man coverage situations against bigger targets. Missed first 3 games of senior season with a shoulder injury.

Best Fit: FS hybrid CB or a nickel corner

Player Ranking (1-100): 66.2 – Really good athlete who can compete as a #4 or #5 nickel back on a team.

Absolutely should get drafted due to his movement skills and coverage ability. It's possible some teams will grade him as a safety. Can be used in a pinch to play some safety. Needs to continue to gain additional strength and bulk to maximize his frame limitations. 6th round player.

21. Lukas Denis S Boston College 5'11 185 lbs

Strengths: Denis is a 2-year starter for BC who really came onto the scene his junior season with 7 interceptions, 2 forced fumbles and 10 passes defended. Versatile defensive back, having played some corner as well in his senior season. Disciplined in his assignment, playing with self-assured confidence. A true ball hawk who is best used as a centerfield type of player with the ability to track and locate the ball mid-flight and disrupt at the catch point. Shows rare key and diagnostic ability with the skill to cover a lot of ground and play with tremendous range. Fluidity in his movement skills, showing the ability to transfer weight to smoothly open up his hips and turn and run without gearing down. Good, strong hands to be able to come up with the ball when given the chance. Turnover conscious, always looking to knock the ball out or create a big play for the defense.

Weaknesses: Lacks great size to be able to hold up as an 'in the box' safety, and can have some trouble bringing down bigger running backs. His lack of size can come into play when in coverage as well, getting boxed out by bigger TE's and possession receivers. Shows hesitancy in run support, attempting to drag down as opposed to using proper form tackling. This hesitancy will affect his routes to the football as well, choosing 'safer' paths to the ball. Quicker in 10-yard increments than 'fast.' Fails to have the long speed to close down running lanes and makeup ground on crossing receivers.

Best Fit: Single-high safety or a slot corner/hybrid safety

Player Ranking (1-100): 63.1 – A good cover guy but lacks the ability to hold up whatsoever in the run game. In every game I watched he missed at least 1 open-field tackle. Teams might only give him a chance at corner in camp. He shows impressive movement/coverage skills to have a chance to make a roster. 6th round player.

22. Delvon Randall S Temple 5'11 210 lbs

Strengths: Randall is a 3-year starter and leader for Temple who has posted incredible ball production numbers in all 3 years with 12 interceptions and 11 passes defended. Randall is built tough with compactness and muscle throughout his frame. A versatile defender who plays as a single-high, cover-3 safety or even as a boundary corner. Ball skills are evident in every game I watched, Randall uses his anticipatory, read/react, and physicality to make consistent plays on the ball. Shows a receivers' mindset with his ability to attack and play the ball in flight. Plays disciplined in the run game, maintaining good body control and decisiveness to come downhill, rarely overrunning plays. For the most part a very reliable tackler.

Weaknesses: Struggles when asked to change direction in space, getting stuck in the mud. Poor pad level in space, failing to keep his pads down. This leads to a lot of really bad whiffs when playing as a single-high safety as the last line of defense. Very average athlete who lacks ideal short-area quickness or long-speed to be effective when lining up in man coverage at the next level.

Best Fit: Box safety

Player Ranking (1-100): 60.1 – Randall possesses an NFL frame and NFL physicality. While he shows some versatility and instincts as a player, he lacks the overall movement skills and consistencies in open-field situations to be trusted on an NFL defense. 6th round player.

23. JoJo McIntosh S Washington 6'1 215 lbs

Strengths: McIntosh is a 4-year starter for Washington and has been a mainstay for the Huskies defense. Built with a prototypical NFL safety physique, showing outstanding girth, muscularity, and length that teams covet. Downhill safety who shows impressive anticipatory skills quickly reacting. Explosive pop on contact, showing the short-area burst to deliver blows. Shows the size and length to shock blockers with his upper body strength and beat the 1st block. Has a good understanding of a variety of coverage assignments, keeping himself disciplined and in-position. Has competed in some big-time college football games, against the best college QBs.

Weaknesses: McIntosh has had limited ball production during his career with only 2 career interceptions. Overly handsy down the field, saw quite a number of plays where he grabs when panicked in man coverage situations. Despite his size, his levels of physicality are inconsistent, most notably in the running game. He fails to accurately and securely wrap up, leading to some terribly missed tackles in the open-field. Lacks the necessary movement skills and change of direction to play in too much space, lacking center field abilities. Shows areas of concern in both man and zone situations, lacking the necessary confidence in his skills.

Best Fit: SS and special teams'

Player Ranking (1-100): 59.2 – McIntosh lacks a "great" quality when it comes to playing safety. Teams will likely fall in love with his size and length thinking they can groom him and at the very least utilize him as a special teams' player. His true next-level role is still not really known and will have to show that he can cover at some level in training camp for a team. 7th round player.

24. Jonathan Crawford S Indiana 6'2 203 lbs

Strengths: Crawford is a long and well-built safety for the Hoosiers who's been a 4-year starter, displaying really impressive ball production numbers. Defensive leader and signal caller for the defense. Has loads of starting experience, starting every game of his college career. Crawford is used quite a bit in man coverage situations in the slot and against receiving TEs. Does a nice job of utilizing his length to disrupt and re-direct routes. An instinctual player who quickly processes and shows really good read/react ability. Shows the ability to lay the wood on occasion, delivering big hits.

Weaknesses: Could make the argument that Crawford was more productive in his freshman and sophomore seasons than his junior and senior years, with more tackles and plays on the ball. Fails to consistently drop low to take out ball carriers, tending to keep his pad level far too high bouncing off runners. Shows some hesitancy in his ability to assist in run support. Gets lost in the mud in pursuit, failing to take adequate and sharp angles to the football. An upright athlete who fails to have the necessary change of direction ability in his hips. Not a great athlete, lacking the short-area burst as well as the long-speed to cover faster receivers.

Lacks the aggression level and functional strength you would expect from someone his size.

Best Fit: Special teams' and backup safety

Player Ranking (1-100): 57.2 – Crawford is a backup safety at the next level who isn't a great athlete, nor a great cover guy. But possesses intangibles and the size teams covet. He's going to have to prove himself on special teams' in training camp. 7th round player.

25. Will Harris S Boston College 6'1 207 lbs

Strengths: Harris is a big, strong and physical safety out of Boston College who displays the muscled-up physique to be a strong safety at the next level. Harris is well liked by the coaching staff and is a team leader. A smart guy who plays football with patience, precision and discipline rarely making a mental mistake. Has a good feel for different coverage schemes and alignments. Utilizes good overall instincts in combination with his ability to take sharp angles to the football, putting him in a good position to make plays in the run game. Harris is a good overall athlete who displays good long-speed, showing the ability to track runners down from behind. A versatile safety showing experience as a single-high, a box safety, Cover 2 or Cover 3. Shows good experience as a blitzer, routinely disrupting the QB.

Weaknesses: A slow mental processor, showing some hesitation. Has some balance issues in space, struggling to change direction and recover if initially beaten. Whiffs far too often tackling. A close but no cigar player, puts himself in a good position, but fails to make plays consistently. A build-up runner, he lacks great initial burst or quickness out of his stance. Really struggles when asked to cover horizontal routes, or redirect his frame.

Best Fit: Strong safety and special teams'

Player Ranking (1-100): 57.0 – Harris is a disciplined guy who is a good athlete, but not great. He lacks great situational and ball awareness to consistently make plays on the ball. Could be a really solid rotational safety for a team, a player who can excel on special teams. 7th round player.

Safeties Top-10 Rankings

1. Taylor Rapp
2. Deionte Thompson
3. Mike Edwards
4. Darnell Savage Jr
5. Nasir Adderley
6. Marquise Blair
7. Darius West
8. Johnathan Abram
9. Khari Willis
10. Sheldrick Redwine

Chapter 15

Conclusion

There you have it, another 2019 draft class done and dusted! In lieu of me basing my guides grading strictly off the tape and making it available to you before the NFL combine even begins, my heights and weights aren't the same as the combine numbers.

The good news is that most of the weights at the combine aren't their true "play weights" either and are generally lower because many players attempt to achieve slightly lower times in the run events. If you would like to have access to the official combine heights and weights, I will be posting the numbers on my website at DTPDraftScout.com.

As always, I greatly appreciate your support. I only did this as a fun side project the very first season and every year since it's grown exponentially. And for that, I truly am more appreciative than you could ever know.

I really hope you enjoy reading this as much as I enjoyed working on it. This guide is literally my life for about 4 months. I put everything I have into it. If you ever have any suggestions or tips on how to make it better for next year, please contact me and let me know.

If you could also do me a simple favor of reviewing this guide on Amazon, it would be greatly greatly appreciated! That means more than you could ever know.

Simply go here:

https://www.amazon.com/dp/B07N3NB91Z

And click "Write a Review" at the bottom of the page. Thanks again guys!! Let's connect either on my website, DTPDraftScout.com or my twitter handle @DTPDraftScout

Let's make this the most fun and enjoyable draft season yet. If you have any questions I would be more than glad to help or assist,

Daniel Parlegreco

DTPDraftScout

Chapter 16

Glossary of Terms and Top 50 Big Board

0 Technique (Zero Technique DT) – A DT who is required to play two different gaps. They are lined up directly over the center. They can be in a 3-4 or a 4-3 system. They are the biggest guys on the defensive side of the ball. They are generally extremely powerful and clog the middle of the field. They generally are not required to rush the passer, nor are they very good at it. They are also called nose tackles as well.

1 Technique (One Technique DT) – A DT that generally is required to take on multiple blockers and open things up for his fellow defensive lineman. They play on either one of the outside shoulders of the center and are not directly over the center like a 0 technique. They generally are also referred to as nose tackles as well. A 1 technique is always partnered up with a 3 technique DT as well. The 1 technique is more powerful, stronger and a better player against the run. The 3 technique is more explosive and a better pass rusher.

3 Technique (Three Tech DT) – Plays on the outside shoulder of either guard. They are the penetrating and more explosive DT that is a better pass rusher. They don't have much responsibility in the way of gap control, and generally are 1-gap players. Think of guys like Warren Sapp and Aaron Donald.

3-4 OLB – Plays mostly on the line of scrimmage but standing up on the outside. These guys are generally your best pass rushers in a 3-4 system. They can be used in coverage at times as well. They are similar to 4-3 DE's but differ because of the defensive scheme your defense employs. 4-3 DE's are required to put their hands on the ground and are relied upon to be generally bigger, longer and stronger against the run. Depending on the defensive coaches and their philosophies, most guys are capable of playing either as a 4-3 DE or a 3-4 OLB depending on what defensive system your team plays.

4-3 OLB – These guys aren't your pass rushers. They consist of both the Will linebacker and the Sam linebacker. The Will (Weak Side) is generally the more athletic, sideline to sideline LB who is faster and can cover better. The Will plays on the weak side of the formation. The Sam (Strong Side) linebacker is the guy that's asked to play closer to the line of scrimmage to play the run more. They play on the strong side of the formation.

Cover 2 – Two deep-lying safeties who each cover half of the field.

Cover 3 – Rather than covering ½ the field like a Cover 2, a Cover 3 requires 3 deep playing guys who each takes a 3rd of the field.

Dime Defense – Has 6 defensive backs on the field, only 1 linebacker and 4 rushers on the line. Used in passing situations or long yardage situations.

JUCO – Transferred from a junior college program.

Mike Linebacker – Quite simply the middle linebacker on your team.

Nickel Defense – Has 5 defensive backs on the field, 2 linebackers and 4 rushers on the line of scrimmage. Used in passing situations or when teams are in 3 receiver sets.

Nickel Linebacker – When a team is playing in nickel, there are 2 linebackers on the field. These linebackers are the best on the team in space, and can really cover and run.

Quick Twitch (Twitchy) – Meaning a guy who is explosive off the snap of the ball. They possess above-average quick-twitch fibers, meaning they are more explosive in their lower bodies.

Rangy – Good length but lacks great bulk on his frame. Almost like a wiry-built guy who lacks the ideal weight on his frame

RPO – A popular new term in the NFL referring to run pass option plays. It's when the QB goes to the line of scrimmage with both a run and a pass play. He generally decides based on the defensive look whether to run or pass

Sam Linebacker (Strong Side Linebacker) – Stronger, bigger guy who is required to play closer to the line of scrimmage. Generally, has more assignments in the run game.

Single High Safety – Deep covering safety who plays deep by himself and covers the entire field. Generally, is a safety who plays with outstanding range and instincts. Think Earl Thomas.

Slot Cornerback (Nickel Corner) – A cornerback who plays inside and covers the receivers closest to the line of scrimmage. These cornerbacks are usually smaller, quicker and more agile.

Sub-packages – Any package which is different from your base defense. Your base defense is either a 3-4 or a 4-3. Every team has sub-packages that are generally required to be used in certain game situations, such as nickel or dime defense. Most teams in the NFL play in their sub-package almost 50% of the time.

Will Linebacker (Weak Side Linebacker) - More athletic outside linebacker who plays on the weak side of the formation in a 4-3 defense.

DTP's Best 50 Players Big-Board

1-Nick Bosa DE

↓

2-Clelin Ferrell DE

↓

3-Ed Oliver DT

↓

4-Quinnen Williams DT

↓

5-Jeffrey Simmons DT

↓

6-Amani Oruwariye CB

↓

7-Rashan Gary DT

↓

8-Josh Jacobs RB

↓

9-Drew Lock QB

↓

10-Cody Ford OG/T

- 11-Byron Murphy CB
- 12-Taylor Rapp S
- 13-Montez Sweat DE
- 14-Noah Fant TE
- 15-Jonah Williams OT
- 16-Christian Wilkins DT
- 17-Kelvin Harmon WR
- 18-Deionte Thompson S
- 19-Greg Little OT
- 20-D.K. Metcalf WR
- 21-Kyler Murray QB

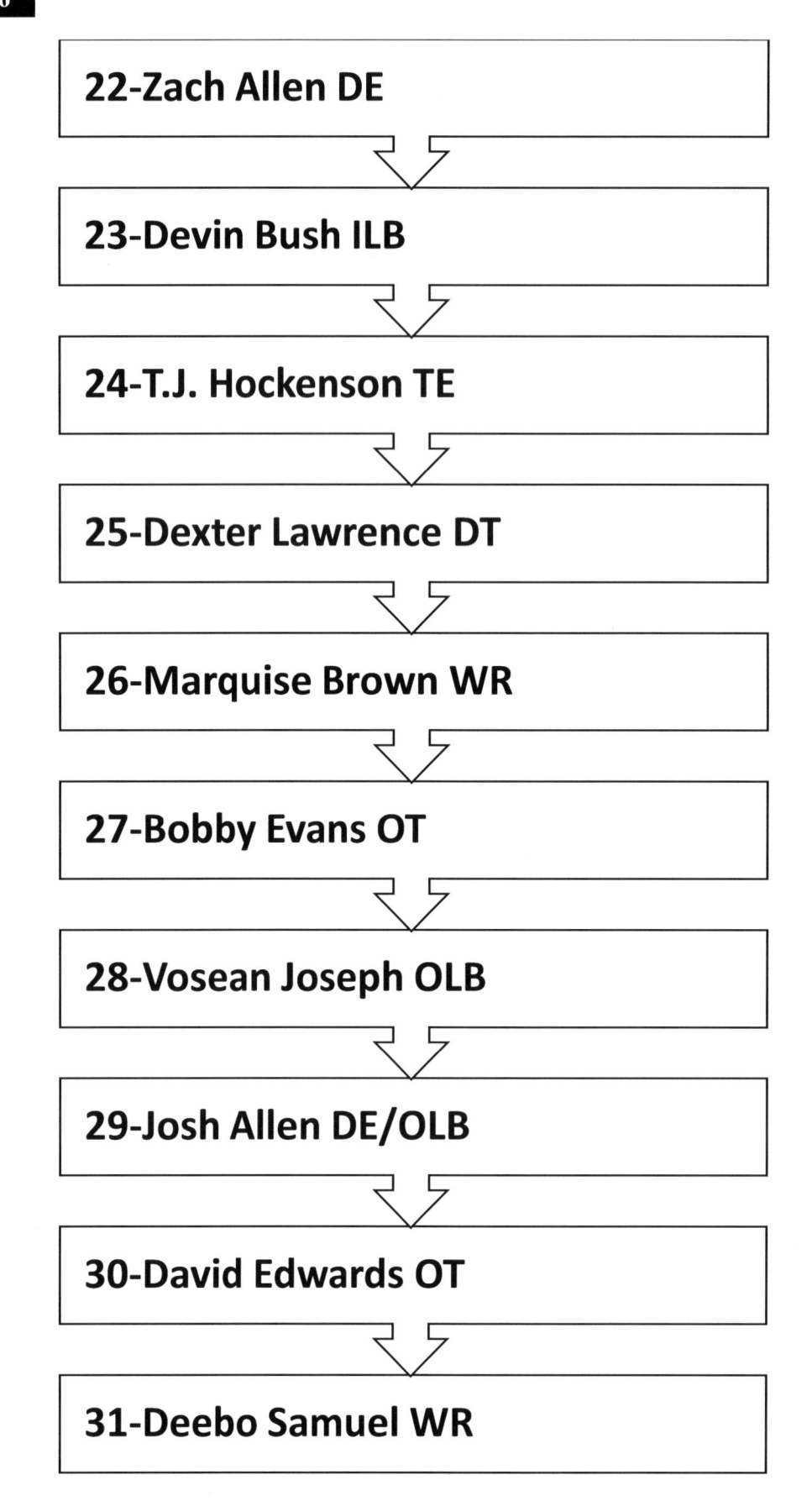

- 22-Zach Allen DE
- 23-Devin Bush ILB
- 24-T.J. Hockenson TE
- 25-Dexter Lawrence DT
- 26-Marquise Brown WR
- 27-Bobby Evans OT
- 28-Vosean Joseph OLB
- 29-Josh Allen DE/OLB
- 30-David Edwards OT
- 31-Deebo Samuel WR

- 32-Jachai Polite DE/OLB
- 33-Josiah Tauaefa OLB
- 34-Deandre Baker CB
- 35-AJ Brown WR
- 36-Brian Burns DE
- 37-N'Keal Harry WR
- 38-Dwayne Haskins QB
- 39-Dawson Knox TE
- 40-Rock Ya-Sin CB
- 41-Riley Ridley WR

- 42-Mack Wilson ILB
- 43-Mike Edwards S
- 44-Daniel Jones QB
- 45-Emmanuel Hall WR
- 46-Greedy Williams CB
- 47-Irv Smith Jr TE
- 48-Charles Omenihu DE
- 49-Antoine Wesley WR
- 50-Chris Lindstrom OG

Printed in Great Britain
by Amazon